Russia in World History

Russia in World History

A Transnational Approach

CHOI CHATTERJEE

BLOOMSBURY ACADEMIC
LONDON • NEW YORK • OXFORD • NEW DELHI • SYDNEY

BLOOMSBURY ACADEMIC
Bloomsbury Publishing Plc
50 Bedford Square, London, WC1B 3DP, UK
1385 Broadway, New York, NY 10018, USA
29 Earlsfort Terrace, Dublin 2, Ireland

BLOOMSBURY, BLOOMSBURY ACADEMIC and the Diana logo are trademarks
of Bloomsbury Publishing Plc

First published in Great Britain 2022

Cover design by Ben Anslow
Cover Image © MHJ / Getty Images

A catalogue record for this book is available from the British Library.

Library of Congress Cataloging-in-Publication Data
Names: Chatterjee, Choi, author.
Title: Russia in world history: a transnational approach / Choi Chatterjee.
Description: London; New York: Bloomsbury Academic, 2022. |
Includes bibliographical references and index.
Identifiers: LCCN 2021036442 (print) | LCCN 2021036443 (ebook) |
ISBN 9781350026421 (hb) | ISBN 9781350026414 (pb) |
ISBN 9781350026438 (epdf) | ISBN 9781350026445 (ebook)
Subjects: LCSH: Soviet Union–Historiography. | Intellectuals–Soviet Union. |
Intellectuals–India. | Great Britain–Colonies–Historiography. | East and West. |
Imperialism–Historiography. | Colonization.
Classification: LCC DK38 .C384 2022 (print) | LCC DK38 (ebook) |
DDC 947–dc23/eng/20211012
LC record available at https://lccn.loc.gov/2021036442
LC ebook record available at https://lccn.loc.gov/2021036443

ISBN: HB: 978-1-3500-2642-1
PB: 978-1-3500-2641-4
ePDF: 978-1-3500-2643-8
eBook: 978-1-3500-2644-5

Typeset by Deanta Global Publishing Services, Chennai, India
Printed and bound in India

To find out more about our authors and books visit www.bloomsbury.com and
sign up for our newsletters.

To Ma (Nonda Chatterjee, educator and novelist, 1938–2012)
Because you saw so clearly, I stumble less often in the dark

CONTENTS

Acknowledgments

A book is never the product of a single mind, and it gives me great pleasure to acknowledge the many, many intellectual debts that I have incurred along the way. Rhodri Mogford at Bloomsbury Academic Press convinced me very early that my project was actually a full-length book and would be poorly served if published as a series of articles as I had originally envisaged. I thank him for his early insight into the shape and form of this book and for his superior powers of persuasion. Laura Reeves has been extremely helpful at every stage of the writing process, and I am grateful to her for keeping me on course with her remarkable attention to time and detail. The reviewers of this manuscript were simply superb, and their suggestions and criticisms were remarkably cogent and helpful in shaping this book.

I have been fortunate to have spent my career in the History Department at California State University, Los Angeles, which is peopled with exceptional colleagues who are as committed to their scholarship as they are to serving our first-generation students. I have learned from them that the historian does not simply write for a circle of fellow intellectuals, but that our work helps our students think more deeply about identity, politics, justice, economics, the nation, the world, and the environment. I thank Stan Burstein, Tim Doran, Chris Endy, Eileen Ford, Kittiya Lee, Enrique Ochoa, Timothy Paynich, Birte Pfleger, Phillip Goff, Sara Pugach, Camille Suarez, Angela Vergara, Mark Wild and Lamont Yeakey for their lively interest in all things historical and political. I especially want to thank Ping Yao, a historian of China; Scott Wells, a historian of the Middle Ages; and Afshin Matin-asgari, a historian of Modern Iran. I was trained as a historian of Russia, but their deep expertise in periods and areas of history other than mine has helped me gain a worldview. Moreover, their intellectual companionship has helped me think more broadly and deeply about global historical processes. This book is a product of our friendship, and as such it reflects our decades-long conversations about history, literature, poetry, cinema, and politics. Afshin has been a wonderful intellectual mentor, and I have enjoyed every argument with him about twentieth-century intellectual history. Thank you for reading drafts of my chapters and providing critical and important feedback at every stage of the project.

Finally, my immense gratitude to my students at California State University, Los Angeles. I wish I could name all of you, but unfortunately I am limited by space. But Miguel Arriola, Ryan Allen, Eric Barnett, Ivan Lorenzana, Jewelyn Mims, Jeffrey Evans, Sergio Maldonado, Stefan Ogbac, Jafet Rodriguez, Moises Ponce-Zepeda, and Katherine Yang deserve a special vote of thanks for sharing their highly original thinking with me. Thank you for always keeping me on my toes, for always challenging me, and for believing that historical research and interpretation matters beyond the walls of the academy. You kept my scholarship engaged and honest, and, most importantly, you pushed me to consider many points of view that I would have overlooked or simply been unaware of in your absence. Thank you for opening my mind and for training me to listen to those who exist outside the charmed circles of knowledge and power.

In the field of Russian history, I have been blessed to have the mentorship and friendship of David Ransel whose feedback on Chapter 3 has been invaluable. I also want to thank Alex Rabinowitch and Janet Rabinovitch for their unstinting support and for always believing in me, even when I was a callow graduate student. Hari Vasudevan read several chapters of the book before passing away suddenly in 2020, an early victim of Covid-19. The scholarly world is poorer without Hari's capacious intellect. Jane Burbank read drafts of several chapters, and her critical advice has been very useful. Steven Marks was an early pioneer in creating the field of Russia in world history. I thank Steve for his extraordinarily inventive scholarship as well as for his irreverence, wit, and love of gardening. Kate Brown's many comparative works have been very influential in various fields of history, and her early interest in my book gave me the confidence to move forward with this project.

Mollie Cavender, Deborah Field, Lynn Hudson, Ali Igmen, Lisa Kirschenbaum, Karen Petrone, Jane Rhodes, and Barbara Walker are the best friends that anyone could ask for. In addition to being accomplished and noteworthy historians, you have been extraordinarily generous with your time. Thank you for reading poorly written first drafts of chapters, for listening to my outlandish ideas, and for always being there whenever I need to talk. I aspire to be a scholar like you someday. Lisa Kirschenbaum's valuable contributions to the last chapter have enriched the volume and provided an important connection to the arguments presented in the first chapter. My deep gratitude to Elena Yushkova for finding documents in the Russian archives. It would have been impossible to write this book without her generous assistance and her extensive familiarity with the Russian archives.

Several institutions invited me to present my research, and I want to thank Alexander Semyonov of the Higher School of Economics in St. Petersburg; Jie-Hyun Lim at Sogang University, Seoul; Ali Igmen of California State University, Long Beach; Joes Segal of the Wende Museum, Los Angeles;

Robert Edelman of the University of California, San Diego; Karen Petrone of the University of Kentucky, Lexington; Sarvani Gooptu of the Netaji Institute of Asian Studies, Kolkata; Mary Neuburger at the University of Texas, Austin; Larissa Rudova of Pomona College; Aviel Roshwald and Ananya Chakravarti at Georgetown University; Ishita Bannerjee at the El Colegio de Mexico; and last but not least, Jennifer Presto of the University of Oregon, Eugene, for their generous hospitality and intellectual support.

Finally, I would like to express my appreciation to my family for their forbearance and patience as the books piled up to dangerous heights in the family room, threatening to obliterate the unwary passerby and the many animals that share our house. I have promised my daughters, Shaheen and Damini, and my son-in-law, Andrew Thieme, that I will never write another book as long as I live. And that when they come home, they will have my entire and undivided attention. My gratitude to my brilliant niece, Ananya Chakravarti, for her passion for historical scholarship and social justice. A big thank you to Kate McGinn for her fine appreciation of all things literary. I admire her capacity for generous listening and envy her beautiful command of the written and the spoken word. You have inspired me to work on my writing, and I hope that we will continue to read many nineteenth-century Russian novels together. Thank you to my sister Rupa Chakravarti for persisting in your Tagorean obsession in the face of all my ill-advised objections; you are far the wiser as a result. Your music, song, poetry, and prose have opened many different vistas and keep me connected to our shared past. Omer Sayeed, my husband, has wielded Occam's razor with uncanny precision for as long as I have known him. If there is any merit in the arguments presented in this book, it is due to his extraordinary capacity for clear thinking and reasoning. Thank you for a lifetime of interesting conversations, long evening walks, and the many shared projects that we have conceived together.

Introduction

This book was conceived as a serendipitous accident on December 9, 2010, on a remote island situated in the middle of the Indian Ocean. Nothing could have been further from the vast Eurasian space of the Russian Empire, either conceptually or geographically. Closer to Thailand than to India, the Andaman and Nicobar Islands are a series of little dots in the endless horizon of the Indian Ocean. People flock there from around the world to enjoy the natural riches of the thickly forested land, sunbathe on the white beaches, and snorkel in the magnificent coral reserves that lie beneath the ocean waves. Most tourists are unaware that their presence is restricted to only a few islands, as this archipelago serves as a key outpost of the Indian navy. Most are equally indifferent to the fact that the Andaman Islands were once a part of the immense ocean-based gulag of the British Empire, and political prisoners transported from British India to the Cellular Jail in Port Blair knew with certainty that they would never return alive to the mainland.[1]

As a historian of modern Russia, I, too, was unaware of the carceral history of the island and would have continued in my ignorance, but for the efforts of my mother, Nonda Chatterjee. A novelist, an educator, and a self-critical Indian nationalist, she was determined that we visit the dreaded Cellular Jail that had housed and killed many, many political prisoners. For all my erudite mother's cosmopolitanism, she knew the difference between the world and the home and was never confused as I often was by the points of superficial convergence.

I went unwillingly, expecting to see faded sepia prints of Indian nationalists on the weathered walls of a colonial era jail. But I was unprepared for the magnitude and the sheer modernity of the sprawling jail ensemble. The Cellular Jail in Port Blair was modeled on the famous Pentonville Prison in London. Built in 1842, Pentonville became the inspiration for progressive prison architecture throughout the world. Prisoners were housed in individual cells instead of being herded together in common accommodations as was customary in the more traditional carceral systems that predated this modern prototype. The Pentonville regime of prisoner isolation was adopted at the Cellular Jail. The prison cells ran sequentially and were housed in enormous wings that radiated from a massive central hall. The Pentonville Prison had four wings, while the newer and much larger Cellular Jail that was constructed between 1896 and 1906 had seven massive wings. The heavy prison walls ensured the complete isolation of the individual prisoners in their cells. The guards from the central tower could watch the prisoners, while the prisoners themselves could only sense and not see the watching eyes of the armed men who ruled their lives. Although the guards could not peer into the individual cells as they would have if the prison was a perfect panopticon, they could monitor the activity of the prisoners in the wings from the main hall, the center of surveillance.

The story got even more interesting as I later learned that Jeremy Bentham, the forerunner of behavioral social sciences, had borrowed the design of the panopticon, the central metaphor in Foucault's theories of discipline and punishment, from his brother, Samuel Bentham.[2] Samuel had been engaged in the service of Prince Grigory Potemkin, a noted statesman, and a military leader but best known as the lover of the famous Russian empress Catherine the Great. A naval engineer, Samuel had designed a panopticon factory to speed up the labor of untutored serfs producing spare parts for the Russian navy. Jeremy Bentham, while on a visit to the Potemkin estate in Krichev, Belarus, in 1786, realized that a system of constant and well-intentioned surveillance was key to increasing labor productivity. Later, he theorized that constant surveillance coupled with deep isolation could also serve as a means of remaking disorderly individuals with the aim of re-incorporating them into society as useful members. Bentham theorized that the architectural reorganization of prison space would lead to compliance, engender self-discipline among the prisoners, and increase their capacity for labor.[3] The intentions were beneficent and the conceptions of social rehabilitation embedded in a particular architectural form were simply brilliant.

The Cellular Jail, however, was not a place of Benthamite rehabilitation. Instead, it was designed to isolate dangerous political prisoners from the Indian mainland for life. As a result, the administration of the Cellular Jail devised its own set of innovations on the original Benthamite plan. In the courtyard of the jail, I saw the small wooden execution hut where the prisoner was hung until the bones of the neck broke under the weight of the body dangling from a noose made from coarse coir rope. Prisoners used the dried husks of coconuts that grew abundantly on the islands to make coir rope, a valuable product of the British prison-industrial complex. The kolu or the oil-wheel looked fairly innocuous until we were told that prisoners were chained to it for hours on end and forced to walk around like beasts of burden under the rays of the boiling tropical sun. The walls of the prison were immensely thick, and so designed that it was almost impossible for prisoners to communicate with each other. But prisoners found a way to speak to each other and to subvert the regime of social isolation and hard labor that tipped many into insanity and led many others to commit suicide. When the guide mentioned that the Cellular Jail had been turned into a university by the highly educated prisoners who taught each other through cleverly designed courses and tutorials, the shock of recognition was complete. Surely, as a Russian historian, I had heard that bit of prison lore before?

On that humid tropical island, I suddenly had a vision of political prisons in the magnificent city of St. Petersburg. The infamous Trubetskoi Bastion Prison in the Peter Paul Fortress was also built on the star design, another variation of the panopticon, to enable constant surveillance of prisoners from a central point of observation. The St. Petersburg House of Preliminary Detention, built expressly to resemble the Pentonville Prison in London, represented the epitome of carceral modernity in the Russian Empire in the late nineteenth century. I remembered reading about young Vera Figner, who had been imprisoned in a lonely cell in the Trubetskoi Bastion after planning the assassination of Tsar Alexander II in 1881. She had fought the onset of madness by devouring works on history and the natural sciences in the dim light of the prison cell, much like the prisoners incarcerated in the Cellular Jail on the prison island.

I came back from my visit with a headache, but at the same time, my mind was buzzing with curiosity and confusion. Had I visited a Russian/ British prison for political prisoners in the middle of the Indian Ocean? Or was I suffering from heat stroke, an affliction very common in the tropics? Could imperial systems of incarceration be so similar when the political systems of the Russian and the British Empires were so vastly different?[4] How could the Russian Empire, where the emperor himself was above the law, unconstrained by either a parliament or a constitution, be compared to the system of parliamentary rule in England where the power of the monarch had been constrained and crippled for at least two centuries? Didn't I know from the innumerable books that I had read in my field over the decades that the Russian Empire (Soviet Union) was backward, autocratic, and oppressive, whereas the progressive nations of Western Europe, especially England, was the home of free trade, common law, civil liberties, and democracy?

The field of Russian history is built around a central assumption: that there is an insurmountable difference separating the free nations of Western Europe and the Russian Empire. As one travels east from Western Europe toward Eurasia, one is taught that the gradient of civilization shrinks exponentially.[5] The idea of Russia as the pathological outlier in the evolution of European nations from monarchy to representative government not only dominates the entire field of Slavic Studies in the West but has also been voiced by many generations of Russian intellectuals. Vasily Klyuchevsky blamed Russian backwardness on its geography. The wide-open Eurasian steppes and the lazy Russian rivers prevented the development of dense European-style cities with their pre-capitalist merchant associations, industrious craft guilds, and their vocabulary of rights and liberties. Lenin claimed that the Russian bourgeoisie, unlike its Western counterpart, was cowardly and therefore unable to fulfill its historical mission of transitioning from a system of autocratic feudalism to modern capitalism and parliamentary rule.[6] The Russian working class, instead of behaving like a true Western proletariat, continued to own land in the provinces and unaccountably insisted on maintaining its close ties to the village community.[7] Paul Miliukov complained that the Russian state was slow to evolve, appearing centuries later than its West European counterparts. Moreover, instead of growing organically from within society, the state was an external graft on the body politic. When the Romanov Empire collapsed in 1917, Miliukov argued that since it was an artificial structure that had failed to integrate the population in a shared vision of the future, the dissolution was pre-ordained.[8] Many Russian intellectuals believed that their inability to become sufficiently Westernized and sufficiently democratic was a result of the Mongol yoke and Russia's contiguity with Asiatic Empires.

But one visit to the massive Cellular Jail on the Andaman Islands upended decades of training, reading, writing, and teaching. What if the history of modern Western Europe was completely different from what we are taught and continue to teach in the field of Slavic Studies? What if the foundational idea in our field, which sees Western Europe as a liberal beacon and a democratic alternative to autocratic and oppressive Russia, is based on our indifference to the history of European Empires in much of the world? If the Siberian prison and exile system, which we had long believed to be a uniquely Russian phenomenon, was but a variation on imperial prison systems developed by other European Empires, could the same be true of other episodes of Russian history?[9] And if we allow this basic fact of comparison between imperial practices in Russia and other European Empires, how does this affect the writing of Russian history in the West?

Having reluctantly abandoned the explanatory schema of a liberal West and an autocratic Russia that undergirds the field of Slavic Studies, I was marooned for a while on a lonely intellectual island, unsure of how to communicate my findings. Finally, building on the scaffolding provided by recent works on comparative imperialism, I devised a set of strategies to bring Russia into world history.[10] The chapters in my book are intellectual bridges that have been built very painstakingly. But in doing so, I have followed a rather idiosyncratic research agenda that I will outline in the second part of the introduction. The book itself connects to three distinct audiences: the field of Slavic Studies, the field of comparative imperialism, and the field of world history.

During the last four centuries, Western Europe was a confusing palimpsest of states that coexisted with extensive overseas empires in the Americas, Asia, Australasia, the Middle East, and Africa. Given the structure of history courses in most universities around the world, it is easy enough to study the history of European nations and ignore their imperial records that matched and, in some cases, surpassed the worst of Russian/Soviet autocratic practices. The contiguous Russian Empire could neither hide the immensity of its imperial holdings nor suppress the ruthless processes of internal colonization that it employed to increase and hold onto its territorial acquisitions.[11] In the late nineteenth century, the massive Russian Empire stretched from the Baltic states in the northeast to eastern Siberia and beyond on the Pacific; Ukraine and the Caucasus in the southwest and across the Caspian Sea into Central Asia bordering China. While Great Britain could switch effortlessly between its twin identities of a liberal nation and an empire, Russia's crimes of empire could not be effaced as easily, especially since it has failed over the course of the centuries to build a democratic state to complement its empire. Perhaps the phrase that Winston Churchill had used to describe the Soviet Union in a radio broadcast of 1939, "a riddle wrapped in a mystery, inside an enigma," could also be applied to the British Empire? How could the country that delimited the royal privilege of taxation through the promulgation of the Magna Carta as early as 1215 create one of the world's most efficient, richest, and most brutal empires that spanned the globe and lasted until the late twentieth century?

This book explores the genesis and impact of a powerful intellectual and political paradigm that has de-coupled the history of Western nations from their overseas empires and posited Russia as the authoritarian alternative to Western liberalism. Autocratic centralization of power, the gulag, forced modernization, and censorship have gained Russia a fearsome reputation. While a huge industry of scholarship and literature has emerged since the eighteenth century in Russia and abroad, to account for these uniquely despotic Russian and Soviet practices, few have considered that they are comparable in many instances to Western European colonial policies. Slavery and incarceration, punitive tax policies and forcible disruption of existing trade routes, deindustrialization and manufactured famines, censorship, population transfers, violent land acquisitions, and the extensive use of state violence to appropriate human and natural resources were ubiquitous in both Russian and West European Empires. Historians have documented the Russian famine of 1891–92[12] when half a million people perished from hunger and cholera, and the Soviet-era collectivization famines of the 1930s when 5–7 million people perished. But in the field of Slavic Studies, we know less about the many famines that took place in Bengal, a rich province of British India in the eighteenth, nineteenth, and twentieth centuries. Tens of millions of people died in famines caused by excessive taxation and rapacious land policies that were instituted by the liberal British Raj. These famines were similar to those endured by Ireland, another English colony.[13] But despite the growing body of scholarship that has been produced on Western European Empires in the last few decades, the binary representation of a despotic Russia versus a liberal West has exerted an extraordinary gravitational pull in the academy, the media, and in international politics. While this political model of Russian oppression has provided intellectual justification for a robust Western foreign policy toward the Soviet Union and post-Soviet Russia, it has also constrained and shaped historical research by perpetuating the so-called uniqueness of Russian history. My book directs the conversation away from an exclusive consideration of Russia's difference with Western Europe and is part of an emerging historical field that places Russia at the crossroads of world history. At the same time it complements and builds on the prodigious scholarship produced by the paradigm of Russia versus the West, or more commonly as it is known, Russia according to the West.[14]

The key difference between Russia and the West European Empires seems to lie in the Russian inability to create a liberal state and a civil society for the Russian people within a larger illiberal empire. In the settler and non-settler colonies of European Empires, the liberties of the citizens were sharply differentiated from the unfree status of the colonized peoples through law, economic regimes, social structures, and institutional mechanisms of violence. In the British, French, and Dutch maritime empires, policies imposed a barrier between the citizens of the privileged metropole, imagined as "liberal nations," and the illiberal colonial periphery. The backwardness of the colonized and their many, many civilizational deficits became the justification for imperialism. Imperialism was an onerous duty; it was noblesse oblige; it was the obligation of European Empires to civilize those they held in thrall in their colonies. But at the same time, European nations represented themselves as independent of their maritime and overseas colonies; and traces of empire were systematically eradicated from West European culture, economy, and political systems.[15] The Russian Empire had also developed a similar vocabulary of duty, obligation, and civilizational mission with key variations, toward their internal colonies.[16] But the physical separation of a liberal Western nation from its illiberal overseas empire was enabled by geography. The contiguous land-based Russian Empire was unable to institute such a political arrangement, especially as it treated the Russian core in a manner very similar to the colonies in the periphery.

A comparison of imperial practices reveals that just as the Muscovite autocracy helped in the colonization of Russia's Eurasian landmass, English liberties and the parliamentary system provided the ideology for the creation of both settler and non-settler colonies in the New World, Middle East, Asia, Africa, and Australasia.[17] While indigenous peoples, peasants, and laborers suffered equally from the depredations of British "liberty" and Russian "despotism," the political liberties of the English nation deflected attention from the harshness of the British Empire. The idea of Russian despotism persists today because of its inability to create a liberal counterpart to its illiberal empire. While the well-documented history of European imperialism[18] has grown exponentially in the last few decades, many continue to compare Western "liberalism" with Russian imperial authoritarianism, effectively assigning to Russia a particular ideological function in world history as the illiberal other.[19]

But if we in the field of Slavic Studies have been working with a romantic and sanitized version of the history of Western Europe, many in the decolonized countries in the Global South in Asia, Africa, and Latin American have ignored the history of Russian/Soviet imperialism as a point of comparison and as a point of reference to understanding their own colonial experiences. In the revisionist Cold War histories of the Global South, Soviet socialism and modernity are routinely represented as the "good" alternative to "evil" Western capitalism and imperialistic modernization.[20] These accounts are for the most part silent about Russian and Soviet imperial practices in Eastern Europe, the Baltics, the Caucasus, Central Asia, and Siberia and therefore are critical only of American and European interventions in the nineteenth and twentieth century. Finally, the field of world history tends to be centered on the empires that Western European countries built in the Americas, Asia, Middle East, and Africa and ignores the many Russian contributions to the history of modern imperialism and modernization in Eastern Europe, the Caucasus, Central Asia, and Siberia.[21]

It is important to remember that the Russian colonization of the massive Eurasian space to the south and the east commenced at roughly the same early modern period as the European explorers traveled west to the New World, and east to India and China via the southern tip of the continent of Africa, intentionally bypassing the empires of the Middle East, North Africa, and West Asia. Moreover, the Russian Empire was built in the immense Eurasian space that had been created earlier by the victorious Asian armies that traveled along the immense distances of the steppes. Rather than split the history of Europe between that of a democratic West and an autocratic East, it is necessary to integrate the Russian imperial experience along with the other narratives of world history to fully understand the emergence of a globalized world in the twentieth century. The European domination of the world in the nineteenth century was only possible because Russia's colonization of Eurasia had helped create an interconnected and Eurocentric global world order. As John Darwin has argued in his book *After Tamerlane*, shared and comparative imperial trajectories offer one of the best ways to understand the history of the world in the last five centuries.[22] And Jane Burbank, a noted historian of Russia, was one of the first to integrate the Mongol and Russian imperial past into world history. The inclusion of the Russian/Soviet imperial experience into world history is one of the key goals of this book.

Russia in World History

To tell a comparative story about modern empires, I have used a two-pronged historical approach: structural and biographical. In the first four chapters, I compare and contrast Russian and British-Indian political prisons and exile systems, historical writing in late imperial Russia and Great Britain, Soviet collectivization of agriculture and the building of the British plantation economy in Kenya in the 1930s, and the British colonization of the Middle East after the First World War and the expansion of the Soviet Empire in Eastern Europe after the Second World War. In the remaining three chapters, I compare the writings of noted intellectuals Leo Tolstoy and Rabindranath Tagore, Emma Goldman and M. N. Roy, and Arundhati Roy and Anna Politkovskaya. As representatives of the postcolonial and postsocialist states that came into existence in the late twentieth century, a comparison of the transnational politics of Roy and Politkovskaya brings the book up to the second decade of the twenty-first century.

Each chapter is built around the lives of exemplary individuals, and the biographical details bring out the human and individual impact of imperial and modernizing systems. The field of world history excels in uncovering global processes, networks, and connections, but individuals are sometimes ignored in the vast abstractions used in this field.[23] In this book, using a reverse strategy, I have used the lives and thoughts of historical actors to illuminate the past. My eccentric cast of characters gives a flesh and blood dimension to abstract historical processes. The chapter on Tolstoy and Tagore unearths forgotten ideas and abandoned visions that have been dismissed by a triumphant and unilateral modernity. These exceptions to the rule not only illuminate the general trends of an era but also remind us that in any historical era there are always alternative ways of viewing the world and of understanding the evolution of global modernity.[24] Sometimes the trajectory of history leads to outcomes that might jar with our contemporary belief systems, but these "aberrations" need to be examined and recorded. Like seeds of endangered plants, counter-modern ideas need to be unearthed, planted, and cross-pollinated in open fields as they diversify the ecosystem and prevent the monoculture of the mind. I unearth the history of those who thought "against the grain,"[25] swam against the tide, and in short acted according to their principles even when everyone told them that they were wrong. The characters in my book challenge the neat and convenient division of the world into the East and the West, progressive and backward, North and South, and liberal and autocratic. By including the history of empires and states in their political writings, Tolstoy's and Tagore's politics blurred the division of the world into a liberal Anglo-American domain and an illiberal Russian sphere.

Roy and Emma Goldman, risking ostracism and oblivion, argued against the Soviet colonization of the global left as well as the Western monopoly of the definition of liberalism. More recently, Politkovskaya and Roy have laid bare the intellectual fault lines that separate the nation and the globe, the home and the world.

Some of my characters such as Leo Tolstoy and Rabindranath Tagore are famous. Others such as religious feminists in Poland and Egypt, Urszula Dudziak, and Zainab Al-Ghazali have attracted little scholarly attention as they challenge academic conventions and consensus about what constitutes history and who gets included in historical narratives. Three criteria have guided my selection process. First, my characters had to exemplify an important historical event or process that distinguished the empire of their origin and provide important insight into the era. Ekaterina Breshko-Breshkovskaia's and Veer Savarkar's experiences in colonial prisons were uncannily similar. Emma Goldman and M. N. Roy represent the visions of the non-Soviet left that were silenced after the Second World War. Finally, Mukhamet Shaykhmetov in the Soviet Union and Noble Laureate Wangari Maathai in Kenya were beneficiaries of a colonial education. They became vocal advocates of colonial modernization that allowed them to escape the rigors of subsistence living.

Second, my characters are complex, and in some cases morally ambiguous individuals whose views changed over time. Both Tolstoy and Tagore profited greatly from their associations with empire even as they denounced imperialism. Veer Savarkar was an advocate of Hindu nationalism and renounced India's cosmopolitan and multicultural history. During her lifetime many Russians believed that Anna Politkovskaya was an anti-national extremist, a phrase that is often used to describe Arundhati Roy in India today. Third, many of my characters represent an alternative vision of organizing the world order. After independence, to the dismay of their liberal counterparts in Poland and Egypt, religious feminists such as Urszula Dudziak and Zainab Al-Ghazali dreamed of building and belonging to a religious ecumene. Vasily Klyuchevsky and George Trevelyan had a dream that to some may seem an impossible one—to rescue the good nation from the hideous coils of imperialism. Tolstoy and Tagore argued that in order to reform the world one has to build an alternative system at home.

In Chapter 1, I return to Leo Tolstoy and Rabindranath Tagore at a critical moment when capitalist and socialist ideologies of modernity and modernization are beginning to unravel. But to reimagine the future, we need an archive of alternative thinking: one that starts with a reappraisal of select thinkers that have been shunned by both the political establishment and the academy. Tolstoy's and Tagore's political ideas are considered to be embarrassing episodes that distract from their otherwise brilliant literary careers, but in the first chapter, I argue that their writings and everyday practices have enormous emancipatory potential in the face of environmental crises, intensifying national competition, and the dilemma of modern selfhood. The novelist and the poet created a powerful vision of our shared humanity based on interconnected notions of self, ecology, and radical nonviolence.

The Siberian prison and exile system have captured the world's imagination as a dreaded system of incarceration designed by the oppressive Russian Empire. Based on a comparison of the prison experiences of Ekaterina Breshko-Breshkovskaia, a member of the Socialist Revolutionary Party of Russia, and Vinayak Damodar Savarkar, a revolutionary and Hindu fundamentalist, I ask two central questions in Chapter 2: How did Breshkovskaia's story about exile and punishment help establish the tsarist genealogy of terror while the sufferings of political prisoners in British India were completely ignored? How and why did the stories of incarceration in the Russian Empire eclipse other brutal systems of punishment designed by European Empires in the late nineteenth and early twentieth centuries?

The strange absence of empire from the history of European nations, and the stranger bifurcation of European history into nation and empire that apparently ran on parallel tracks without intersecting or even casting a shadow on the other is the subject of Chapter 3. I compare the historical writings of the British historian George Trevelyan, who, in a masterly sleight of hand, detached the history of the English nation from the British Empire. In Trevelyan's oeuvre, the empire was an extension of homegrown British trading practices with a few regrettable incidents that marred its benevolent expansion worldwide. Vasily Klyuchevsky created a compelling narrative about the Slavic people whose peregrinations to the north and then across the steppes of Eurasia resulted in a colossal empire. Unlike Trevelyan, Klyuchevsky did not sanitize the history of the imperial state. Writing in the conditions of strict censorship, he argued that the Russian peasants were the greatest victims of the absolutist state. But like Trevelyan, Klyuchevsky also ignored the violence that was wreaked in the peripheries of the empire on non-Russian peoples.

The intellectual frameworks of socialism allowed a variety of intellectuals to define a distinctive sense of selfhood. Many believed that membership in a socialist community provided a secular moral vocabulary, an acute historical consciousness, and a chance to live what both men and women perceived to be an engaged and useful life. Moreover, socialism also offered a way to link self-development with the building of a global community, one that demanded accountability from both the state and markets. But while the vast majority of the revolutionaries read their own lives through the nexus of state power, some were fellow travelers, and an even smaller minority claimed that Soviet policies and official communist parties represented a total perversion of the ideologies of socialism and anarchism. In this chapter, I analyze the works of notable revolutionaries, Emma Goldman and M. N. Roy, who courageously challenged the Leninist/Stalinist appropriation of communism, and offered a decentralized model for the global left.

The Stalinist collectivization campaign of the 1930s, along with the Great Terror, constitutes one of the darkest chapters of Soviet history. As a ruthless Soviet Union built collective farms and state-owned farms, millions of peasants lost their land and were turned into a captive and cheap labor force for agriculture and industry. A highly authoritarian system of internal passports and security services controlled peasant mobility, turning them into second-class citizens. In Chapter 5 I compare the collectivization campaign in the Soviet Union to the massive land grab that occurred in the British colony of Kenya in the 1930s when the vast majority of the native inhabitants were stripped of their land and relocated to Native Reserves that were specially created to contain them. Kenyans living in these reserves then became sources of cheap labor for the highly profitable plantation economy. I assess the terrible human and environmental impact of both socialist and capitalist forms of industrial agriculture on pre-modern societies. But I end the chapter by analyzing the memoirs of Mukhamet Shayakhmetov and Wangari Maathai. While they were highly critical of Soviet collectivization and the British plantation economy, they nonetheless valued Western education and became ardent advocates of modernization in their postcolonial nations.

Recent historiography has redefined the Cold War as a global war instead of an exclusively Soviet-American conflict. In chapter six, I revisit the Cold War through the old-fashioned lenses of European imperialism. The flurry of nation building that ensued in Eastern Europe after the First World War in the former lands of the Austro-Hungarian, Romanov, and Ottoman Empires has overshadowed the vast extension of the British and French Empires in the Middle East in the first half of the twentieth century. I compare the Anglo-French division of the former lands of the Ottoman Empire in the aftermath of the First World War with the extension of the Soviet Empire in Eastern Europe after 1945. The two world wars provided opportunities for further imperial expansion for these seasoned world powers. I end the chapter by comparing the process of decolonization in Poland and Egypt, one that gave religious feminists such as Urszula Dudziak and Zainab Al-Ghazali a chance to voice radical visions of the future as they transitioned from empire to nation.

In the seventh and final chapter, I analyze the writings of journalists and activists Anna Politkovskaya and Arundhati Roy from two opposing perspectives: the nationalist critique generated from sections within Russia and India that see Roy and Politkovskaya as "tools of the West," and the self-understanding and self-articulation of Roy and Politkovskaya who claim to function outside the boundaries of the nation as global citizens. Where should a woman's allegiance lie: to herself, to her family, to the nation, or the world? In the last part of the chapter, the eminent historian Lisa Kirschenbaum answers important questions about historical philosophy, methodology, and the politics of writing transnational history when one lives in a globalized world that is unaccountably regulated by borders, passports, and national jurisdictions.

Kirschenbaum adds a valuable perspective that is in contrast with some of my political views expressed in this chapter. Her robust defense of transnational scholarship and politics echoes and reflects some of Tolstoy's and Tagore's ideas that have been presented at the beginning of the book. The last chapter ends on a note of uncertainty and non-resolution that reflects my own mental state and my mixed feelings toward the strange coexistence of strong nation states and currents of globalization. I am mulling over the various ways to understand the world, and more importantly, considering the most useful ways to inhabit it. Rather than present the final word on the competing claims of the nation and the world, I offer arguments and perspectives for each side in the hopes that it will help the reader think more deeply about geopolitical arrangements, political obligations, and the rights and duties that come with membership in a polity. Instead of thinking about the nation and the world in binary terms, we are better served when we think about these interrelated concepts in an intellectual continuum. There is nothing to prevent us from building a sturdy home with strong bridges that connect us to the world. Almost a century ago in his novel *The Home and the World*, Tagore reminded us that it was impossible to choose one over the other, and, more importantly, no one should be forced to make that terrible choice.

The best conversations like the best friendships are based on the ability to speak rationally about matters that we may disagree about. A monochromatic world where we all agree in self-righteous union would be a lot like living on the moon: boring, predictable, and most certainly, asphyxiating. Our world is immeasurably enriched by the inclusion of diverse points of view and I hope that my audience will enjoy the array of personalities, opinions, interpretations, and facts presented in this book.

1

Tolstoy and Tagore

Principles of Global Thinking

Despite my best intentions, one way or the other, bearded prophets have ruled my life. Rabindranath Tagore, the Noble Prize-winning poet laureate of Bengal, was one such formidable presence, and the ascetic image of the handsome man clad in dark robes cast a very long shadow over my "childhood" and "youth." The main thoroughfare of the city of Kolkata was named after Tagore; his ancestral home in Jorasanko, Kolkata, was a site of pilgrimage as was his educational center Shantiniketan, in Bolpur. During the winter months, the broken pavements of Kolkata rang with his music, poetry, dance-dramas, and plays, as cultural venues, big and small, competed to perform the works of Tagore. His songs blared from loudspeakers, and his photographs hung in street corners, stores, and homes were adorned with fresh garlands of flowers daily. Every child could recite his poetry, every woman could sing his songs, while every man knew his novels intimately. And what annoyed me most was the way in which people closed their eyes reverentially whenever Tagore's name was pronounced, as if invoking the name of a deity.

I grew up in a household whose adoration of Tagore bordered on the fanatical. My grandparents could recite chapter and verse from his novels and plays, and my sister and my mother conducted entire conversations in Tagorean song and verse at both lunch and dinner! I was the lone holdout, countering their admiration for this progenitor of modern Bengali culture with juvenile and ignorant sarcasm. I fled the close confines of this dense literary culture for the wider steppes of Russia, hoping to find broader vistas. Unfortunately, and to my deep regret, I found that Russians had produced both Tolstoy and a comparable Tolstoyan cult slightly before that of Tagore.[1] In Russia too people tended to close their eyes reverentially whenever the name of the great bearded man was invoked. They asked me again and again if I had visited Iasnaia Poliana, and had I indeed read Tolstoy's great novels. In Russian? I dutifully plowed through *Anna Karenina* and *War and Peace*, without hearing the magic in the words or deciphering the meaning in the characters as they struggled with history and daily life. Instead, I turned with relief to the didactic texts of a semi-bearded Lenin. Here was a man with a plan, clear and direct, with no obfuscation about self-realization, no confusing moralizing, and a simple recipe for modernizing the world while also creating socioeconomic equality, plenty, and freedom. What could possibly go wrong in the aftermath of 1917 when it was obvious to everyone but the most obtuse and reactionary that the state could undertake modernization and redistribution more efficiently and equitably than greedy capitalists?

My graduate education in the United States taught me that almost everything went wrong once the communists came to power. Party leaders morphed from wordy intellectuals into bloody dictators. The ruthless modernization of industry and agriculture resulting in millions of casualties also led to bleak barracks-style communism, to use Trotsky's immortal phrase. Finally, the Soviet Union ran out of juice, money, ideas, and defenders. It collapsed in an ignominious heap in 1991, and few came to hear Gorbachev on December 25, 1991, at the Kremlin when he officially pronounced the Soviet Union dead. Meanwhile, there was another man with a plan waiting in the wings of world history. Clean-shaven Milton Friedman and his many acolytes at Chicago, Princeton, and Harvard, and in the centers of power in Washington, Nairobi, Cairo, New Delhi, Beijing, and Mexico City to name only a few, having triumphantly buried communism, proclaimed that the logic of capitalism and the "free market" would usher in a world of plenty and freedom. Riches made at the top, facilitated by the policies crafted by compliant and pro-globalization politicians, would eventually trickle down lifting all boats worldwide. And during the 1990s and early 2000s, we witnessed the incredible miracle as hundreds of millions of people worldwide were lifted out of absolute poverty, especially in Asia, Africa, and Latin America.[2] Consumerism was the new panacea worldwide, and the more we borrowed and the more we spent, the more we were contributing to global prosperity. The global recession of 2008 created a rare moment of clarity when we realized that capitalism, like socialism in its early stages, did initially create spectacular growth rates and did ameliorate absolute poverty.[3] But then like socialism it stalled and only the additions of new markets, cheap labor, or "free" natural resources could sustain the initially high growth rates. Neoliberal structural reforms created new jobs throughout the world via new global supply chains, but they also created monumental inequality, concentrating resources and riches at the very top that elected officials struggled to ameliorate, very ineffectually I might add. Scientific and technological innovations coupled with automation disproportionately skewed rewards toward entrepreneurs, technologists with advanced intellectual skills, hollowing out the vaunted middle class in the West while the rising middle class in Asia became the engine of world economic growth.

The division between the right and the left, between capitalism and communism, has created the chimera of an unbridgeable and fatal binary opposition that has defined politics, economics, and culture in the twentieth and the twenty-first centuries. But if one looks more closely at this so-called chasm, one finds that both communist and capitalist states are uncritical advocates of a certain mode of economic modernization based on resource extraction, factory production, organized labor, financial systems to regulate capital flows, urbanization, centralized state power, and imperialism. Both ideologies are invested in a category of selfhood that is based on individualism, material self-fashioning, and self-fulfillment through achievement and accumulation. Socialism and capitalism are profoundly anti-nature and work with the fatal self-deception that man does not exist within the ecology of nature, but can take unthinkingly from nature to create the spaces of modernity. Both entertain an impoverished vision of environmentalism as the preservation of national parks, and nature reserves, and continue to believe mistakenly, even though the evidence accumulates daily, that present-day modernization and consumerism are both desirable and sustainable worldwide.

These two systems of modernization are totalitarian in their denunciation of other ideologies that explain selfhood, community, and the universal and have dubbed them utopian and anti-modern. This exclusionary political vision has profoundly shaped the academy where we are trained to consider only those intellectuals who have accepted the basic premises of industrial modernity as an undifferentiated good, and as the only possible goal for all of mankind. We dismiss those who question or challenge the inevitability of the global spread of industrial modernity and label them as utopians, anarchists, cranks, pacifists, tree-huggers, impractical dreamers, feminists, environmentalists, and the most deadly of all academic insults: civilizational and religious thinkers. We banish them summarily from the stern departments of history, political science, economics, and philosophy to those more receptive to unorthodox ideas such as literature, religious studies, ethnic studies, and women's studies. When we do summon these thinkers, it is to illustrate their general irrelevance to the contemporary world. In the words of a recent commentator, "the social changes of the last few decades have made the whole outlook of these thinkers (Tagore, Iqbal, and Liang Shuming) seem quaint and quixotic."[4] Less tactfully, Martin Malia opined, "Tolstoi's [sic] 'mature' solution to the enigma of life may therefore be interpreted either as a neurotic regression into infantilism or as a true transcendence of carnal contingency, depending on one's point of view."[5]

The unraveling of intellectual systems in the twenty-first century that have created and sustained capitalist and socialist ideologies of modernity and modernization affords us an unparalleled opportunity to reimagine the future. But in order to do so, we need to create an archive of alternative thinking, a new corpus of intellectual history that can lead us beyond the rehashing of arguments on the right and the left, and about the various ways to conceptually grasp the world. These include arguments about the market versus state control of the economy, capitalist versus state-sponsored development, class war versus meritocratic hierarchy, liberalism versus totalitarianism, individualism versus community, and my least favorite and perhaps the most oxymoronic phrase ever created: nature versus civilization as if civilization is or ever can be distinct from nature. In this first chapter, I will argue that the pathways to the future start in the recent past with thinkers such as Tolstoy and Tagore, literary giants, but whose political ideas were deeply misunderstood, mocked, criticized, satirized, and for the most part ignored by the literati, academics, and politicians who have controlled the dissemination of their views since their death. Today most seem to agree that Tolstoy and Tagore were rather deficient in their understanding of politics and economics and that their forays into these realms are considered to be embarrassing episodes that distract from their otherwise brilliant literary careers.[6]

Drawing inspiration from Isaiah Berlin, probably the only scholar in the world who has analyzed the political thought of both Tolstoy and Tagore, but alas in separate essays, I challenge the academic wall that separates Tolstoy's and Tagore's 'brilliant' literary legacy from their 'puerile' political thought.[7] By relabeling the categories of the literary and the political we can create an alternative global archive, unearth a genealogy of counter-modernity, and rediscover an intellectual tradition that challenges the pre-eminence that modern ideologies of the right and the left have enjoyed for more than a century. Tolstoy's and Tagore's ideas have enormous political and emancipatory potential in the face of climate change, the economic ravages of global modernity, and the dilemma of modern selfhood that can only express itself through acts of egotism, accumulation, and violence. More importantly, their canon of political thought has the radical potential to move us beyond the debates between the right and the left, the division of the political and literary, east and west, north and the south, and the division of historical time between modernity and backwardness.

While Tolstoy's influence on Gandhi has been well documented through their correspondence and through scholarship on the subject serving to cement Indo-Russian relations, few have compared Tolstoy and Tagore as influential political thinkers whose ideas have the power to shape world politics in the twenty-first century. Tolstoy died in 1910 at the height of his global prominence. Tagore was drawn into the international limelight in 1913 when he received the Nobel Prize for literature for his slender volume of poetry, *Gitanjali*, a prize that unaccountably eluded Tolstoy, at that point in time the far more accomplished man of letters of the two. Even though their lives overlapped for several decades, Tolstoy died before Tagore's poetry was translated into English. Tagore, a master of erotic allusions and the imagery of desire, was unimpressed by Tolstoy's strictures on women and sexuality in the *Kreutzer Sonata*. He wrote rather uncharitably, "tried to read Anna Karenina. Could not go on, found it so unpleasant. I can not understand what pleasure can be had out of such a sickly book. . . . I cannot stand for long these complicated, bizarre, perverse goings-on."[8] Although Tolstoy and Tagore failed to develop a personal relationship, intellectually they reached very similar conclusions about politics and statecraft, self and universality, and nature and modernity.

Despite their predilection for black robes and unkempt beards that conjured up images of Eastern prophets, Tolstoy and Tagore were neither Eastern thinkers nor anti-modern champions of religion and traditionalism. And they exhibited considerable discomfort with their roles as religious prophets.[9] They were cosmopolitan intellectuals who profited handsomely from the global literary marketplace that European imperialism created in the late nineteenth century and from the capital land markets. But for some reason, they stopped midstream in the course of their brilliant careers to take a closer look at the orthodoxies of modernity, both from the right and left, that even during the course of their lifetimes was becoming insurmountable. Tolstoy and Tagore were cantankerous and cussed men, opinionated and vainglorious to an inordinate degree. They were absurdly sensitive to the stings and barbs of public opinion even when they intentionally challenged the popular nostrums of the day: be it imperialism, nationalism, religious and racial chauvinism, economic modernization, and revolutionary violence. They abhorred the unfreedom that membership in any organization or social milieu necessarily imposes and refused to join a political party.[10] They reserved the right to speak even when their audiences could not or refused to understand them. Though they were deeply wounded by the many attacks that were leveled at them in print and in person, they pursued their lonely quest till the bitter end of their long-lived lives: speaking the political truths that few around them wanted to hear. Finally, they created a new model for elite behavior that was unprecedented for its time and one that merits urgent reconsideration.

Tagore and Tolstoy were powerful men who defied the might of the British and the Russian Empires openly and with contumely. Such was their global fame that, while their works were censored and banned, neither government was rash enough to attempt to imprison them or silence them permanently. Despite the many accolades and the material rewards that they received during the course of their careers, both remained to the very end tormented, perverse, and vocally anti-establishment figures, searching in vain for that inner peace and contentment that eluded them their entire lives. They were lonely men, for the most part, finding rare companions among the multitudes that thronged them. But their inner demons as well as the sufferings that they witnessed led them to roam in wide intellectual pastures, experiment with different modes of expression, and produce works of great intellectual complexity that were expressed in highly accessible prose and poetry.[11] They died unquiet deaths, deeply apprehensive about the future. Tolstoy died in 1910 before the carnage of the First World War and the Russian Revolution, afraid that unchecked imperialism would lead to a global catastrophe. And Tagore, who had witnessed the devastation of the First World War, deeply dreaded the onset of the Second World War. He died in 1940 fearing that India might only gain a nominal freedom and that it would lose its spirit of tolerance and the profound syncretism of its cultural traditions.[12]

Tolstoy and Tagore were the products of two parallel and competing empires that fought unceasingly for the control of Asia and the Middle East during the nineteenth and the twentieth centuries, and the profits from their imperial associations, as well as imperial citizenship, rendered them acutely sensitive to and conscious of the many ways that power functions. The Tolstoy family had served the mighty Russian state as noblemen for many generations, while Tagore's grandfather had more recently amassed a fortune by participating in imperial commerce and the lucrative British-run opium trade in Asia. Both took for granted ancestral estates, the comfort of educated extended families, retinues of servitors, and an assured position in Moscow, the seat of the old Russian nobility, and Calcutta, the capital of British India, even as they despised urban life. Fame came easily and early, and neither had to struggle to engage the attention of their eager and appreciative audiences. Tolstoy and Tagore furnished the cultural content of Russian and Indian nationalism with their novels, songs, and poetry, but they soon tired of what Tagore was to call "these narrow domestic walls" and Tolstoy "the boring and vulgar Anna Karenina." They fled the limited Russian/Indian nation that they themselves helped create with their literary masterpieces, for more global visions of the future.[13]

Tagore and Tolstoy saw themselves primarily as universal thinkers who engaged in serious conversations about a global counter-modernity that they tried to articulate throughout their lives. Voracious readers and ardent bibliophiles, they drew deeply on the literature, philosophical writings, and political activities of Western philosophers, poets, socialists, anarchists, environmentalists, and religious thinkers (Proudhon, Thoreau, Henry George, Adin Ballou, John Ruskin, William Morris, Paul Valery, Henri Bergson, Kant, Schopenhauer, Shakespeare, Milton, Shelley, and Keats to name only a few); on classical and religious texts of various traditions: Christian, Buddhist, Confucian, Islamic, Indic, and Sufi; and on a variety of folk and indigenous traditions. They curated a world cultural heritage visible today in Tolstoy's library at Yasnaia Poliana and Tagore's library at the Jorasanko Thakurbari. They also created a powerful vision of humanity based on nested and radically interconnected notions of self, community, and nature, and insisted inconveniently for their times that all political and ethical solutions had to be universal in their application.

Tolstoy and Tagore rejected the notion that the Russian Empire or the Indian state could prosper at the expense of their enemies, or that it was possible to accumulate unlimited material wealth without violating the rights of others, or that the spaces of modernity could be built at the expense of the natural environment. Tolstoy emerged as a fierce critic of state power, capitalism, and imperialism in an age of unbridled Russian and European military conquest. He lashed out at the Tsar, liberals, Slavophiles, the Russian Orthodox Church, revolutionaries, and socialists. And Tagore, to the immense anger and incomprehension of his compatriots: nationalists, socialists, and religious leaders, who formulated the "derivative discourse" of Indian nationalism against an oppressive British Empire, subjected the concept of the nation and nationalism to a sustained and perceptive critique throughout much of his life.[14] Their timing was ghastly, their frankness insupportable, but they refused to sacrifice their vision of global justice in the name of pragmatism and expediency, or give in to the insistent demands of racial, religious, or national communities. But when is it ever a good time to speak truth to power?

Their rebellious personalities and propensity to flout social and intellectual norms stemmed from their aristocratic backgrounds, their lack of formal schooling, and their lack of formal religious instruction. Tolstoy flunked out of Kazan University early in his career, and Tagore, who was sent by his father to study law in England, spent his time reading and writing excellent poetry instead. They were dismayed by the institutional training, regurgitation, and rote memorization that seemed to be so prevalent in modern educational systems and worried that it would suppress creative and independent thought among the youth.[15] Tolstoy fitfully experimented with popular education his whole life at Yasnaia Poliana, producing a wonderful corpus of children's literature in the process. Tagore, in addition to writing children's literature that has nourished generations, first set up a school, Santiniketan, then a university, Viswabharati, and finally, a center for rural reconstruction in Sriniketan: institutions that still exist on his father's estate in Bolpur, West Bengal.

Tolstoy rejected the authority of the Orthodox Church, the Russian monastic establishment, and reinterpreted the very Gospels in his bid to find the real Christianity, shorn of accretions by structures of authority. Tagore came from a family of iconoclasts. His father, Debendranath Tagore, had created a new religion, so critical was he of the orthodoxies of Hinduism, and Tagore himself mercilessly lampooned Hindu fundamentalism in his famous novel, *Gora*, and the power of the priestly class in his play, *Biswarjan*. They also hated the literary establishment, composed of universities, scholars, professional writers, and journalists, believing that the academic separation of art and life, knowledge and wisdom, intellectual convictions and daily life, and religion and spirituality was profoundly immoral and a major impediment to real progress. Tolstoy and Tagore argued that this modern disjunction between poiesis, the art of imagination, and praxis, the ability for the practical execution of ideas, was the single greatest threat to both civilization and nature.

Tolstoy and Tagore rejected the power of the scholar and priest, of ritualized and archived knowledge, and looked for answers in the world of nature, in observations of human behavior, in reason, in global knowledge, and their own experiences. They believed that literature should be more than a description and analysis of the flaws of human nature and society. And they were in turn deeply criticized for trying to make their literature into an instrument of individual transformation and social change.[16] Coincidentally, Tagore and Tolstoy were married to conventional women who were many years younger than themselves. While Mrinalini had the good sense to die early and relieve Tagore of her humdrum presence, Sonya, depending on whose side you take, either harried Tolstoy to his grave on account of her jealousy, and anger, or saved the Tolstoy family from penury by intervening against his more grandiose gestures of generosity. While Mrinalini sold her jewelry to provide funds for Tagore's experimental school in Santiniketan, Sonya tried without success to draw her husband back from what she believed to be Tolstoy's senseless religious and political experiments on himself and his family.[17]

Intentional Selflessness

Tolstoy and Tagore were ruthless in their self-introspection, offering to a bemused public their moments of despair and weakness, ungenerous thoughts, and intemperate desires. Tolstoy shared his every weakness, sexual longings, melancholia, and every selfish action in his diaries and fiction. Tagore, the more private of the two, used his poetry, novels, songs, and paintings to probe the dark recesses of his soul without identifying himself in the self-lacerating manner that Tolstoy adopted. They suffered from intense bouts of depression and existential despair throughout their lives and, in their continual restlessness longed for inner peace, stasis, fleeting moments of transcendence, and even death. Toward the end of their life they believed that only death would calm their internal turmoil, and rather than fear death, they passionately longed for a final release from their spiritual and emotional sufferings.[18]

Tolstoy and Tagore believed that all ethical and moral prescriptions must begin with an honest consideration of the canvas of the self. But self-reflection and self-scrutiny were not only a means to improve the self and to create a better and improved version: richer, more successful, more popular, more important, and more powerful. Tolstoy identified the problem of selfhood early in his life. In his diaries, along with the demands of his intemperate sexuality, he identifies vanitas or the insistent demands of his ego as the prime cause of his suffering.[19]

In *My Confession* (1882), Tolstoy repeatedly ridicules his younger self that pursued perfection only for the sake of distinguishing himself from his contemporaries, or sought distinction and fame among his social circle. Tolstoy confronted the problem of the self acutely at the height of his career when he had achieved unimaginable fame and success, and when there were few laurels left to win in the world.[20] He recorded his existential despair, much in the manner of Augustine's and Rousseau's confessions as Irina Paperno has so brilliantly demonstrated. In *My Confession* and *Notes of a Madman* (1897) Tolstoy notes with utter consternation that there are no rational reasons for his despair as he is of sound mind and body, owner of a large estate, a happily married husband, and father. He realizes to his extreme horror that the prospect of acquiring more of what he already has in terms of additional acreage of lands, of gaining unimaginable fame surpassing that of even Gogol, Pushkin, and Shakespeare, does not bring him any additional comfort or happiness. His mid-life depression deepens as Tolstoy realizes that he has achieved all the goals that he has set himself, and does not even know what it is that he, Tolstoy, wants from life. Tolstoy contemplates suicide as a possible option, but he keeps returning to the three consequential questions that he then tries to answer for the next three decades of his life. Who am I? Why do I live? What must I do?

Tolstoy's readings in the scientific disciplines confirm the essential meaningless of life while his readings of the Old Testament, Buddha, and Schopenhauer remind him that death is inevitable.[21] Tolstoy identifies four ways that people customarily use to deal with one's impending mortality. Most of us postpone the problem of life and death out of sheer ignorance. Interestingly, Tagore also writes about the trope of ignorance, but in a less judgmental way than Tolstoy, who attributes the quality of ignorance primarily to young women. Tagore understands ignorance as *avidya*, a concept derived from the Upanishads. According to this tradition, *avidya* is neither intentional nor a result of innate female stupidity as Tolstoy alleges. Rather, it is a state of consciousness during which we, having failed to engage in serious self-scrutiny, lack knowledge of our true self. Lack of self-knowledge then forces us to rely on the incorrect version of our self that society and our egotistical vision reflects back to us.[22] In Tolstoy's classification the second way to deal with questions of life and death is epicurean; in which we luxuriate in our material acquisitions and feel proud about our achievements until we face the prospect of impending death. Lacking spiritual resources and community we die screaming like the protagonist of his famous short story, "The Death of Ivan Ilyich" (1886). The third option is to commit suicide rather than wait for death. While self-annihilation is the path of the coward, the fourth is possibly the worst choice. It is the path of weakness when we know full well how our life story is going to end, but go through the motions anyway keeping the fiction of our immortality alive. Instead of taking remedial action to alleviate our inner torments and prepare for a good death by living a good life, we wait endlessly for nothing.

Faith was the last option, and Tolstoy candidly says that his faith is both experiential and intentional.[23] Faith assuaged momentarily his anguish and spurred him onto further action, and in Tolstoy's canon, God, like nature, functioned as a metaphor for intentional selflessness. These were both imaginative and physical locations that afforded temporary respite from the incessant demands of the self where Tolstoy experienced temporary freedom from fear: fear of the essential meaningless of life, fear of failure, and the fear of dying. Tolstoy, although he deeply envied those who had unquestioning faith, could never bring himself to believe unconditionally in the omnipotent God, the trinity, and in the creation myth that sustained millions of laboring folk. Tolstoy admired the credulous faith of the poor, but like his own brilliant but tortured creation, *Father Sergius* (1911), Tolstoy found it difficult to sustain prolonged meditation and prayers in his own life.

In the short story "Where Love Is, God Is" (1885), Tolstoy shows quite clearly that we create the "god effect" in society through intentional acts of kindness (another location for selflessness), when we in effect become our brother's keeper. To his surprise, Tolstoy did not find answers to his three questions in the practices of the Orthodox Church, or the monastic establishment, or even in the divinity of Christ. Tolstoy argued with bitter and biting wit in both *Kingdom of God Is Within You* (1893), and in his novel *Resurrection* (1899), that he could not join any religious institution that rejected universality, or one that bred chauvinism, intolerance, and ethnic particularity. Tolstoy claimed in many of his writings that the Russian Orthodox Church cooperated with the state to sustain the system of economic inequality, and compliantly put forth mountains of propaganda to legitimize the institutional violence that the Russian state exerted through prison, courts, police, and armies. Not surprisingly, the Orthodox Church excommunicated Tolstoy in 1901, a decision that it has yet to reverse a century later.

Refusing to accept almost two millennia of ecclesiastical practice and commentary, Tolstoy in his characteristically imperious and ruthlessly independent fashion rewrote the very Gospels, presenting Christ's truth anew for modern times.[24] In his *Gospels in Brief* we find a demystified, a demythologized, and barely recognizable Christ. Neither the Son of God, nor the sacrificial lamb who gave his life for his believers, nor the bearer of the Holy Spirit: but a most rational man. Jesus, in Tolstoy's estimation, offered simple solutions to the problems of selfhood, global inequality, and violence through his five commandments: do no ill to others (Google's logo), do not covet another's partner, refuse to take oaths of any kinds (or refuse to legitimize any political authority or hierarchy), do not resist evil (as violence begets violence), and do not discriminate between fellow men and foreigners.

According to Tolstoy, religious rituals, faith in God, or even the tantalizing prospect of life after death that the acceptance of Christian sacraments promised, distracted one from Christ's simple but powerful injunction: to love your neighbor as yourself.[25] How did one go about doing this and what were the practical ways to achieve this seemingly impossible goal? How did the implementation of this extraordinarily simple but horrendously difficult precept affect one's sense of self as a physically bounded entity: one who is taught to live for self-gratification and self-fulfillment alone? Tolstoy sought selflessness as a final act of desperation that was borne of intense emotional suffering. He wanted to relinquish the enormous burden of the many selves that he had acquired: the nobleman, the military officer, the wealthy landowner, the provincial administrator, the family patriarch, and even the brilliant man of letters. The dictum to love one's neighbor as oneself has usually been interpreted as an act of altruism or an act of religiosity, but in Tolstoy's philosophy, intentional selflessness offered a respite, a momentary cessation from the insistent calls of one's ego, the drumbeat in one's ears, the racing heart, the panic in the dry mouth that ultimately threatens to strangle the self.

Unlike Buddha, Tolstoy did not achieve inner peace even though he achieved enlightenment of a sort. But more remarkably for his age and time, he tried to implement the truths that he gained from his readings and self-reflection into the rhythms of his daily life. What commentators found magnificent in his fiction, for example, the famous mowing scene in *Anna Karenina* when Levin the idealistic landowner works in rhythm with his peasants in the fields, seemed less impressive in real life. When Tolstoy donned the peasant blouse it appeared to many including his wife Sonya to be artificial and affected. When Tolstoy became a vegetarian to protest militarism and violence, donated the sales of his nonfiction writings to various social causes, sewed his shoes, completed his self-assigned "bread labor" in the fields, or even emptied his chamber pot to minimize exploiting the labor of others, he incurred the wrath of his family and his social circle. Generations of literati such as Ivan Turgenev, Vladimir Nabokov, Boris Eikhenbaum, A. N. Wilson, Gary Saul Morson, and more recently Rosamund Bartlett and others are still puzzled and irritated by the simple fact that Tolstoy, like Socrates, tried to live by his principles. They would have Tolstoy write, think, and lecture about principles in time-honored and time-approved academic fashion, instead of trying to live them howsoever unsuccessfully. The complete break between one's daily life and art, the lack of correspondence between personal words and deeds, belief and action, knowledge and application is celebrated, advocated, and actively encouraged by a triumphant modernity that feeds on this radical displacement in human consciousness between cause and effect, text and context, and reading and being. It is the equivalent of recycling bins and trashcans in our public spaces: receptacles that shield us from the origins and consequences of the material and emotional waste that we generate daily and preclude any troubling thought about the destination of our mountains of garbage.

While Tolstoy was trying to fuse philosophy and daily life, he was also a bit of a killjoy and believed rather unreasonably that one should renounce all earthly pleasure. Tagore on the other hand, like an unapologetic bee, gathered honey where he could, in sensuality and the contemplation of physical forms, in the paradoxical savagery and the sweetness of tropical seasons, in the unselfconscious joy of children's play, in the bacchanalian reversal of social hierarchy, and intellectual creativity. He sought joyfulness to counteract the intense despair brought on by personal losses (the death of his beloved sister-in-law, his wife, two of his children, and even that of his grandson). The many intemperate attacks that Indian nationalists, politicians, and literary critics, at home and abroad, leveled at him throughout his life were extremely painful, even though it was often Tagore's unorthodox views that invited such extreme and critical responses. This was further compounded by external events such as the terrible conditions in India under a rapacious British rule, the growing communal violence in a nationalist Bengal, the horrors of the First World War, growing totalitarianism in Europe and Asia, and the relentless militarism that was sweeping the globe at the turn of the twentieth century. The different forms of wistfulness, melancholy, sorrow, grief, and anguish recur constantly in Tagore's oeuvre, punctuating even his most flagrant songs of joy: "I un-slip my heart in torrents of bliss, but the soul cries forlorn."[26] Why were these moments of joy so few, the spring blossoms so transient, and the rain showers on the parched and cracked earth so rationed and so episodic? What prevents us human beings from inhabiting more completely the pleasure gardens of their imagination? More perceptively, the poet asks, is pain the most necessary component of pleasure? Can we experience moments of happiness only when they puncture the periods of our most intense suffering?[27]

In *Sonar Tari* (Golden Boat, 1894), a brilliant and enigmatic poem, young Tagore offers a partial answer to this paradox. A farmer sits in his rice field isolated by the rising waters of the monsoon-swollen river. A golden boat appears on the horizon steered by a mysterious but vaguely familiar figure.

The boat approaches the bank and the farmer gives generously of his harvest, but when he wants to climb aboard the boatman demurs, claiming that there is no place for him. The poem can be read as a parable of modernity, where the worker is dehumanized, and the products of his labor expropriated without due compensation. But at another level, it is also the plea of a naïve young poet who wants the world to accept both his poetic contributions as well as himself, the creator. In a letter to a critic, Tagore provided a wistful explanation for the poem. "Take all I have. I have labored only for you; my happiness lies in giving to you. Take all I have. But do not cast me aside, do not forget me: preserve my impress in my work."[28]

But at a later stage, especially in a series of essays entitled *Atmaparichay* (Self-Knowing or Self-Introduction) that were published posthumously in 1943, we find a more mature Tagore who is beginning to overcome his desire for love, fame, and social acceptance and, more importantly, to realize the poverty and shallowness of his desires. Rather than withdraw from the world in anger and pain upon facing rejection, he is learning, albeit haltingly, to hew his solitary road and to realize the possibilities inherent in limitless travel. The poet no longer desires to compel or beg the world to recognize his existence, but like a waterfall making its way to the ocean,[29] he wishes to explore the world. Intentional selflessness in this instance is not an annihilation of the self, but an unimaginable expansion of the possibilities and the contours of the self. The poet's ambition is limitless: he reaches out to grasp the entire universe, and like William Blake, he wishes "to see a world in a grain of sand and heaven in a wildflower" (Auguries of Innocence). The outward-looking self becomes a bridge that leads to discoveries, new knowledge, and unmoored and torrential creativity that does not require a public seal of approval to acknowledge its originality. The artist becomes a medium through which universal truths are enunciated, a body that registers a thousand sensations, eyes that can see myriad wonders, a voice that sings a transcendent song of joy, and a mind that roams freely through the immense universe. Freed from the iron cage of our incessant self-regard that continuously seeks the approbation of others, we contemplate the world with reinvigorated senses. "I seek the unknown in the midst of the known, and a song is born of my wonderment" (*Akash Bhora Surjo Tara* [Skies Laden with Stars], 1924). While the poet uses the word "*bismaye*" (wonderment) to describe his mental state in the refrain of this poem, Tolstoy used the verb "udivliat" (to wonder) to describe Alyosha's final state before his death, in his brilliant short story "Alyosha the Pot" (1905).

Tolstoy, who advocated the practice of love as a cardinal rule both in philosophy and in politics, and sought unconditional love throughout his long life from his friends and family members, gave us very few examples of the varieties of love in his fiction.[30] In Tagore's oeuvre, we find that the experience of love in its many incarnations: carnal, divine, maternal, obsessive, fetishistic, self-serving, and selfless, but regardless of the form, love for another sets the self on its outward journey.[31] He presents us with the infinite ways that love can breach the levees and dykes surrounding our bounded self.[32] Tagore drew from the images of love that are omnipresent in classical Indian literature, art, and mythology, especially from the plays of Kalidasa, and the poetry of Jayadeva that celebrates the Radha-Krishna love cycle so central to the Indian literary classics as well as the popular imagination. But he also found the same emotional register of self-transcendence and ecstasy in the Sufi verses by Hafiz and Rumi, the Bhakti cult poetry of Dadu, Kabir, and Lalan, in the lyricism of Wordsworth, Keats, and Shelley, and the songs of the wandering Hindu and Muslim minstrels (baul) of Bengal. Tagore struggled his whole life to fashion a universal language of communication and realized that his poetic imagination like a mighty river was rendered more powerful still by the conjoining of distant tributaries.

According to Tagore, "a poet is a true poet when he can make his personal idea joyful to all men." In order to do so the poet has to find the appropriate means of communication. "This common language has its own law that the poet must discover and follow, by doing so he becomes true and attains poetical immortality."[33] Tagore believed that our personal joy is but a reflection of cosmic joy, and he expanded on the concept of a joyful universe that he found both in the Upanishads and in the lyrical descriptions of nature found in Vedic hymns. According to the Taittiriya Upanishad the world is born of bliss, sustained by joy, and will return inevitably to a state of *anandam*. Tagore differentiates between the states of happiness and joy: arguing that the former is timid and self-contained, discriminating, and rule-bound, while the latter is transcendent, wild, anarchic, and all-encompassing. Happiness is selfish in wishing to preserve its meager gains for oneself, while joy scatters its stores of abundance recklessly, heedless of the future. Can the experience of *anandam* or transcendental bliss be understood either in a nonmystical or a non-metaphysical way? Where is this fountain of eternal delight and, more importantly, how do we fashion a self that is ready to drink from its lucid waters?

Tagore, like Tolstoy, was unmoved by organized religion and ritual from an early age, and he cast away the sacred thread that marked his Brahmin status, publicly marking his noncompliance with the caste system in India. But he meditated daily on the Gayatri Mantra, a chant from the Rig Veda that enjoins us to seek the wisdom that allows us to comprehend the glory and magnificence of this unbounded universe.[34] Tagore repeatedly invoked his "Jiban Debata" (Lord of My Life), a concept that he never could quite articulate, although he drew it from the folkloric concept of "maner manush" (man of the heart) that was so prevalent in rural Bengal of his time. But more interesting is the boon that Tagore asks of this unknown deity. He begs the deity, "I the ever old you take again as new. Bring me within life's bond, I pray, the wedding tie renew."[35] Tagore did not fear death or old age per se but he feared losing his capacity for elation and wonder. To be unable to feel joy or the intimations of ecstasy appeared to him a state more terrifying than death itself. But unlike Tolstoy with his powerful biblical commandments, Tagore refuses to give us the key, the word, and the path, claiming that he is neither a theologian nor a philosopher, merely a poet.[36] But he implores us to adopt a path that attunes our impoverished senses to the music of the spheres.

Principles of Global Thinking

After 1991 with the onset of globalization it has become fashionable to study world history and literature, comparative economics and politics, and global ecosystems and weather patterns. But Tolstoy and Tagore, with their poor sense of timing, enunciated principles of global thinking at a historical period when concepts of universalism were under fierce attack from competing empires and emerging nation-states. By the late nineteenth century European Empires, forgetting their history of classical, Christian, and Enlightenment universalism, developed elaborate categories of class, race, and civilizational thinking to justify their brutal invasions of the Americas, Eurasia, Asia, and Africa. Colonized countries in response to systems of cultural imperialism that were imposed through the media, educational systems, and bureaucratic practices defended the most retrograde elements of their culture, and fabricated "authentic pre-colonial pasts."[37] These then became the justification and basis for extreme national chauvinism and postcolonial authoritarianism. Thus the caste system that had been an elastic social arrangement through the ages, child marriage, ritual compliance, and even the protection of cows suddenly became crucial to Indian identity. National pride among colonial and postcolonial people rested on a disavowal of history that corresponded in equal measure to the ahistorical arrogance of the colonizers. History became a game of political football between academics and politicians both in the empire and the metropole.

The fifth commandment in Tolstoy's typology was that one should not differentiate between countrymen and foreigners. The love for one's fellow beings had to be applicable universally like Kant's Categorical Imperative, or it was doomed to failure. Tolstoy had a fine understanding of the linked and essentially relational nature of the state, violence, and imperialism from his experiences as a landowner and from his brief service in the Russian military in the Caucasus and, in the 1850s, in Crimea. Tolstoy had been deeply troubled by his military experiences and refused to romanticize imperial conquest as a mere adventure and the quest for freedom, or even legitimize it as a civilizing mission that was intended to modernize primitive and backward peoples.[38] Tolstoy also refused to distinguish between good and bad empires, and was equally critical of eastern and western European imperialism. He thundered against the colonization of both the Caucasus and Africa, the military interventions in the Ottoman lands, the Russo-Japanese War, and the horrendous massacres in the aftermath of the Boxer Rebellion. In one of his last political essays written in 1908, Tolstoy wrote sarcastically and perceptively,

> But one has only to free oneself from the superstition that justifies violence to be horrified at all these crimes which have been committed and are being committed ceaselessly by some nations against others, and still more to be horrified at the national moral stupidity resulting from that superstition, according to which the English, the Russians, the Germans, the French, and the Americans can talk—in the face of the frightful crimes they have committed and are still committing in India, Indo-China, Poland, Manchuria, and Algeria—can talk not only about the threats of violence confronting them but the need to protect themselves against these threats.[39]

In his little-known masterpiece *Hadji Murad* (composed between 1896 and 1904 but published posthumously in 1912), Tolstoy wrote about the many subtle ways that imperialism degraded both the conqueror and the conquered. Unlike Joseph Conrad's infinitely better-known novel *Heart of Darkness* (1899) that presents the horrors of imperialism through imperial speech and the imperial gaze alone, Tolstoy presents Hadji Murad as a complex human being: as a man of action and guile, inflicting violence throughout his life, and dying by the sword in biblical fashion. Murad in Tolstoy's novella becomes the legitimate subject of literature whereas we have to imagine the humanity of the "natives" in *The Heart of Darkness* and salvage it from the ravages of imperialism.[40] Hadji Murad negotiates with the Russian military to strengthen his position within the tribal structure of the Caucasus, and when he fails in his bid to unseat Shamil, the ruling Chechen warlord who held up the Russian military advance through the Caucasus for decades, he chooses the terms and conditions of his inglorious death. In Tolstoy's hands, the tribal leader emerges as a complex and layered man, replacing the one-dimensional portrait of the "fanatical Muslim" that was so popular in nineteenth-century European popular literature, and that we have reprised so effortlessly in the aftermath of 9/11.[41] Hadji Murad, killer and hunted, friend and betrayer, aggressor and victim, worries about the well-being of his family, makes friends among his Russian captors, inspires his supporters, and calculates his options while negotiating with Russian administrators with clear-eyed vision. In his story, Tolstoy compares the "modern violence" of the Russian Empire to the "primitive violence" expended by the tribes of the Caucasus. Modern violence eradicates forests, the source of human sustenance, while primitive violence kidnaps people for ransom and beheads traitors. Tolstoy's sophisticated and complex roading of the situation elides both intellectual paradigms commonly used to understand imperialism: that of beneficent conquest saving a backward people through modern means, or the postcolonial fantasy of evil aggressors and blameless victims. In Tolstoy's fine-grained short story we see an unequal encounter that sets in motion unending cycles of violence powered by the horrific appropriation of natural resources. But Tolstoy must have believed that the wound of imperialism could be sutured by human understanding, otherwise, why would he fight for the global cessation of violence.[42]

Anticipating both Gramsci and Foucault and in consonance with anarchist ideas of his time, Tolstoy argued that the state created systems of coercion, as in armies, schools, and prisons for two reasons. One was internal: the state needed the levers of violence to legitimize and maintain the unequal social and economic systems that redistributed the fruits of one's labor from the producer to a parasitic elite class. Tolstoy wrote at length about armies, police, and prisons, institutions that perpetuated a horrendous cycle of violence on its people as well as those who were drafted to serve in them. Second, states invariably used their military resources to expand their territory, grab more market share, extract resources, and enslave inhabitants of other regions. Tolstoy became a bitter and brilliant critic of Russian imperialism and in an acerbic essay on the Franco-Russian alliance of 1894, he satirized the means through which states, international diplomatic systems, and the clerical establishment[43] induced the creation of national consciousness and patriotism. In his opinion, the love for one's "country" was an utterly spurious and inauthentic emotion. Tolstoy, writing in satirical and savage repetition and expanding on a subtheme in his monumental *War and Peace*, described how people were taught to love their country and hate their enemy while participating in parades and festivals, waving flags, singing songs, and offering toasts. The Franco-Russian elite gloried publicly in the love of their country while dining on fine viands and drinking French wines, but it was the poor peasant who was drafted into the army, torn from his field, forced to leave loved ones, and kill people that he neither knew nor hated.

While Tolstoy agreed with the Russian revolutionaries that the redistribution of land was the only way to secure social peace and equality in Russia, he differed with them on their use of violence to reach their goals. Since violence begets violence, revolutionaries in power, in Tolstoy's opinion, would inevitably behave in a manner similar to the oppressors that they overthrew, a fact that has been more than validated in the aftermath of 1917. One has to break this chain of unending violence that begins when humans start to appropriate more than their share of resources and then erect coercive systems to safeguard their ill-gotten gains. In *What Then Must We Do* (1887), when overwhelmed by the poverty, homelessness, and misery among the urban poor in a rapidly modernizing Moscow, Tolstoy cautioned his fellow elites to voluntarily give up their resources or face revolutionary upheaval and chaos. Later, Tolstoy, like Norbert Elias, argued in his seminal *The Kingdom of God Is Within You* (1893) that the civilizing process and the acquisition of power and wealth would have a softening effect on the greed of the elites, no doubt referring to himself. While Marxist theory fixated on the first step of the proletarian revolution—the violent expropriation of the propertied class as a necessary step toward creating a just and equal society—Tolstoy, more revolutionary than the Marxists, appealed directly to the elites to stop their mindless accumulation of property at the expense of others. He claimed that it was human greed that led to the exploitation of others at home and abroad. Tolstoy regarded the islands of "civilization" amid the oceans of "poverty" as a catastrophic and unsustainable situation created by the greedy behavior of the few, while Tagore created the concept of social property to be earned by non-exploitative means and used for the benefit of mankind.[44]

Tolstoy believed that he had to live a frugal life rather than simply preach about it, but he also realized how hard it was to separate his daily life from the exploited labor of others. Tolstoy created a powerful anti-model of elite behavior and as he became a global celebrity by the beginning of the century his powerful message began to resonate worldwide. As a young man in London, Mohandas Gandhi, the future leader of the movement for Indian independence, read Tolstoy's ideas about using the self as a canvas for political experiments with deep interest as he struggled to formulate his vision of *satyagraha*, the struggle to achieve self-mastery and become an advocate of truth and nonviolence. It is important to remember that Tolstoy claimed inspiration from people that he met such as the peasants Bondarev and Sutaev, who gave away their property to lead righteous lives,[45] and he spoke in concert with other major counter-modernist and anarchist thinkers such as Petr Kropotkin, Henry David Thoreau, Ralph Waldo Emerson, and Jane Addams in the United States; William Morris and John Ruskin in England; and Liang Qichao in China, to name only a few.[46] John Ruskin's powerful set of essays entitled *Unto the Last* (1860) that critiqued capitalism and argued for the establishment of agricultural cooperatives based on labor and equality inspired both Tolstoy and Gandhi.

Tagore was an integral part of the Indian nationalist movement that grew rapidly during the infamous British attempts to partition Bengal in 1905 in order to weaken the growing mass movement. He even created many of the songs, slogans, and poetry that inspired millions of Indians to rise up against British rule. But Tagore soon realized that many inequities were being practiced in the name of Indian nationalism: poor Muslim peasants were forced by Indian nationalists to boycott cheap British products and buy expensive swadeshi (home-made) goods instead. When he realized that Indian nationalists were neither above planning terrorist attacks nor above instigating Hindu-Muslim violence to achieve their goals of political freedom, Tagore became an ardent and spirited critic of Indian, Western, and Japanese nationalism during their heyday. Tagore argued that the nation and its disciplinary apparatus: schools, armies, and prisons, and the cult of nationalism concentrated unprecedented power and resources effectively in the hands of the state. But the process of state formation, whether in its liberal or totalitarian incarnation, also created a deformed and unthinking individual who continuously expanded the sphere of unfreedom by supporting political decisions made in the name of the enormously powerful nation-state. Tagore identified incipient totalitarianism, a desire for sameness in both the formation of the nation-state in the West and in the elaboration of national consciousness in colonized countries, a concept that he was to develop in two powerful novels that were composed almost eighteen years apart, *Home and the World* (1916) and *Four Quartets* (1934), that was written after his visit to the Soviet Union.[47]

Tagore even criticized Gandhi, who he held in great personal esteem, for advocating that every Indian use the spinning wheel for thirty minutes a day, as he abhorred the imposition of sameness in the name of an imaginary nationalist unity.[48] He argued like Tolstoy that the nation contained the germs of imperialism and the nation was essentially a proto-imperialist institution. Its existence served to legitimize and deflect attention from imperialism, a natural extension of bellicose nationalism. He shocked and outraged Indian nationalists by refusing to acquiesce to the political fiction gaining momentum in much of the colonized world in the early twentieth century: of the binary opposition between a good nation and an evil empire. In his critique of Japanese aggression against China in the 1930s, Tagore compared the chauvinistic nationalism that powered Japanese aggression abroad to a process that happened in early centuries among European Empires. He claimed a human identity that was both larger and deeper than any political affiliation and argued that all forms of the state were necessarily transient. Even though Tagore publicly renounced his British knighthood after the infamous Jallianwala Bagh Massacre in 1919 when British troops fired on unarmed Indians, he, like Tolstoy, continued to extol his deep personal friendships with intellectuals, artists, and politicians from around the world. He invited scholars, artists, scientists, musicians, and other eminent personalities from countries around the world to spend time at his three institutions: to engage in research, scholarship, and teaching. Tagore believed that individuals could create supranational relations that would sow the seeds for the global civilization of the future, where human identity and not their national party card would be the mode of identification.

Through his numerous visits to Europe, the United States, and countries in Latin America, Middle East, and Asia, Tagore presented an alternative to "imperial travel" and "imperial eyes." As a colonial subject abroad in the seats of power in the West, in universities such as Oxford and Harvard, in conversations with famous intellectuals such Romain Rolland, W. B. Yeats, and Einstein, and even on a short visit to the White House in 1930, Tagore disproved imperial pronouncements about native backwardness and primitiveness that necessitated military interventions overseas. But in his travels that were facilitated by imperial roads, railways, and steamships, Tagore refused to represent either the modern Indian nation or an ancient and mystical India. Instead, throughout his life, Tagore struggled by means of his poetry, art, and his educational initiatives to articulate and elaborate the concept of a capacious and modern Indian civilization—one that could present a global, ecological, and humanitarian alternative to sectarian, racial, and national identity.[49] In his poem entitled "He Mor Chitto" (Pilgrimage to India, 1910), calculated to infuriate every Indian nationalist, living or dead, Tagore audaciously displaces the central narrative of conquest from Indian history. In the process, he deprives both the violent and nonviolent strands of Indian nationalism of their very reason for existence. Instead, the poet reimagines the waves of invasion that have rolled over the Indo-Gangetic plains through the time-thickened centuries as successive chapters in travel and pilgrimage. He names the many peoples who have arrived on the plains of India: the Dravidians, the Aryans, the Persians, the Greeks, the Mongols, the Chinese, the Muslims, and most recently, the Christians from the West. They have commingled to create a composite and racially impure music and civilization, inspired by a landscape of "austere and meditative mountains" and plains captivated by "prayerful rivers." Tagore argues that India's essence lies in its inspiring geography and ecology, and only those who love this sacred environment and labor to conserve and protect it have the right to call themselves citizens and patriots. The poet, not content with dispensing with race, national, and ethnic particularism, also challenges social and religious hierarchy as he exhorts the Brahmin (the elites) to cleanse his soul and grasp the hand of the other, as a way to consecrate a new "religion of humanity."

While Tolstoy and Tagore refused to join a political party, they did not refuse to participate in politics. But they did so in their idiosyncratic and individualistic ways that redefined the very nature of modern politics as a tool devised to mobilize masses in support of a leader and a political party. Believing as they did that real change would come when empowered and enlightened individuals acted on their truths, they practiced a politics of selfhood that was anchored in an attempt to find a correspondence between words and deeds. The public performance of intentional selflessness was intended to challenge social conventions and religious and academic discourses that saw inequality at home and imperialism abroad as both natural and normal. They also argued that political convictions that were born out of knowledge, rational inquiry, and a reflection on one's experiences were more important than those that were taught by a state, educational institutions, or elites. Real change did not come through coercion and fear, nor was it born through violent revolutions that invariably replaced one oppressive group with another. Tolstoy even claimed that representative democracy only enlarged the circle of elites without fundamentally erasing exploitation, oppression, or inequality. Tagore argued that India needed social change in the villages, patient work, that dismantled the structures of caste and class that perpetuated rural poverty, debt bondage, and the oppression of women. He said that economic development in the countryside was more important than the attainment of political independence. Tagore called on peasants to form land and craft cooperatives, landlords to invest in the education and welfare of their tenants, and on everybody to revive the rich and syncretic popular culture that had sustained the psychological and emotional link between people and the land for centuries, the intellectual and spiritual basis of true environmentalism.[50] Through his rural agricultural foundation, Sriniketan (that was started by Leonard Elmhirst with monies donated by the American heiress, Doris Straight), that sought to make self-reliant and strong villages, his school at Shantiniketan, and his university, Viswabharati, Tagore tried to accomplish his gargantuan goals with little fanfare or ceremony. Ultimately, both intellectuals practiced a patrician code of frugal living and global thinking that became an uncomfortable reproach to the luxurious lifestyles of their fellow elites. Their quest to change elite behavior was a large political task, one that grows more urgent with every passing day.

Nature Is Not and Never Can Be a Category

In the final section of this chapter, I analyze Tolstoy and Tagore's understanding of nature as it formed the third leg of their definition of selfhood. As they came to maturity through the early days of industrial modernity in Russia and India, they were fascinated and repelled by the accelerated processes of socioeconomic change. Both men were deeply interested in science but feared that technology and scientific knowledge were being used to thoughtlessly multiply the production and circulation of arms and goods. Tagore argued that science should be used to create a more humane and just society that was embedded in and not exploitative of nature. He greatly encouraged experimentation with breeding sturdy livestock and poultry, combining European and Indian strains, at Sriniketan. And Tagore even sent his son-in-law to the University of Illinois, Urbana Champaign, to master the modern methods of agriculture.

As landlords with agrarian roots that went back generations, Tagore's and Tolstoy's understanding of nature was complex: utilitarian, ethico-moral, sensual, spiritual, and not merely aesthetic. They did not think about nature in the modern mode of occasional, passive, and ultimately futile spectatorship. Nature was the crucible of everyday life: one that enjoined frugality, self-reflexivity, creativity, equality, and joy. Only in nature did one realize the full dimensions of oneself, and nature, like love, engendered a profound and embodied selflessness.[51]

For Tagore, nature was not an analytical category. He usually slept in an open verandah to catch the very first rays of the rising sun. He gloried in the torrential monsoon rains, and even the fierce heat of the midday tropical sun did not send him indoors for shelter and relief. For Tolstoy, his long walks through the Russian plains and forests was another name for self-conscious living, and well into his late seventies "he strode the earth like a petty colossus," and thought little of undertaking lengthy pilgrimages on foot to distant Russian monasteries. Both men hated the city, be it Moscow or Kolkata, and they condemned urban spaces as parasitic and unequal: one that enjoined hierarchy, difference, and alienation. Tolstoy believed that man's estrangement from nature was the root cause for the modern epidemic of violence, and Tagore feared that urban spaces stunted independent thought and diminished our capacity to experience moments of transcendence that are anchored in the everyday.

They argued that the village and not the city was the key to the prosperity of both human beings and the wilderness. The parasitic city, instead of draining and impoverishing villages, should be a source of ideas and provide material sustenance to its surrounding.[52] The village was the eco-tone, a highly productive zone, where two different ecosystems, the forest and the fields met to produce new forms of life and sociability. The village is an eco-frontier, an essential place that opens our modern eyes to the impact that human production, consumption, and waste have on the natural environment. Proponents of modernization were spectacularly ill-equipped to understand these ideas that were borne of a deep familiarity with natural spaces, and believed naively and as it turns out disastrously, that nature could be exploited endlessly for the benefit of cities. Neither Tolstoy nor Tagore romanticized the peasant or village life, and as landlords, they knew well the peasant capacity for irrationality, laziness, violence, and even resistance to adopting labor-saving technology.[53] But the village functioned as a metaphor in their writings, and they anticipated many of the ideas that are to be found in the modern concept of deep ecology. The fundamental premise of deep ecology is that humans are but a tiny part of vast and constantly mutating ecosystems, and as such we should take from nature according to our needs rather than according to one's desires and greed. Tolstoy and Tagore argued a century ago that rather than "conserve nature" (a stance of complete and ignorant hubris), we should align ourselves to our natural world through observation, work (bread labor), sensory immersion, and cultural and religious practices. Only then will we gain the elemental consciousness that we are but a small link in a complex and endless chain of being and existence.

But there were subtle differences in Tolstoy's representation of the village and Tagore's concept of the "tapovan," or the forest of spiritual retreat. In Tolstoy's fiction, we find that feudal exploitation is the key trope in his understanding of the Russian village. Every human encounter is vitiated by the parasitic relationship between the landowner and the peasant. As he aged Tolstoy to his growing horror realized that every aspect of his daily life depended on the uncompensated labor of peasants. It was only in the forest that Tolstoy experienced true community and, not surprisingly, he sought to refashion the Russian village along those lines. In his powerful short story "Master and Man" (1895), Tolstoy shows very clearly that the violent snowstorm is responsible for creating a feeling of radical equality between the servant and the master. The hitherto exploitative master, Brekhunov, when faced with imminent death in the frozen woods chooses to cover the body of his servant with his own, an act of altruism unimaginable in less natural circumstances. Paralleling the arguments of his famous contemporary Peter Kropotkin, Tolstoy in many of his short stories shows us that living in nature enforces a measure of cooperation and equality, whereas the parasitic city allows us to pretend that social and economic hierarchies are natural. In the novella *Cossacks*, the Russian nobleman is unable to create a meaningful relationship with the inhabitants in the Cossack village, no matter how hard he tries. But when Olenin goes hunting with Uncle Yeroshka, the aged and poor Cossack, the social and economic barriers fall away. In the forest there is no nobleman or a poor Cossack; the latter is transformed into a highly skilled master of natural space and guides the nobleman through the forest to the manner born. Tolstoy asks in the short story "How Much Land Does a Man Need" (1886) and it turns out that we need only six feet; that is all the land we need when we die.

Tagore throughout his life was haunted by the image of the tapovan, the ashram, or the famed hermitages in the forests of ancient India where much of Indian philosophy, religion, statecraft, and literature were produced.[54] The tapovan could be a site of meditation for ascetics and sages, but more often than not they became small, self-sufficient, forest-based communities. The inhabitants were united and disunited by a shared quest for knowledge. And for more than three millennia, the ashram offered an alternative to urban life in India. The Indian epics Mahabharata and the Ramayana are constructed around the binary opposition of power, pleasure, and material accumulation concentrated in cities, and the spiritual power that one gains in the forest when one is separated from material wealth and loses the desire to grasp the levers of power. The innate sensuality of the tropical seasons and the immense biodiversity of the tropical forests fed the emergence of a vast array of spiritual and intellectual practices, philosophy, and self-discipline that we now understand under the umbrella term of yoga. The idea of the tapovan, a place of radical nonviolence, where one's days are spent in meditation, labor, both physical and intellectual, and the contemplation of beauty in its many forms, has played a formative role in molding Indic consciousness through the ages.

Tagore tried to recreate a tapovan at Shantiniketan, where he supervised the planting of hundreds of fruit trees, fragrant vines (many, many varieties of jasmine), and other flowering and medicinal plants. He created new holidays so that his students could celebrate the different seasons of nature and establish a meaningful and perennial relationship with the natural environment surrounding their institution. Tagore argued that the forest, usually represented as a place of exile and sorrow in the Indian epics such as Ramayana and Mahabharata, was our real home. As an antidote to urban living and modernity, the forest served as a haunting and powerful literary subtext in many of his literary works. Tagore reread Indian classics and brilliantly inverted the trope of exile to make his point. He argued that exile in the forest denoted a topos of "creative unity" and it would be wrong to associate it exclusively with loss, heartache, and nostalgia. When Rama and Sita, the main characters from the epic Ramayana, are sent into exile into the forest, they do not bemoan their fate. They find life in the forest to be infinitely richer, so much so that they even feel guilty about the deep pleasure that they experience during their days in exile. Tagore claimed that Kalidasa, the classical Indian dramatist from the fifth century, juxtaposed the poverty of city life to the spiritual and sensual richness of the forest hermitage in his famous play, *Shakuntala*. Unlike many other conservative thinkers who lamented the loss of Indian culture and civilization under centuries of colonization, Tagore's robust engagement with the present prevented him from wallowing in nostalgia for a vanished Indic civilization. He believed that everyone could and should create a tapovan in the present, a bounded space that offers comfort and inspiration to weary travelers in their journey for self-knowledge. Indeed, Tagore argued that one can only claim citizenship in this world when one treads lightly on the land: creating gardens replete with flowers and fruits that nourish the imagination and shelter the body.

Conclusion: Liminal Men?

During the last century, Yasnaia Poliana and Shantiniketan have evolved into sites of spiritual and intellectual pilgrimage that draw hundreds and thousands of visitors from across the world. Why do people come and what do they seek as they wander through these worn and well-trodden spaces? There are many other noble estates in Russia, far richer, far grander, and more sumptuous; the shabby furnishings, the crooked paths and the minimalist landscaping at Yasnaia Poliana pale by comparison. And in India, with its wealth of giant architectural assemblages, what does Shantiniketan have to offer to the modern tourist? Are we drawn by the presence of these two literary giants alone, or are we seeking with them and through them alternative modes of living, being, seeing, and thinking?

Tolstoy and Tagore were fearlessly original because their conception of selfhood was larger than the system of social rewards and punishments designed to imprison us. They were outspoken because they knew that their truth was their own truth, not one that was dinned into them by propaganda, ritual, habit, or violence. They argued that politics must move beyond modern, imperial, national, and socialist frames to include other roads to freedom: roads that emerge from self-reflexive thought that lead to self-sustaining communities worldwide. They insisted that all knowledge must be based on a rational analysis of personal experiences that connect the I, the community, and the ecology in a single continuum. They believed that in the quest for a perfect state or society, neither the individual nor freedom of thought should be sacrificed. They were suspicious of those that desired power and refused any position other than that of moral authority. Finally, they argued that it was only in nature that we were cured of our unnatural greed, our desire for accumulation, and our self-destructive egotism that creates hierarchical and exploitative societies. And it is only in nature that we realize to our utter relief that we were but an insignificant fragment of a rich and complex world. Bereft of their conceptions of transcendent selflessness and cosmic joy, our modern ideas of happiness and self-fulfillment are but pale and attenuated shadows that we stalk grimly through the many distorting mirrors of ourselves.

Tolstoy and Tagore tried to live their lives according to their ideals but were only mortal after all, with many flaws, eccentricities, and weaknesses that continue to evoke our curiosity decades later. In the end, neither man was able to walk away from fame and fortune, even though the open road beckoned powerfully throughout their lives. Tolstoy's deep fascination with spiritual wanderers and pilgrims manifests itself in many of his literary works, from *War and Peace* to *Father Sergius*. And we know that Tolstoy, like Princess Maria Bolkonskaia of *War and Peace*, stood for hours conversing with pilgrims while they traveled on the road from Moscow to the famed Monastery of the Caves in Kiev.[55] On several occasions Tolstoy undertook lengthy pilgrimages himself, traveling on foot as an ordinary peasant and dossing down in flea-ridden peasant huts at night. Tagore sang that his freedom lay in the sky, in the fields, and the dusty paths (*Amar Mukti Aaloy Aaloy*, 1926) but like Tolstoy he was unable to give away all his private property. They were liminal men in liminal times, but they had glimpsed a richer world outside the prison walls of the home, the nation, and the ego. It is a well-known fact that poets, whether living or dead, always have the last word in any conversation. In one of Tagore's most powerful songs, one that still resonates today, the poet urges us to walk alone.

Ekla Chalo Re (1905)

If no one comes when you call, walk alone
Walk alone, walk alone, walk alone, o walk alone
If no one speaks to you, o hapless one
If all avert their faces from you, if all are afraid
Then speak your mind fearlessly, alone.
If everyone turns back, o hapless one
If no one follows you down the darkened path,
If no one looks back in their flight away from you
Then tread the thorny path with your bleeding feet
And walk on alone.
If no one holds a lamp for you, o hapless one
If all shut their doors when you seek shelter from the stormy night
Then light your own ribs from the lightning flame
And walk alone . . .

(TRANSLATED BY RUPA CHAKRAVARTI)

2

Imperial Incarcerations

Ekaterina Breshko-Breshkovskaia and Vinayak Damodar Savarkar

The story of Ekaterina Breshkovskaia, a populist, propagandist, and passionate advocate for the Russian peasantry who spent many years in Siberian exile and captivity, was an odd choice to pique the interest of the American reading public at the turn of the twentieth century. But the dramatic events in her life, including her participation in the famous populist crusade of 1874, four years' imprisonment before her trial in 1877, and a five-year sentence in the Kara mines in Siberia, followed by fourteen years in exile seemed irresistible for journalists looking for stories about the "evil empire," and to American progressives looking for role models abroad to add moral urgency to their political tasks at home.[1] Breshkovskaia, Babushka, or the "Little Grandmother of the Russian Revolution," as she was commonly referred to, fit the bill in ways that Sofia Perovskaia and Vera Figner, more morally ambiguous heroines, could not. After all, she had never tried to assassinate either the Tsar or any senior officials in the tsarist bureaucracy. Breshkovskaia, like the American abolitionists, had been convicted of nothing more than engaging in propaganda among the world's most downtrodden people: the Russian peasants. Her romantic noble past, the Christian aura of self-sacrifice that permeated her renunciation of an aristocratic lifestyle, and her dedication to the welfare of the poor sat easily within the dictates of Victorian gender norms of the late nineteenth-century Western world. And even if Breshkovskaia had abandoned her son and her husband to pursue revolutionary dreams, her temporary lapse in maternal feelings was easily repurposed as a story of sacrifice: a tale of a mother who put the well-being of the Russian people above her own happiness![2]

But there was more to Breshkovskaia's harrowing saga. Her story of captivity and exile symbolized not just the narrative of a brave woman and her quest for freedom and justice; it also highlighted the perversity, the innate lawlessness, and the vast repressive capacity of the Russian Empire. With its autocratic government, ubiquitous secret police and poorly developed legal system that failed to either recognize civil liberties of the individual or undertake progressive penal reform, the Russian prison and the Siberian exile system provided a durable synecdoche, a metaphor, and a shorthand description for the shortcomings of the empire itself.[3] Reading Breshkovskaia's story today, we can see the tentative lineages of the Stalinist gulag that arose in the middle of the twentieth century, as well as the shadowy outlines of a literary topos that was going to be populated in the subsequent decades by the lives of its victims. When Evgenia Ginzburg, Varlam Sholomov, and Aleksandr Solzhenitsyn created and occupied the distinctive terrain of the literary gulag archipelago with character types and unforgettable story lines, they drew extensively on the generic conventions of memoir literature and fiction about nineteenth-century revolutionaries' prison experiences.[4] For some observers the creation of the Soviet gulag in the aftermath of the Bolshevik revolution seemed an extension and an elaboration of a system of incarceration that had been designed in the tsarist era. Russian prisons and Siberian penal colonies continue to provide a rich vocabulary for state-sponsored oppression despite their overwhelming differences in scope, intention, and impact from the infinitely more repressive and gargantuan system of Stalinist labor camps. Although the gulag does not rival the impact that the Holocaust has had on modern Western consciousness, Anne Applebaum has argued it is its closest and most immediate rival for a archetype of evil.[5]

While Breshkovskaia basked in the glow of American public attention and received widespread sympathy for her many sufferings while in exile, Vinayak Damodar Savarkar, another anti-imperial activist, equally devoted to the cause of India's peasants (surely among the most downtrodden people in the world), was engaged in battle against an empire that combined surveillance, incarceration, and a global system of imprisonment and penal exile far more efficiently than the Russian Empire could ever aspire to. The *New York Times*, the *Nation*, the *Atlantic Monthly*, the *Outlook*, the *Survey*, and many other prestigious newspapers and journals covered Babushka's travails with fawning attention, but Savarkar's case attracted little sympathy, approbation, or even interest. Savarkar's story had as many dramatic possibilities as Babushka's. Starting with Savarkar's arrest in London in 1910, his escape from a British ship and recapture in Marseilles, the involvement of the Court of Arbitration in The Hague about his illegal extradition to India by British authorities despite his plea for asylum, and the harsh sentence that condemned him to imprisonment for fifty years in the dreaded Cellular Jail, located on the Andaman Islands in the Indian Ocean, Savarkar's life could as easily have been interpreted as a tale of imperial incarceration, like that of Babushka. But few journalists chose to pursue either the literary or the political possibilities of Savarkar's saga.

In this chapter I compare the prison experiences of Breshkovskaia and Savarkar and the public discourses generated by their cases. I ask three questions: How did Ekaterina Breshkovskaia's story about exile and punishment cement the tsarist genealogy of the Soviet gulag in the Western consciousness? Why were the sufferings of political prisoners in British India as exemplified by Savarkar's life completely ignored in the pages of the same press that expressed endless concern for freedom of speech, expression, and political representation? How and why did the Russian system of imprisonment and exile eclipse similar systems of punishment designed by the British Empire in India?

Informed by the writings of Hannah Arendt, Aimé Césaire, and Jawaharlal Nehru, intellectuals who recognized the similarities between totalitarian and colonial systems, I argue that the savagery of the Holocaust and the gulag should be studied alongside the brutal violence of imperialism.[6] The moral indictment of totalitarianism whether in its fascist or communist incarnation has exercised a stronger hold on the popular imagination and academic research agenda than the story of European imperialism.[7] Few have analyzed the two phenomena as interwoven and connected strands in modern global history, preferring for the most part to tell the history of Western Europe separately from the world that it colonized. Analyzing the English language texts published in the aftermath of the political internment of Breshkovskaia and Savarkar as coterminous phenomena that happened in the same frame of world time, I argue that while the system of exile and incarceration became a metaphor for the Russian Empire, comparable crimes committed by the British Empire were effectively managed in the realms of political and historical discourse to dull their full import. Locating the sins of modernity in the flesh and the blood of two historical actors allows us to understand the reasons for the resounding success of the stories of incarceration in the Russian Empire, and the relative obscurity or even absence of the same in the British Empire, even after the waves of decolonization in the post–Second World War era, and the formation of independent postcolonial states.

The Russian prison and exile system was notorious both within the empire and abroad and evoked widespread fear and horror with stories of intemperate floggings of female prisoners, and noblemen broken by torture and interrogations. Tales were told of sadistic guards and members of the ubiquitous secret police who arrested innocent people without due process and incarcerated them for lengthy periods of time in hideous prisons and labor camps. Recent historical research, as well as testimony from prison memoirs, has mitigated some of the harsher aspects of its fearsome reputation. It appears that, unlike the common criminals, political prisoners in the Russian Empire had various privileges that included access to books and journals, and enjoyed considerable freedom of movement within the districts of eastern and western Siberia. Exiles intermingled freely with local populations, at whose homes they were billeted, built schools and libraries, and pursued revolutionary agendas, all the while receiving a stipend from a highly inefficient prison bureaucracy that provided little if any oversight.[8] Escapes from Siberia were such common occurrences that even the *Times* of London commented on the poor policing methods employed by the Russians and accused prison administrators of colluding with the prisoners.[9] Nobody, on the other hand, had ever managed to flee the British Cellular Jail and reach the Indian mainland alive. Based on the model Pentonville Prison in London, the Cellular Jail was designed to incarcerate political prisoners indefinitely within its massive walls, and the administration made few attempts to institute the Benthamite programs of rehabilitation and reformation of criminals that were so popular during this period in the countries of Western Europe. When Surendranath Bannerjee, editor of the *Bengalee* (and my great, great grandfather), India's influential English language journal, published accounts of physical torture and hard labor that drove prisoners to suicide and insanity in the Cellular Jail in 1912, it ultimately led to an official inquiry into the prison conditions.[10] But the uproar that ensued from this exposé of prison practices found few echoes in the liberal press of either England or the United States, and political prisoners continued to be incarcerated in the Cellular Jail till the onset of the Second World War. Unlike the stories of Breshkovskaia, Leo Deich, Nicholas Chaikovski, Peter Kropotkin, Vera Zasulich, and Vera Figner that gripped the Western imagination so powerfully,[11] information about the extensive system of British penal colonies that were built in the nineteenth century in the Indian Ocean is sparse. Histories of the prison islands of Singapore, Malacca, Penang, Andaman Islands, Mauritius, and Aden and those of the numerous prisons located on the mainland of British Burma and India are hard to come by and, in contrast to the Russian case, historical research into the British maritime gulag is still in its infancy.

Ekaterina Breshko-Breshkovskaia

Ekaterina Breshko-Breshkovskaia became an international celebrity primarily due to the good offices of George Kennan, an accomplished American journalist and author of the bestselling two-volume account of the Siberian exile system. Kennan's journalism propelled the Russian prison system to world consciousness.[12] The blockbuster sales of Kennan's books were helped by his electrifying public speeches, which he delivered at venues across the United States and England. Dressed in the rough garb of a Russian prisoner with chains binding his hands and feet, Kennan enthralled audiences with his harrowing tales of the sufferings that he had witnessed in Siberian prisons.[13] Kennan, who had intended to write a sober and objective account of Russian prisons at the outset of his Russian journey, fell completely under the spell of the Russian revolutionaries. Their aristocratic manners, easy command of European languages, and humanist erudition were wildly at variance with popular images of bomb-throwing anarchists in the Western penny press. The Russian intelligentsia proved irresistible for even a hard-bitten and initially pro-tsarist journalist such as Kennan.[14] What upset him the most was the contrast between the European manners of the political exiles and the Asiatic conditions of their captivity. Surrounded by Siberian natives, there were few if any refined people for the prisoners to consort with. Breshkovskaia later recalled that staying at a hamlet on the Chinese frontier among the Buriats was the worst of her eight-year exile in Seleginsk. "I grew almost frantic with loneliness, and to keep my sanity, I would run out on the snow shouting passionate orations, or even playing the prima donna, and singing grand opera arias to the bleak landscape, that never applauded."[15]

Kennan's descriptions of Breshkovskaia seem as vivid today as in 1889 when they were serialized in the *Century Magazine*, and later reprinted as two volumes in 1891. Kennan singled out three qualities of Breshkovskaia that resonated with her legions of Western admirers: her courage in challenging the Russian state; her moral fortitude in facing extended periods of imprisonment and exile with equanimity and transcendental calm; and her continued dedication to the cause of Russia's freedom despite her personal sufferings. According to Kennan,

> Almost the last words she said to me were: "Mr. Kennan, we may die in exile, and our children may die in exile, and our children's children may die in exile, but something will come of it at last." I have never seen or heard of Madame Breshkovskaya since that day: but I cannot recall her last words to me without feeling conscious that all my standards of courage, of fortitude, and of heroic self-sacrifice have been raised for all time, and raised by the hand of a woman.[16]

Breshkovskaia spent almost twenty-two years in prison and exile but after returning to European Russia in 1896, she plunged back into politics linking up with former revolutionary colleagues. She became one of the founding members of the Socialist Revolutionary Party that advocated a socialist peasant revolution in Russia. Breshkovskaia expressed few qualms about the adoption of political assassination as the preferred policy for the Socialist Revolutionaries, even though she herself served primarily as a propagandist.

An impassioned and gifted speaker in public, Breshkovskaia was a divisive and polarizing figure within the Party. While she could speak to crowds of peasants with ease and fluency, she lacked the qualities of either a theoretician or a party organizer. But her tales of heroic self-sacrifice and her sufferings while in prison and exile made her the perfect candidate to woo public opinion in the West and raise funds in the United States. Ernest Poole, a Progressive-era journalist closely associated with the "gentlemen socialists" in the United States and a champion of settlement work with the urban poor, met Breshkovskaia in Russia in 1904. His essays on Babushka initially appeared in the Outlook, and they were subsequently published as a composite pamphlet.[17] Based on conversations with Breshkovskaia, Poole emphasized that very early in her life Breshkovskaia was deeply moved by the sufferings of the Russian peasants and tried to give away her material possessions, despite her mother's admonitions about her profligate generosity. She rejected her noble surroundings and tried to improve the conditions of peasants both ·on her father's estate and in the western province of Chernigov, currently located in Ukraine. In Poole's account, Breshkovskaia's socialist ideology was refashioned as a Christian missionary narrative that was eagerly consumed by her American readers. Lurid stories about serf floggings and the cruel treatment of peasants sounded familiar to American readers of Uncle Tom's Cabin and other influential abolitionist texts. The vicious social order of autocratic Russia, which refused to engage in reform or countenance civic initiatives from an educated public, provided sound justification for Breshkovskaia's radical political choices. Autocratic repression validated Breshkovskaia's participation in the populist crusades of the 1870s, when thousands of Russian students and radical activists streamed into the countryside ostensibly to educate peasants. In reality, these activists intended to raise a peasant army for a socialist revolution aimed at both toppling the tsarist regime and preempting the onset of capitalism in the Russian countryside.[18]

When Breshkovskaia arrived in the United States in the autumn of 1904 for a speaking tour sponsored by the influential American Society for the Friends of Russian Freedom, she met many important intellectuals and activists including the founders of Hull House and Henry Street Settlement, Jane Addams and Lillian Wald respectively, as well as the eminent suffragist Alice Stone Blackwell.[19] Breshkovskaia's magnetic personality, her sense of political urgency, and the aura of genuine sanctity that enveloped her drew many Americans into her orbit. Several gentleman socialists, including Arthur Bullard and William English Walling, were fascinated by Breshkovskaia's populist and socialist politics, and they traveled to Russia to report on revolutionary events in the following years. Breshkovskaia spoke at numerous gatherings including at the Faneuil Hall, in Boston, and Copper's Union, in New York, and her presentations at public rallies received thunderous ovations. The events of Bloody Sunday in January 1905, when tsarist troops fired on a peaceful procession of unarmed workers in St. Petersburg, made American audiences even more receptive to Breshkovskaia's charges against the Russian Empire[20] and led to an outpouring of material and moral support. At the end of her journey throughout the United States, Breshkovskaia had collected over $10,000 that she used to procure a shipload of arms for delivery to Russia.[21] Her audience, unaware that their generous gifts were being used to fund armed uprisings, and also unaware of the full extent of Breshkovskaia's radical politics, continued to offer unconditional support for Babushka during the course of the next two decades.

The American public believed that Babushka was a veritable saint who was engaged in a crusade for freedom and justice against the Russian autocracy.[22] The articles in the press were remarkably similar as few journalists undertook any investigations into the political conditions in Russia. For the most part they were content to repeat Breshkovskaia's versions of her own life as one of self-sacrifice and unwavering dedication to Russia's poor, embellished with clichés about the harshness of Siberian prisons and the lawless nature of the Russian autocracy. Breshkovskaia was commemorated in poetry and an ardent admirer wrote about her

You are too great for pity. And after you
We send not sobs but songs; and all our days
We shall walk bravelier [sic] knowing where you are.[23]

Upon her return to Russia, Breshkovskaia was arrested in 1907 and exiled to Siberia for another seven years at the age of sixty-five. Her American friends sent her money, warm clothes, and continued to keep the story alive in the media until her release in 1917. In 1918, Alice Stone Blackwell published an English-language autobiography of Breshkovskaia based on Poole's account as well as Breshkovskaia's published interviews with the famed Jewish-American writer Abraham Cahan. Blackwell also included copies of her own correspondence and those of other eminent Americans with Breshkovskaia.[24] In 1931, another version of Breshkovskaia's memoirs was published by Stanford University Press to glowing reviews, under the auspices of the Committee on Russian Research at the Hoover Library that had been created by the noted historian Frank Golder.[25] Because of her sharp opposition to the Bolshevik ideology of rapid modernization, Breshkovskaia found it prudent to leave the Soviet Union especially given the widespread repression of Socialist Revolutionaries during the civil war. During her last visit to the United States before going into self-imposed exile to Prague in 1919, she called for the liberation of Russia from the Bolsheviks and called for American help and intervention.[26]

While few of Breshkovskaia's political writings were translated into English, her life story of repeated imprisonments and inhumane treatment in prison and Siberian exile over a period of nearly thirty years was a sturdy narrative bridge, connecting the tsarist autocracy to the Soviet Union. Breshkovskaia's incarcerated body wracked by pain, her noble soul humiliated by sadistic guards, and her ability to build a moral community within the prison walls lay at the epicenter of a powerful set of images about Russia and the Soviet Union. The treatment of political prisoners in the Russian Empire formed the basis of a powerful historical and philosophical discourse about the absence of law, legality, and civil liberties in both Russia and the Soviet Union, and Breshkovskaia's autobiographies provided literary form and political scaffolding for subsequent stories of imprisonment in the Soviet Union. The freedoms of the West were predicated to a large extent on the existence of the Siberian system of exile and the gulag in the East.

Vinayak Damodar Savarkar

In contrast to Breshkovskaia's anodyne legacy, Savarkar is a complex figure in Indian history, and it is with trepidation that I take up his journey through the independence movement of India. Accused of fomenting anti-Muslim prejudices and communal violence through his philosophy of Hindutva that roughly translates as India the land of Hindus, and his close ties with right-wing organizations such as the Rashtriya Sevak Sangh and the Hindu Mahasabha, Savarkar has been much reviled by secular intellectuals and liberal journalists in India. Suspicions still linger about his intellectual influence on Nathuram Godse, the Hindu fundamentalist who assassinated Mahatma Gandhi, and Savarkar's intellectual legacy is divisive for India's ruling political party, the Bharatiya Janata Party (BJP), even though his ideas form the basis of their ideology. However, Savarkar, before his metamorphosis into a Hindu nationalist,[27] spent eleven years in solitary confinement in the Cellular Jail in the Andaman Islands, was subsequently imprisoned in jails on the Indian mainland, and kept under house arrest until 1937 for another sixteen years. He was an important member of the militant generation of freedom fighters in India that rejected the impassioned journalism and petitioning that elite leaders of the Indian National Congress engaged in in the late nineteenth century. Savarkar advocated armed uprisings against the British authorities in pursuit of Indian independence and like the Russian revolutionaries believed that acts of spectacular violence would rouse the masses against the injustice and illegality of British rule. Unlike the first generation of Congress leaders such as Gopal Krishna Gokhale, Dadabhai Naoroji, and Bannerjea who used journalism and education to raise public awareness in their quest for Home Rule, the new generation of Indian revolutionaries, led by Bipin Chandra Pal and Bal Gangadhar Tilak and operating in the provinces of Bengal, Maharashtra, Madras, and Punjab, were radicalized by philosophies of anarchism, nihilism, and militant nationalism. They combined these secular imports with a homegrown religious cult of an imaginary Mother India, drawn from influential fiction written by the novelist Bankim Chandra Chattopadhyay, and an assortment of religious texts and practices, whose sufferings were to be redeemed by the sacrifices of impassioned martyrs.[20]

Savarkar's generation rejected the British narrative of a liberal empire that granted unity to a historically divided India and brought progressive modernity in the train of conquest. They were determined to engage in armed anti-imperial struggle like the Russian and Irish revolutionaries. Not surprisingly, they provoked a fierce campaign of repression from the British administration during which many were executed and many more imprisoned either in the Andaman Islands, or in the many other prisons that were built in cities such as Calcutta, Lahore, Hazaribagh, Buxa, Allahabad, Madras, and Yerawada, among others. British jails in India were a massive colonial enterprise. The jails held millions of prisoners over the years of British rule and were highly profitable for the ruling authorities. Prison laborers produced a variety of goods connected with the leather, jute, cotton, woolen, and timber industries, as well as skilled handicrafts such as carpets and rugs.[29] Savarkar's memoir titled *My Transportation for Life* is an important text in the genre of prison literature in British India.[30] It was initially serialized in *Kesari*, an influential Marathi language newspaper that was founded by Bal Gangadhar Tilak, a nationalist leader who was arrested several times during his political career, and finally incarcerated in Mandalay Fort, Burma, at the age of fifty-two for a six-year term.

Born into a family of gently decaying but elite Chitpavan Brahmin landlords in the district of Nasik, Maharashtra, in 1883, Savarkar received a good education in Ferguson College, Pune, while pursuing his goals of national regeneration and national independence. He formed the secret society Abhinav Bharat or New India, which was modeled on the activities of his hero, Giuseppe Mazzini. Initiates had to swear an oath of dedication to Mother India, and many of the rituals resembled those that were popular among nihilist societies in the West. Savarkar continued his impassioned advocacy for Indian independence even after being admitted to the Honourable Society of Gray's Inn, in London, to study law in 1907.

The year 1905 marks an important revolutionary watershed in Russian history, when the Tsar faced mounting insurgency not only from workers and peasants but also from the expanding middle class, sections of the clergy and the nobility. Sporadic mutinies in the armed forces almost brought the Russian Empire to its knees. It was an equally fateful year in the history of Indian independence.[31] If 1905 was the dress rehearsal for the Bolshevik revolution of 1917 in Russia, as Trotsky argued, in India it was an important milestone on the road to independence. In 1905, Lord Curzon, the British Viceroy, partitioned the province of Bengal, allegedly for administrative purposes. However, this imperial ruling was interpreted as a challenge to the growing nationalist movement that was headquartered in the capital city of Calcutta, home to a class of wealthy professionals, civil servants, landowners, and intellectuals. The partition of Bengal drew vociferous protests, street demonstrations, and mass burnings of British-made goods. While some patriots revived indigenous manufacturing (swadeshi) as a way to put economic pressure on British manufacturing, others argued that only armed struggle would rid the country of the British.

In 1908, Khudiram Bose and Prafulla Chaki threw a bomb at the carriage of British Magistrate Kingsford, known for imposing harsh sentences on nationalists arrested for seditious activities. But the bomb missed its mark, killing the wife and daughter of a British barrister, Pringle Kennedy, instead. In the aftermath of what was known as the Alipore Conspiracy Case of 1908, young Khudiram Bose was summarily hanged, and many of his associates were sentenced to life imprisonment at the Cellular Jail. This was the beginning of many other conspiracies and armed insurrections that resulted in the exodus of a generation of young men to prisons on the mainland, as well as to the dreaded Andaman Islands and the Mandalay Fort prison in British Burma.[32] The lengthy incarceration of these young men, many from highly educated families, not surprisingly led to the publication of a spate of prison memoirs in the aftermath.[33]

The British government was manifestly unnerved by the quick transition from the peaceful politics of the Indian National Congress to the revolutionary activities that were spawned by the swadeshi movement. Targeted assassinations of high-ranking government officials; the publication of anti-British pamphlets, fiction, and journalistic broadsides; and the fomenting of disaffection among workers and peasants—all considered to be just and even praiseworthy by sympathetic observers outside the Russian Empire—were dubbed as "sedition" and "civil unrest" in British India by the Anglo-American press. The British government used a variety of repressive measures including surveillance, widespread censorship, a ban on the printing of anti-British literature, pre-emptive arrests, rigged trials without jury, lengthy incarcerations, and the widespread use of physical torture in order to contain the movement for Indian independence and discredit the Indian nationalists within India and abroad.

Upon his arrival in London, Savarkar took up residence at India House, a hotbed of radicals and nationalists, where Lenin was reputedly a visitor.[34] He supplemented his voracious readings in history and political philosophy, by writing a biography of Giuseppe Mazzini, a hero among Indian nationalists who admired Mazzini's unswerving dedication to the cause of Italian unification against Hapsburg despotism. This book was soon banned by the British authorities, but Savarkar was engaged in writing an even more incendiary history text the entitled *Indian War of Independence*.[35] By its very title, the book challenged the reigning British interpretation that the uprisings of 1857 (a series of revolutionary upheavals that convulsed Northern India and in the aftermath of which the British Crown took direct possession of the area formerly ruled by the East India Company) were nothing more than a series of mutinies by sepoys or enlisted soldiers. Through the process of historical exegesis, Savarkar created a rich genealogy and justification for the revolutionary activities of his generation. The book, which marked a significant historiographical and political rupture in modern Indian intellectual thought, was banned from being imported into India as it was considered to be highly seditious and even dangerous. Despite the ban, the book found its way to India just as banned texts circulated in the Russian Empire with impunity, and it was considered essential reading for nationalists until Savarkar's ideology was discredited in the aftermath of Gandhi's assassination.

Savarkar exercised considerable influence over the hundreds of Indian students studying in London and his message of revolutionary violence proved to be increasingly attractive to a new generation of Indians. In 1909, Gandhi and Savarkar held tense debates in the India House about the relative merits of the tactics of ahimsa or nonviolence that Gandhi claimed was a founding principle of Indian civilization. Savarkar used copious counter examples from Indian history, and religious texts such as the Mahabharata and the Bhagavad Gita, to claim that armed struggle and violence was an equally legitimate Indian response to colonization. The strained relations between the two men continued till Gandhi's death as they were bitterly divided not only on the interpretation of Hinduism, but also about the methods and form of nationalist struggles.[36]

In 1910, Savarkar was arrested in London on charges of sedition and for procuring arms to wage war against the King. He was implicated in two cases: the Nasik Conspiracy Case in India, in which a high-ranking British officer was assassinated, and a more scandalous one in London, when Savarkar's friend and associate Madan Lal Dhingra shot Sir William Curzon Wyllie, aide-de-camp to the Secretary of State for India and suspected by many of mounting close surveillance on Indian students in London. At his trial Dhingra, a bon vivant scion of a wealthy family, and a student at an engineering college, said, "I am surprised at the terrible hypocrisy, the farce, and the mockery of the English people. They pose as the champions of oppressed humanity—the peoples of the Congo and the people of Russia—when there is terrible oppression and horrible atrocities committed in India."[37]

While Dhingra, unrepentant to the very end, was executed at Pentonville Prison in London, Savarkar, after a dramatic bid for escape from his ship at Marseilles, was recaptured. The court in The Hague, after intense pressure from British authorities, refused Savarkar's appeal for asylum and ruled that his recapture in France by British authorities was legal. He was brought to trial in India where under colonial law Savarkar could be sentenced more harshly for sedition than if he had been tried in the courts of London. In 1911, Savarkar was sentenced to two consecutive terms of life imprisonment in Cellular Jail on the Andaman Islands for fifty years, and his property was forfeited.[38]

The Andaman and Nicobar Islands, where thousands of indigenous inhabitants perished from exposure to syphilis and other infectious diseases brought by the colonists, had served as a penal colony from the 1850s. The prison population swelled in the aftermath of 1857, and many convicts died, like those in Siberian exile, clearing the jungle in order to build a colonial economy based on the cultivation of sugarcane, betel nuts, tea, rubber, and coconut.[39] Cellular Jail, built by convicts to house almost 700 prisoners in solitary confinement, was conceived as a Benthamite panopticon in the late 1890s. With seven different wings radiating from the central guard tower, it was an impressive monument to British aspirations to penal surveillance within the Indian Empire. In the steamy equatorial jungle, the heat, suffocating humidity, mosquitoes, and other insects combined with bureaucratic regimentation of every aspect of daily life, including the regulation of personal hygiene, made life a living hell for the inmates. The grueling labor that inmates were forced to perform led many to suffer physical and mental breakdowns, while some unable to bear the prison routine committed suicide. Prisoners were not allowed to possess writing materials and were allowed to write home only one censored letter a year, an occasion that afforded them intense joy.[40]

Western-educated Indians who had failed to protest against the British pacification of "criminal tribes" in the nineteenth century or against the large-scale atrocities conducted against the mutineers of 1857 that included mass killings or against the punitive campaigns against Wahabis in the 1860s, many of whom were exiled to the Andaman Islands, were galvanized by the imprisonment of Bannerjea in 1893 and Tilak in 1897 and again in 1908.[41] Arrest and incarceration of scions of educated and upper-class families created the same uproar in India as the exile and executions of noblemen and women in Russia. The Cellular Jail became home to many political prisoners from 1906 onward, as the British government was desperate to isolate and confine Indian radicals and control their dangerous views about self-rule and Indian independence.

While Gandhi's and Nehru's prison memoirs have found a respectable place in the Western literary canon, those by Savarkar, Aurobindo Ghosh, Manabendranath Roy, and Barindra Kumar Ghosh remain unexamined for the most part.[42] For a student of Russian history, trained to decode Russian and Soviet prison memoirs, Savarkar's account of his transportation to penal servitude is very familiar. Like his Russian counterparts, Savarkar arrogantly denied the validity of the British-Indian legal system, and claimed it lacked the authority to try him. As a lawyer in training, Savarkar used his memoir to indict the corrupt administration of Cellular Jail and by extension the colonial system. The narrative commences with his transportation to the Andaman Islands and, rather than defend himself against the charges that were leveled against him, Savarkar makes clear that the burden is on the British to explain the legitimacy of their occupation of India.

Savarkar provides minute details of physical and mental torture, beatings, endless supervision, and surveillance that the prisoners were subject to. Unlike Russian prisons, where noble-born political prisoners were accorded a variety of privileges, Indian political prisoners were forced to engage in hard labor that included picking oakum until their hands bled. Prisoners were also chained to the oil mill like beasts of burden for hours at a time. Even though they dropped from exhaustion while being forced to move in circles while yoked to a wheel (kolu) in the intense equatorial heat, there was little relief afforded from this labor regime. By forcing prisoners to engage in hard labor, authorities believed that the daily routine would break the spirit of prisoner resistance and install feelings of inferiority and subordination. Savarkar's meticulously detailed account convinces the reader of the utter inhumanity of the British imperial project. He uses pen pictures of David Barrie, the Irish administrator of Cellular Jail, and of vicious Muslim guards from the North West Frontier Provinces to show that the British rule rested on an array of collaborators, victims, and accomplices who unthinkingly perpetuated the imperial system as they misrecognized their own position in this hierarchy. Savarkar's virulently anti-Muslim ideology that is visible today in the policies of the Hindu nationalist parties was shaped in part by his prison experiences.

Savarkar, like Breshkovskaia, believed that he had two major obligations in prison. He conducted a constant internal battle to prevent himself from falling into lassitude and despair. Second, he felt that it was his duty to continue his role as a propagandist, explaining to guards, fellow convicts, and British administrators that the occupation of India was profoundly illegitimate. Like his Russian counterparts, Savarkar, a well-educated man, turned to literature, history, philosophy, and poetry as tools of political struggle. Spectacular feats of memory that included remembering hundreds of pages of poetry and prose, history and economics, prevented him from committing suicide. The continual accretion of knowledge, an important weapon in the quest for truth according to the Bhagavad Gita, and his creative literary activities allowed Savarkar to continue his fight from behind the bars and compose poems, political treatises, a memoir, and many songs in his head. It is important to note that British authorities denied inmates writing materials and only allowed limited access to a library stocked with pacifist texts after many years of sustained agitation and hunger strikes by the prisoners. Russian prison authorities unthinkingly allowed political prisoners unlimited access to books, journals, and writing materials, and Lenin, Trotsky, and many others were able to write their political texts and conduct research for their incendiary publications while housed in prison. In fact many of them, including Trotsky, regarded their solitary imprisonments as sabbaticals that allowed them to compose their revolutionary treatises.[43]

Savarkar was inspired in his struggle by thinking about the prison experiences of famous prisoners, such as Peter Kropotkin, John Bunyan, and Walter Raleigh. Despite prohibitions, prisoners managed to communicate with each other even though they were housed in solitary confinement. With great difficulty, Savarkar organized a mini-university for his fellow convicts and wrote his lecture notes on whitewashed walls of his prison with his fingernails, or so he claimed. He gave talks on European and Indian history, focusing on revolutionary heroes such as Napoleon, Mazzini, Russian revolutionaries, as well as heroes of Indian history who resisted both British and Muslim rule. Savarkar claimed that he built a political movement within the prison walls, and a utopian society that offered a vision of future India: an ethical community bound by knowledge and righteousness, but also an intensely hierarchical one that included an elite leader and his narrow band of associates. Ordinary people could join this community by expressing devotion to the cause and engaging in selfless acts of labor and love, which included washing Savarkar's clothes.

Perceptions of Imperial Incarcerations: Nation and Empire!

Neither Savarkar's case nor his subsequent account of his prison experiences drew much Western sympathy or interest. *The Times* of London published numerous articles condemning the calls by French socialists, especially Jean Juares, to grant Savarkar asylum in France. Young Guy Aldred, friend, anarchist, and editor of the *Herald of Revolt,* called for Savarkar's freedom and wrote angry editorials about the monstrosity of a fifty-year sentence that was awarded on the basis of unsubstantiated charges, but his editorials received very little publicity.[44] Sir Henry John Stedman Cotton, a British administrator and widely regarded as a friend of India, vigorously disputed rumors in print that he approved of Savarkar's methods.[45] *The New York Times* appeared relieved that the Court at Hague ruled against Savarkar's request for asylum while other publications briefly reported on the facts of his trial.[46] Neither Savarkar's lengthy imprisonment nor the publication of his memoirs drew much international interest. In this last section I advance a few preliminary ideas about why the system of Siberian exile sullied the reputation of the Russian Empire beyond repair, while the British were able to sustain similar penal practices in the colonies till the middle of the twentieth century with relative impunity.

The Siberian exile system should have been equally uninteresting to a cosmopolitan American reading public as the British maritime gulag, but generations of talented Russian propagandists and their Western sympathizers turned it into a unique prototype for imperial incarceration. Tales of political imprisonment and the exile served as a formidable Western weapon against the Russian Empire for both British politicians and Russian revolutionaries.[47] Sergei Kravchinsky and Kropotkin published numerous articles in the Anglo-American media indicting the system of Siberian exile and the inhumane treatment of Russian political prisoners.[48] Organizations such as the American Friends of Russian Freedom and the British Friends of Russian Freedom carried on their crusades against the Russian Empire in the West with skill and persistence. Generations of Russian revolutionaries, such as Alexander Herzen, Pyotr Lavrov, Nicholas Chaikovskii, and Kropotkin, and subsequently the Russian Marxists found in England a congenial home for their anti-tsarist propaganda.[49] Their ability to openly publish revolutionary tracts that were circulated in the United States, to win adherents, and raise substantial sums burnished the liberal credentials of England and its much-vaunted freedom of the press. The work of propagandists was supplemented by outstanding works of Russian fiction and ethnography such as Feodor Dostoevsky's *House of the Dead*, Leo Tolstoy's *Resurrection*, and Anton Chekhov's *Sakhalin Diaries*. These works, which brutally indicted the tsarist system of exile and punishment, reached a wide public by means of felicitous Western translations. Finally, the Russian intelligentsia, unlike their Western counterparts, failed to create a legitimizing narrative of colonization and conquest, and discursively separate the Russian nation from its Empire.[50]

That the Russian Empire lagged behind its Western counterparts in possession of military technology and industry is a well-known fact; less well known is the story of how the Russian Empire lost the information wars with its British rival. Unable to manage the international fall-out from the news published about the incarceration and oppression of political prisoners, the Russian autocracy lost all legitimacy in the eyes of a censorious world that was predisposed to condemn its every initiative. The British, on the other hand, were able to successfully manage the occasional criticism and the infrequent embarrassing story about ill-treatment of its subjects in various parts of the empire, and postponed the full-throated outcry about its colonial practices in the international arena till well after the Second World War. Richard Popplewell has shown that with limited manpower and despite an aversion to creating an investigative force modeled on Russia's dreaded Third Section of the Imperial Chancellery, British authorities were able to contain the activities of Indian revolutionaries and terrorists within India and squash conspiracies hatched in England, Europe, the United States, and Japan with relative ease.[51] The Russian Empire was unable to suppress the nationalist movements in the western borderlands, Caucasus, and Central Asia and imperial unrest played a major role in its dissolution during the First World War. Millions of colonial soldiers and laborers sustained the British war effort and played an important role in ensuring its victory.[52]

Anti-Russian propaganda also helped England play the "Great Game" (immortalized by Rudyard Kipling in his novel *Kim*) against the Russian Empire that edged dangerously closer to the Indian subcontinent after the Russian conquest of Central Asia in the second half of the nineteenth century. British authorities deployed a successful network of spies and native informants in the Northwest Frontier Provinces of the Indian subcontinent and tried to prevent the ingress of revolutionary literature. Unlike the Bolsheviks, who vigorously supported Indian nationalists and communists, the Russian Empire did not subsidize Indian nationalists as pawns in their fight against the British in Central Asia, Iran, and Afghanistan. Indian freedom fighters were inspired by Russian revolutionary literature and even learned the techniques of bomb-making from Russian nihilists in London and in Paris, but few Indians found in either St. Petersburg or Moscow a congenial home to draft their plans for independence as Russian revolutionaries did in London.[53]

While the use of force by Russian revolutionaries was occasionally deplored by the Western press, there was a tacit acknowledgment that the use of violence against an unjust and repressive government such as the tsarist autocracy was fundamentally legitimate and the culture of the gun and the bomb in which thousands of Russian officials perished during the first decade of the twentieth century was romanticized and whitewashed.[54] In the case of India, however, the Anglo-American press refused to accord to Indian revolutionaries the moral right to use violence as a weapon in their search for independence, and the revolutionary situation in India was usually described as sedition or civil unrest.[55] Most commentators deplored the use of violence by Indian nationalists, instead of indicting the British authorities as purveyors of violence against the nationalist movement. Locke's theory of rebellion against tyrants justified the violence used by Russian revolutionaries against the autocracy, but in the case of India a Hobbesian understanding of

British rule justified its monopoly of violence and its repression of "native unrest." According to the Anglo-American press, India was unfit for self-rule and thus advocates of revolutionary violence were never considered to be romantic revolutionaries like the Russian nihilists. Instead they were regarded as seditious agents disrupting the tenuous civil peace that the British authorities had enforced on a fractious and backward society. The British Left was surprisingly timid in its advocacy of Indian independence, even as Kier Hardie, Member of Parliament for the Labour Party, denounced the "Russian methods" of the British Raj in India.[56]

The possibility of such invidious comparisons with the Russians had crossed the mind of the British themselves and in a letter from 1908 Sir John Morley, Secretary of the State for India, wrote "that a tide of strong opinion might one day swell in U.S.A. about our rule in India, of the same kind as had prevailed here (in England) about Austria, Russia and the Turks."[57] There was much anxiety in England about the sharp criticisms leveled at the British Empire by eminent Americans such as William Jennings Bryan, who claimed that the British rule in India was worse than Russian despotism.[58] American travelers were appalled by the impoverished state of India under British administration, as were members of the American diplomatic corps.[59] But these minority views focused for the most part on the British economic exploitation of India, and remained silent about the endemic political repression of nationalists and revolutionaries. Theodore Roosevelt's appraisal that British rule in India was for the most beneficent, well intentioned, and in the best interests of an ancient but backward society that was ill-suited to democracy and modernity prevailed for the most part in educated American circles.[60] Indian nationalists in the United States such as Har Dayal Singh, M. N. Roy, Taraknath Das, and Virendra Chattopadhaya drew support from many American progressives and radicals such as Agnes Smedley, but also received scrutiny from the State Department. At the urgent promptings of the British authorities, many revolutionaries were arrested and then deported after the First World War.[61] Few in the United States demanded that the Wilsonian Program of national self-determination be applied to India or the other British colonies in the aftermath of the First World War.[62]

Under the terms of the Defence of India Act of 1915, the Rowlatt Act of 1919, and subsequent legislation, the British government in India was able to arrest people without a warrant, hold them indefinitely in detention, and hold trials in camera without the presence of the jury. British authorities censored and shut down newspapers at will, imprisoned activists for distributing leaflets, subjected under trial and underage prisoners to severe physical torture and detained them indefinitely without due process. The police attacked peaceful political processions of workers and peasants savagely with weapons, and the imposition of martial law in disaffected provinces of India was a recurring theme under British rule.[63] It was only during the interwar period, when Gandhi employed his tactics of satyagraha, an imaginative amalgamation of Hindu asceticism and Tolstoyan pacifism, and the images of mass arrests and beatings of peaceful protesters were widely published, that the pendulum of Western opinion slowly swung in favor of Indian independence. Gandhi's selection of nonviolence as a mode of nationalist politics should be reconsidered in the light of political practices that were actually possible under the oppressive conditions of British colonialism.

The romantic Russian nihilist, the staple of American and British pulp fiction, never found an Indian equivalent.[64] Generations of revolutionary youth in Bengal, Punjab, and Maharashtra who, like their Russian counterparts, enrolled in secret societies, hatched conspiracies, built crude bombs, looted banks, and raided armories to liberate India and inspire her millions to rise up against British rule were neither celebrated nor even humanized for popular consumption in Western discourse. Breshkovskaia, the Little Grandmother of the Russian Revolution and a woman of European origin, was a figure that many could relate to in the West, but Savarkar and Khudiram Bose were irrational natives who were unable to appreciate the benefits of British rule or respond in a "reasonable" and "civil" manner that the imperial authorities could understand. Categories of race and gender undoubtedly played a major role in the construction of different political imaginaries but a sustained analysis on this score is beyond the scope of this chapter.

In public commentary on the Russian Empire, the Siberian exile system became a metaphor for unjust state-sponsored terror and violence. In the British Empire, to the contrary, the acts of violence by Indian nationalists overshadowed the vast array of repressive measures used to silence and kill them. The history of British prisons, surveillance, executions, torture, mass imprisonments without trial or jury, censorship of the press, and the widespread use of violence by the armed forces under martial law was quietly buried under an avalanche of news about civil unrest, mutiny, treason, murder, and mayhem that increasingly justified authoritarian British response during the wars of independence in Ireland and colonies in Asia, Africa, and the Middle East. The exile of thousands of Irish men and women to penal colonies in Australia and Tasmania, where many perished from hunger in the early nineteenth century, and the exterminations of many thousands of Boers in concentration camps in early-twentieth-century South Africa did little to sully the reputation of the "liberal British Empire."[65]

Autobiographies published by Irish and Indian political prisoners, which rival that of their Russian counterparts in both literary merit and in the sensitive explorations of liberal subjectivity, did not lead to the creation of a grand narrative about a "British Siberia," one that effaced other, more progressive legacies of the British Empire. The existence of multiple sites of incarceration, and the widespread use of coercive labor regimes in Asia, Africa, and the Caribbean, failed to cast a shadow on the parallel existence of a liberal English nation, the home of democracy, civil liberties, and an unparalleled literary heritage.[66] It remained splendidly isolated from the seamy side of administering and profiting from an empire. Individual stories about systematic oppression in different parts of the empire never coalesced into a single narrative powerful enough to challenge the pervasive myths about the supposed "rule of law" promulgated by British imperialists in the colonies in Asia and Africa. Around the world, imperial publics, including many native elites located in British colonies, continued to believe that the British occupied much of the world to spread the ideals of enlightenment, to institute good governance and principles of free trade, to modernize, uplift, and save backward peoples who could not be trusted to rule themselves. The contiguous land empire of Russia prevented it from perpetuating the British fiction of an English nation, politically liberal and based on individual rights and liberties, and apparently independent of a highly authoritarian empire overseas that subsidized its magnificence. While the British were able to discursively unhinge the liberal English nation that defended the rights of free-born Englishmen from a global network of coercive labor regimes and prisons in its empire, the Russian Empire was never able to create a Russian nation that was separated from its many imperial misadventures. The tsarist autocracy became a victim of its even-handed repression of Russians and the colonized alike and Alexander Etkind has argued that Russians, instead of being a privileged ethnicity within the empire, suffered the most under tsarist and Soviet rule.[67]

While research into the Siberian prison system and the Soviet gulag continues[68] in the twenty-first century, there have been very few attempts to file for reparations or even create a catalog and history of the British penal system in the colonies from Asia, Africa, and to the Caribbean. The publication of Carolyn Elkin's book in 2005 created a media storm because she not only detailed the horrific treatment of participants in the Mau Mau movement for independence in Kenya at the hands of British colonizers but also used the word "gulag" in connection with the British Empire.[69] Historian Niall Ferguson criticized the sensationalism of Elkins's claims and replied that it was "equally egregious to compare the suppression of Mau Mau with Stalin's Terror."[70] But Elkins's book has emboldened other critics; and in 2011, Richard Gott published his richly documented account of British repression in its imperial colonies in the eighteenth-century period, followed by Kwasi Karteng's *Ghosts of Empire* and Pankaj Mishra's *Ruins of Empire*.[71] These publications have opened new areas of inquiries for historians, politicians, and plaintiffs. In 2013 the British Foreign and Commonwealth Office in London issued regrets, but not an apology for the widespread torture of the Kikuyu people during the Mau Mau rebellion and offered modest monetary reparations.[72] But these are very tentative and hesitant gestures that barely begin to address the problems of widespread incarceration, as well as the coercive labor regimes in British plantations, mines, and factories around the world.[73] Unlike the Soviet publication *Katorga i ssylka* and the Soviet organization All Union Society of Former Political Prisoners and Exiles that existed till 1935 and lavishly cataloged the prison history of the Russian Empire, less attention has been paid to the experiences of prisoners of the British Empire. The activities of martyrs and freedom fighters are enshrined in the national histories of the nations that emerged in the twentieth century, but despite the existence of a British Commonwealth and the records of a Colonial Office in London, these histories recount the relations of the colonized and colonizer in individual postcolonial nations rather than create a composite account or histories of captivity and incarceration across the British Empire.[74]

Differences in language, culture, uneven diplomatic ties, and the self-interest of ruling elites that have inherited the British discursive mantle of progress and modernization have dictated the ways in which the past is remembered in postcolonial states. While former political prisoners and freedom fighters have received modest pensions and are acclaimed on government holidays such as Independence Day and Republic Day, India can ill-afford to publicize stories of British prisons as many of the same buildings today are used to house political prisoners under the Terrorist and Disruptive Activities Prevention Act that was applied to all of India in 1985, and whose illiberal provisions were subsequently amended and reenshrined under the Unlawful Activities Prevention Amendment Act in 2004, and then again in 2008.[75] Ironically, the repression of left-wing activists in the central and eastern part of India and the extra-judicial treatment of separatists in Kashmir and terrorists in the northeastern and the northwestern parts of India continues to be justified by the Indian government as lawful responses to "mutinies," and "unrest," and "riots." Terms inherited from the British Empire continue to shape many policies in an independent India.

It is not my intention to minimize the atrocities of the Russian system of exile and punishment and compare it favorably to the British one, but merely to point out that in many cases the tsarist system was not sui generis. The suppression of political dissent and independence movements contrary to both historical discourse and popular assumption was neither a Russian invention nor a monopoly but a common imperial practice that was widely used by colonizers in the modern world such as the Spanish and the Portuguese in the New World, Asia, and Africa; British, French, and Dutch in the New World, Asia, Africa, and the Middle East; the United States in Latin America, the Pacific, and the Philippines; the Japanese in China and Korea; and the Ottomans in the Middle East and Southern Europe.[76] Putting the Russian prison and exile system in comparative global perspective allows us to rethink the intellectual binary of a repressive Eastern Europe and a liberal Western Europe that is central to our understanding of the history of the twentieth century.[77]

3

The Empire Vanishes as the Nation Remains

Vasily Klyuchevsky and G. M. Trevelyan

Vasily Klyuchevsky, the son of a poor parish priest from Penza, an agrarian province in the Russian Empire, and George Macaulay Trevelyan, born of a long line of landowners, eminent intellectuals, and high-ranking British civil servants, never met and in all probability had never heard of each other during the course of their illustrious careers. But if the plebian and the aristocrat had ever walked into the bar together (probably somewhere in Afghanistan where the secret agents of the British and the Russian Empires played the deadly great game in a zone poorly demarcated by imperial lines), they would have realized that they lived in a remarkably convergent and congruent universe, for the most part. Being exemplary public intellectuals, Klyuchevsky and Trevelyan worked tirelessly to create an evolutionary story of how the Russian and the English nation came into existence, one whose skeletal structure, musculature, and emotional tissue endure today.[1]

They chose to tell the story of a nation at a historically odd moment, the late nineteenth and early twentieth centuries; this was a period when the Russian Empire at the apex of its power dominated the enormous landmass of Eurasia, including the recently annexed Turkestan or Central Asia, and when the British Empire ruled not only the oceans but significant parts of the continents of America, Asia, Africa, Middle East, and Australasia. Were Klyuchevsky and Trevelyan simply provincial as many metropolitan intellectuals are in their inattention to their country's interactions with the wider world? Were they tone-deaf nationalists in the age of empire? Or did they choose to significantly downplay the ways in which colonialism and imperialism affected the history of their respective nations for reasons that were best known to them?

A reconsideration of Klyuchevsky's and Trevelyan's scholarship is important for two reasons: first, they helped create a sense of imperial nationalism among citizens, one that resonated widely during the height of the Russian and the British Empires. More importantly, their works have endured through the twentieth century and continue to provide an important basis for national identity in post-imperial time and space. The ideology of imperial nationalism or the sense of belonging to a strong nation within the larger empire can service many political functions. National identity provides an intellectual and emotional matrix around which people can cohere, identify, and build spatial and virtual communities. A strong nation often manifests itself in territorial expansion and colonization. During the life of the empire, imperial nationalism distinguishes the center from the periphery and provides legitimacy for imperial occupation. Defeated colonial elites often adopt the national cultural system of the colonizers that they perceive to be "superior" and inadvertently provide the sustenance for imperial expansion. This body of knowledge offers recuperation in the aftermath of imperial collapse as citizens based overseas or at the periphery can come finally "home." Finally, post-imperial nationalism serves as the basis of a successful post-imperial foreign policy. Colonial elites who have been reared in the traditions of imperial nationalism are often slow to understand the local customs and manners of their own people and continue to look toward their adopted Mecca. The creation of imperial nationalism that is ground in profound amnesia about the actual workings of empire is thus a powerful ideological tool that serves both the nation, the empire, and the post-imperial nation.

Unlike the extensive literature that exists on the evolution of the nation and nationalism, the traditions of imperial nationalism and post-imperial nationalism have received little critical attention as a conjoined phenomenon, with a few noteworthy exceptions cited later.[2] Klyuchevsky's and Trevelyan's texts, as well as their long afterlife, offer an extensive chronological canvas on which we can trace the evolution of these twined concepts that are doubly illuminated when placed in comparative perspective. As scholars have argued, empires and nations are not antithetical political entities that necessarily succeed or precede each other in neat progression. More often than not they are interrelated political formations that exist in the continuum of time and space. The evolutionary change of political formations over time is often more revealing than historical snapshots or definitions derived from moments of stasis.[3] A successful empire is built on a strong nation that exists at its core, and strong national sentiments provide the ideology and legitimacy for the successful imperial trajectory of any political formation, be it nation or empire.

A nation is a product of many forces, political, economic, cultural, that work at both the elite and the popular level. Klyuchevsky and Trevelyan argued that the nation is formed above all by a self-conscious people who believe that they embody a set of distinctive values and characteristics that have been forged in the shared knowledge of a past. This identity is further nourished by the remembrance of common experiences that have taken place in a bounded and geographically distinctive space. Rivers and dales, forests and plains, beech trees and birch trees, the Tatar thistle and the daffodil, all play a role in forming our ideas about a nation.[4] Klyuchevsky's and Trevelyan's writings were part of the political process of nation-making, as they saw themselves primarily as citizen-scholars. Instead of offering a structural/deconstructive analysis of nations and nationalism as detached and cosmopolitan observers, they wrote histories that became the building blocks of national identity. Their writings were intended to strengthen national bonds through a constructive dialogue with the past, rather than tear down the nation for the sake of progressive ideas, the demands of transnational capital, or other, more worldly considerations. Trevelyan's and Klyuchevsky's vast intellectual capacity for nation-building explains their continued relevance in the twenty-first century. Both would have fundamentally agreed with Ernest Renan's dictum that "a nation's existence is . . . a daily plebiscite, just as an individual's existence is a perpetual affirmation of life."[5] And they believed that the historian's job was to teach audiences how to participate in the "daily plebiscite" of nation-making in the mode of reason (as thoughtful citizens), but also in the emotional register of home-making.

Our historical memories are neither random nor disorderly; they are usually plotted on a recognizable storyline. The history of a nation can be seen as exploitative, oppressive, heroic, or as nothing more than a series of contingencies and lucky accidents. Furthermore, it can be told in imaginative ways as a tragedy, a farce, a comedy, a melodrama, a satire, or as a romance: in epic or prosaic key.[6] But irrespective of the literary mode used, the story of the nation only becomes "real" when it gains resonance, depth, and recognition among a sufficient number of people who then together form an ideologically charged and politically active community. Klyuchevsky wrote that "a people acquire a government when feelings of unity find expression in political links, and in elite power and laws. In a state, people not only become political, but acquire a sense of historical uniqueness, a national character, and a consciousness of their world significance."[7] In other words, Klyuchevsky argued that nation-making was more than a process of internal state formation as it offered an identity, a position, and a mode by which one could interact with each other as well as with the outer world. But the path from a consciousness of one's national significance in the world to imperialism is a fairly short one.[8]

Trevelyan in England and Klyuchevsky in Russia, independently of each other, are credited with creating the genre of social history in their respective countries. But in reality, this intellectual endeavor was a supreme act of political intervention by senior scholars and thoughtful nationalists who realized that the increasingly fractious elites in Russia and England were failing to cohere the people around an idea of a shared past. Trevelyan and Klyuchevsky argued that the past was inextricably rooted in a shared sense of geographical space, and the experiences that arose in that distinctive ecology. They were well aware that while national self-consciousness led to the birth of the nation, national greatness had manifested itself in colonization and empire building in England and Russia. But Klyuchevksy and Trevelyan realized that while imperial glory was transient, it was important that the nation itself survive the upcoming and inevitable apotheosis that loomed on the horizon. They also believed that the post-imperial nation could form the basis of a more ethical future, or better still, inspire selfless and altruistic behavior, much like the one that they modeled.

The national histories that Trevelyan and Klyuchevsky wrote became an important spiritual and intellectual resource in the times of trouble that followed the decolonization of the British, Russian, and Soviet Empires. Unlike the postcolonial nation that has the swaggering confidence and the aggrieved virtue of a long-oppressed victim and underdog, how can a post-imperial regime recuperate the original virtues that led to the creation of a strong nation in the distant past? Instead of merely declining into an amorphous cosmopolitan polity, was it possible for the mighty Roman Empire to become a spartan republic again? Could Little England and post-imperial Russia seek meaning once again in the virtues that led to their founding? Can historians and the discipline of history recuperate a people and a nation, in the aftermath of national and imperial collapse? Finally, is there any intellectual justification for the continued existence of a nation in the face of cosmopolitan criticisms leveled by Marxists and post-structuralists? Advocates of neoliberalism, transnational capital, and global governance are today equally dismissive of the idea of a nation, but Trevelyan and Klyuchevsky would have argued that in order to understand the world you need to first build a home.

George Macaulay Trevelyan

Trevelyan spent much of his life writing history, but at some distance from the academic professoriate. Inherited wealth in the form of a steady income and landed estates gave him considerable financial independence, and it allowed him to escape the increasing professionalization of the discipline that he noted with increasing disquietude. Trevelyan worried about historians who put their expertise and knowledge ahead of their political and civic duties. Among Trevelyan's circle of friends and family members, history was usually written by those who made it or those that were close enough to people in power to have a strong personal opinion on matters of national importance. As such the tone was engaged, passionate, bitter, or even emotional and self-righteous like that used by his revered grand uncle and infamous India-hand Lord Macaulay in his five-volume *History of England*. But it was rarely bipartisan, detached, scholarly, and, god forbid, anti national. As Trevelyan said numerous times, history was not a science even though it was based on the verification of facts and extensive research. It was impossible to establish a set of infallible historical laws that could be used to explain the entirety of the past and/or the varieties of human behavior. He disagreed with both his mentor John Seeley at Cambridge and the famous Cambridge historian J. P. Bury about the fetishization of methodologies imported from scientific disciplines.[9]

In 1903, despite having been elected to a fellowship at Trinity College, Cambridge, Trevelyan turned down the position to pursue the writing of a narrative and literary history that would inspire civic nationalism and create a sense of wonder about the past. But Trevelyan, who was addicted to archival research, also hoped to provide intellectual training in the evaluation of historical facts and interpretations to a wider public.[10] Strangely enough, he did not believe these goals to be necessarily incompatible, and but at that stage of his life, Trevelyan thought that they could be best pursued at a distance from the university system. Later, Trevelyan would return to Cambridge in 1927 when the conservative Prime Minister Stanley Baldwin appointed him as the Regius Professor of Modern History. He served in that capacity till 1943 when Winston Churchill appointed him as the Master of Trinity College, Trevelyan's alma mater. During the interwar period when lamps were going out not only in Europe (as Sir Edward Grey had said describing an earlier era) but more importantly across the British Empire, both the university and the public needed Trevelyan's authentic, cultured, and passionate voice to reassure them that come what may there would always be an England.

Starting in 1899, Trevelyan taught on and off at the English Working Men's College, an institution of higher education that was started by Christian socialists in London.[11] Like Klyuchevsky, Trevelyan learned to write for a broader public by actually consorting with its members and learning from firsthand experience how ordinary people relate to the past. Trevelyan taught courses in both history and literature at this institution as he believed that it was impossible to understand one discipline without the other.[12] Also, he believed that one acquired a deeper knowledge of English history by studying its great literary heritage. Trevelyan argued that the institutions of higher education such as the Working Men's College were not merely a place where upper-class men from Oxford and Cambridge could perfunctorily discharge their obligations to society and then retire to the ivory tower with a clean conscience. But much like the nation, these institutions offered an opportunity to cultivate the true "spirit of friendship and good fellowship, as the basis of liberal education."[13] He suggested that elite historians who are "doomed forever to know no other class but their own"[14] should seek an opportunity to participate in the intellectual and social equality that arises from being united in the common endeavor of learning about the nation's past. Trevelyan, who had descended from generations of the landed gentry, realized that it was dangerous to argue and debate only with members of your social circle and ignore the people who stand outside the doors of the manor. As every landowner knows, pitchforks, normally used by peasants to turn the drying hay and straw, can very easily become weapons of war when communication breaks down between the lord and the peasant.

Finally, Trevelyan, more so than Klyuchevsky, believed in the romantic power of the historical narrative. Trevelyan's ability to inspire a fascination with the past stemmed from his ability to write in poetic and evocative prose, a rare gift among historians. As a writer of distinction, he thought that it was impossible to understand English history in the absence of English literature. Literary works not only birthed the nation, but the English language itself offered a key to understanding the evolution of England. Literature alone depicted individuals in such a way as to make that particular period of history exciting and even unforgettable. Trevelyan, who had a fine understanding of the relationship between history and historical fiction, not surprisingly regarded Tolstoy's *War and Peace* as "the greatest of all historical novels."[15] And his remarkable work *English Social History* was a homage to famous historical novelists such as Leo Tolstoy, Walter Scott, and Rudyard Kipling, who in their time had also pressed history and fiction into the service of the nation.[16]

In the section that follows, I will analyze Trevelyan's best-known work, *English Social History: A Survey of Six Centuries,* from the perspective of nation-making and end with an analysis of Trevelyan's understanding of British imperialism. It was published first in the United States in 1942 and then reprinted in the United Kingdom in 1944.[17] The wartime paper shortages delayed the publication of Trevelyan's history in its home country. The book sold almost half a million copies, and it went on to enjoy considerable success not only in the United Kingdom but in the larger Anglophone world. It was translated into innumerable languages.[18] Generations of readers in the colonies such as India were entranced by Trevelyan's work and today *English Social History* is a required text in undergraduate courses in English literature at both the Calcutta University and the Benaras Hindu University. But we, postcolonial people, struggled to reconcile his descriptions of a free and bucolic England with the brute facts of imperialism. The sharp disjuncture between decent English people and evil British imperialists was incubated in the pages of Trevelyan's history and continues to exist as a paradigm for understanding the history of the island.

It is important to remember that Trevelyan's *History of England* (1926) and its successor *English Social History* were written in the vortex of vast and violent international wars that changed the global patterns laid down by several centuries of European imperialism. On the one hand, Trevelyan's passionate defense of English civil liberties and freedoms was written in response to his fears about the inexorable rise of fascist and Bolshevik authoritarianism in Europe. More importantly, *English Social History*, in which Trevelyan drew freely upon his former works, was written during the early years of the Second World War when it was apparent to all but the most dimwitted that the sun was setting inexorably on the British Empire. Within twenty years of India's independence in 1947, the mighty British Empire would be all but dead, thereby changing the destiny of the world for better or for worse. Trevelyan wrote at a time when he was anxious about the survival of England itself and had a few thoughts to spare on the worldwide empire that had contributed so greatly to its war efforts.

While Trevelyan's famous peer and fellow Harrovian Winston Churchill tried unsuccessfully to revive the idea of the British Empire by rhetorical bombast and an unscrupulous appropriation of American military might and superpower status, Trevelyan created the unforgettable image of England where a sturdy yeomanry, a locally rooted gentry, and a solid middle class built a nation of common law and common sense. Civil liberties that were born of peasant movements,[19] and national and anti-Latinate religious thought, were codified in independent universities, towns, legal associations, guilds, and the Parliament. Great Britain was a nation of commerce and of brilliant intellectual endeavor, both literary and scientific. These three seams of gold reinforced each other to form a durable bedrock. The book also provided a vision of a kindly but fundamentally fair people who muddled through the centuries with the liberal application of compromise. The English were held together by an ineradicable attachment to their land and their enduring love for the surrounding seas.

Trevelyan's lyrical and sharp-eyed descriptions of the English countryside were based on his lifelong love of walking in the countryside. He was passionately committed to preserving the land not just for a tiny class that owned the huge English estates, but for everybody. Trevelyan, an indefatigable walker like Tolstoy, thought little of completing a forty-mile brisk walk through the hills and the dales. Geographical nationalism was at the core of his identity and historical practice, and Trevelyan's deep love for a nation that was born at the confluence of the land and the sea shone through every page that he inscribed. When Trevelyan described the "whiff of freedom" that blew off the northern moors, it was not a mere poetic conceit. Instead, it was a description written by someone who had known the landscape of Northumberland at a visceral and intimate level.

David Cannadine, in his excellent biography, has chronicled Trevelyan's work for the National Trust, an organization that was devoted to the preservation of not only the historic estates of the aristocracy but also the coastlines, lowlands, fields, and wildlife preserves of England.[20] Trevelyan advocated unceasingly for the expansion of Youth Hostels throughout England so that city-bred youth could experience the spirituality and the solace of nature, and develop an attachment to the land and the soil. If he recorded the English past in the pages of his history books, Trevelyan wanted also to preserve the landscapes where the history took place and where he had learned to be an Englishman. Like the early environmentalists such as Tagore and Tolstoy, Trevelyan instinctively understood that there had to be symmetry between the city, the fields, and the forests. He dreaded the time when unchecked urbanization in the name of modernization would lead to the destruction of the landscape that birthed a nation.

England, according to Trevelyan, was not made by monarchs, the state, ruthless capitalists, or imperialists. Instead, peasants and farmers, women of various social classes, anti-papal dissenters, university students, vagrants, and workers played a key role in creating this eccentric nation.[21] Paraphrasing the Duke of Wellington's original saying, Trevelyan wrote that "the battle of Waterloo was won, not on the playing fields of Eton, but on the village greens of England. The men who fought in the ranks on June 18, 1825, were little educated but they had the qualities of country bred men."[22] Moments of class war and social divisions were not omitted from his narrative, as is evident in Trevelyan's masterly descriptions of the English Civil War and the Glorious Revolution, but they always resulted in some sort of compromise with the minimal shedding of blood.[23] Strangely enough, civil wars and civic uprisings, for the most part, resulted in the strengthening of the English national fabric, and it was due more to the pragmatism of the lower orders rather than the intelligence of the elites.

Trevelyan was probably either being facetious or self-deprecating when he famously opined in his introduction that "social history is a history of a people with politics left out," as *English Social History* was anything but an apolitical text. The downplaying of high politics, the inattention to the doings of statesmen and aristocrats was completely intentional in the maelstrom of the Second World War when the preservation of social unity was of the utmost importance. Above all, the book created a palpable sense of national history being embedded in the intentional acts of everyday living: in small towns and villages, on the lonely heaths and the moors, and in the fens and the forests.

Generations of readers have been mesmerized by Trevelyan's close-grained descriptions of rural life: of peasants' snaring the lords' overfed pigeons feasting on their grain fields, the complex cheesemaking operations of the dairymaids, the scientific labors of blacksmiths, and the gradual destruction of the open field system of agriculture and the commons. The mosaic of the text is composed of unforgettable details of everyday English life in small towns and villages. Trevelyan's countryside is permeated by arts, crafts, and industry: the weaving and spinning of cloth, the making of bread, the brewing of strong beer, and the building of ocean-worthy ships. The countryside comes alive with the labor of farmers and workers, the activities of tradesmen and artisans, the viral ideas of small inventors, and the political practices that arise from strong and opinionated communities. The colleges of Oxford and Cambridge to the contrary are somnolent and anti-intellectual, beset by drink and gluttony. But they have one saving grace: they are fiercely independent and can be depended on to join the good fight against overweening efforts of centralization. Finally, Trevelyan was very prescient in his attention to the social history of women, women writers and intellectuals, and their immense contributions to the making of a nation.

England, unlike Germany, was not grounded in a primordial nation of mythic folkways and epic poetry. Instead, Trevelyan argued, the island detached itself from a cosmopolitan and Franco-Latinate global order to form a nation during the fourteenth century, the age of Chaucer.[24] A distinctive Englishness emerged when the land had absorbed the conquering Norman (Scandinavian elite that had adopted the Latinate culture of southern Europe) and the Anglo-Saxon (Teutonic) peasantry that had absorbed the Celtic folkways and memories of an older time. A fused English polity had been created through a "mingling of the races."[25] The new nation manifested itself in several ways: one through the emergence of an extraordinarily rich and poetic English language that we find in literary works such as *Canterbury Tales* and *Piers the Plowman*. Subsequently, through the centuries, Trevelyan found literary nationalism at work in the works of Shakespeare, Marlowe, Spenser, Milton, Dryden, Wordsworth, Alfred Tennyson, and Thomas Hardy to name only a few. The works of Scottish writers such as Walter Scott and Thomas Carlyle strengthened the nation. Trevelyan's tracing of national development through literary works was extraordinarily innovative for its time and presents a model of how a historian can yoke wayward and usually cosmopolitan poets and artists to the nationalist cause.

Second, the medieval peasant uprisings against feudalism and the demands for economic freedom, according to Trevelyan, were the most characteristically English demands of all time.[26] This resulted in the movement away from Norman-style royal centralization and led to the rise of an independent yeomanry. This class created the institutions of local government and their demands for representation culminated in the formation of the English Parliament. Anti-feudalism was complemented by anti-clericalism and the rise of the national Anglican Church, another key part of Englishness. The growth of towns based on the free trade in cloth resulted in what Trevelyan calls early capitalism, and the strengthening of guilds, legal associations, and universities allowed it to become an all-encompassing phenomenon. And finally, the English attacks on France during the Hundred Years War (1337–1453) cemented the growing sense of nationalism. While the existence of an external enemy such as the French, the Spanish, the Dutch, and the Russians was always the necessary condition for the successful flourishing of English nationalism, and it formed the backdrop of many self-congratulatory comparisons in Trevelyan's texts, the enemy never became a focus of murderous rage or genocidal intent.

Unlike Wordsworth and the romantic poets, Trevelyan never idealized an Edenic countryside. The English countryside was an industrious one, brought to life by what he, Trevelyan, referred to as early capitalism even though he did have serious reservations about the social effects of the Industrial Revolution and the Machine Age. He associated the growth of the cloth trade with the creation of the English nation and wrote approvingly of the establishment of the joint-stock companies and a strong Royal Navy during the Tudor period. Francis Drake and Walter Raleigh were not simply unscrupulous pirates who raided the Spanish Armada of ill-gotten treasure from the Americas, but their actions were key to understanding English success in the larger world. Commerce, sea power, and colonization were the reasons for England's wealth, and these in turn provided for her national safety. The colonization of the Americas and the West Indies was carried out by "freedom-loving people," who also happened to be extremely creative in their ability to make a profit from the trade in slaves, the plantation economy, commodities, and finished goods.

The narrative of the orderly fusion of the Norman elites and the Anglo-Saxon lower classes was mirrored in Trevelyan's account of the absorption of Wales. If Scotland and Ireland proved to be more troublesome, Trevelyan did not spend too much time on either the Border Wars with Scotland or on Britain's brutal conquest of Ireland. After all, Trevelyan's uncle, had administered the relief works in Ireland 1845–7 during the Great Famine when over a million died due to government inaction. Charles Trevelyan had sanctioned a policy of non-interference in the name of laissez-faire politics. Trevelyan, commenting on ruthless English activities in Ireland and the expansion of the slave trade on the Gold Coast, wrote that they "failed to see what dragon's teeth they were helping to sow."[27] But it is quite clear from his vast oeuvre that Trevelyan was an advocate of imperial nationalism. Although Trevelyan disagreed with his Cambridge mentor, John Seeley, about how history should be researched and written, he had internalized the latter's advocacy of a "Greater Britain" as a means to extend English national achievements throughout the globe. And Trevelyan, like Seeley before him, emphasized the commercial basis and liberal intent of British imperialism, rather than the crude military desire for annexation, militarism, and glory.[28] In the works of both the professor and his student, the British Empire was created in an accidental and haphazard manner and resulted from attempts to extend trade routes and commercial ventures throughout the world. It would seem that imperial ambitions or military glory played little role in the acquisition of empire. Finally, Trevelyan argued that British imperialism was also an attempt to institute principles of good government on backward peoples and prepare them for eventual self-rule.

The African slave trade was self-evidently abhorrent, but Trevelyan spends more pages describing the triangulated transatlantic trade in rum, sugar, iron, and cloth than delving into the experiences of those being transported on British slaving ships. In the *History of England* (1926) Trevelyan details the activities of abolitionist William Wilberforce and how the British banned the slave trade globally. He does not dwell on the role that individual Englishmen played in the expansion of slavery and the enormous profits that the storied ports of England reaped from these activities. Trevelyan argues that the British went to India primarily as traders, to procure the products of the East, with little desire to colonize or settle. The collapse of the Mughal Empire and the anarchy that followed forced the British to take on an imperial role in the subcontinent. In his *History of England* Trevelyan is even more complimentary about British efforts to spread what he refers to as "good governance" in India even though he admits that it was a mistake to use purely autocratic efforts in ruling this populous land. In retrospect, he felt that more efforts should have been made to involve representation from local constituents in India.[29] Similarly, the colonization of Canada, Australia, and New Zealand was seen as a providential way to dispose of the excess population of England, with little thought about the impact that colonization had on the original inhabitants of the land. Finally, Trevelyan's complete silence about late nineteenth- and early-twentieth-century British imperialism in Eastern and Sub-Saharan Africa and its role in the division of this enormous continent is surprising for a historian who had strongly criticized British conduct in Egypt in the 1890s, and in South Africa during the Boer Wars of the early twentieth century.[30]

It is hard to read sentences such as these: "on the whole, our supremacy in the oceans and along the shores of the world was used in the Nineteenth Century on the side of peace, goodwill, and freedom,"[31] in the light of our postcolonial knowledge about European imperialism. And Trevelyan's enormous inattention to the widespread misery and violence of empire has rightly provoked condemnation and irony from later historians such as Bill Schwarz.[32] But Trevelyan, writing during the Second World War, wrote as a frightened nationalist, not as an objective historian, and even less as a confident imperialist. He was trying to preserve what he termed "Englishry," English values, and England itself at a time when it was far from clear who would emerge victorious during the Second World War. At the end of the book, Trevelyan ruefully acknowledged that he had completely ignored the history of the British Empire in his text, and was at a loss to explain why "the consciousness of the Empire of which we had become the center, lagged far behind the reality."[33] But studied indifference to Empire, both as a historical paradigm and as a narrative strategy, was Trevelyan's biggest gift to the post-imperial English nation. Trevelyan's fundamental belief that England's history was a peculiar product of internal processes notwithstanding the worldwide presence of the British Empire was not a singular interpretation. The widespread intellectual and political consensus that the history of England was separate from its imperial trajectory enabled it to survive the wars of decolonization that followed in the twentieth century with minimal loss of reputation and relative impunity. If England escaped its postcolonial denouement due to the politics of the Cold War, Trevelyan's reputation suffered terribly in his own country. In anticipation of the coming onslaught from the academy, Trevelyan burnt all his papers shortly before his death in 1962 at his home in Cambridge.

Vassily Klyuchevsky

In terms of chronology, Klyuchevsky lived at an earlier time and died almost fifty years before Trevelyan, but I have decided to place his biography in the second part of the chapter for reasons that will soon become apparent. Like Trevelyan, Klyuchevsky was a man of the provinces who belied the label of provincialism with his comprehensive understanding of the sweep of Russian history. He was born in Penza to a poor clerical family in 1841, and he lost his father, a priest in the Orthodox Church, at the age of nine. Klyuchevsky wore the marks of his modest origins and upbringing with pride throughout his life. Like many sons of the clergy of this seminal period in Russian history, he decided to use his seminary education from the Penza Theological Seminary for secular purposes. Klyuchevsky's shift from an institution of religious education to a secular one was a part of larger processes that marked the advent of modernity in the second half of the nineteenth century in Russia.[34] Klyuchevsky successfully cleared the entrance examinations at the prestigious University of Moscow and enrolled in the department of history.[35]

In Moscow, Klyuchevsky was thrown into a maelstrom of intellectual ferment. He was fortunate to be trained by an exceptional historian, Sergei

Soloviev. Like Klyuchevsky, Soloviev was a scion of a priestly family, and both professor and student brought their ethical and moral considerations to the discipline of history. Soloviev was the famed author of the dull but justly famous twenty-nine-volume *History of Russia* and his prodigious research in uncovering primary sources brought a strong measure of professionalism to Russian history. But it was his student, Klyuchevsky, who was going to provide the brilliant interpretative frameworks for understanding Russia's past. Klyuchevsky's version of Russian history continues to be compelling even a century later.[36]

After Soloviev's death, Klyuchevsky succeeded him at the University of Moscow in 1879 as a professor of history. Although he spent the rest of his life at this eminent institution, Klyuchevsky like Trevelyan felt that it was important that he share his academic findings with a wider audience. Throughout most of his career, Klyuchevsky lectured simultaneously at institutions as diverse as the Moscow University, the Moscow Theological Academy, the Alexandrine Military School, the university level Higher Courses for Women, and the School of Painting, Sculpture, and Architecture. Aspiring historians, scientists, lawyers, medical students, artists—in short, a vast cross-section of the educated public in Russia—arrived early at packed auditoriums to hear the master speak his vivid pen pictures of the past into life. Klyuchevsky's lectures were a rare combination of big picture thinking, source-based analysis, and performance art so extraordinary that many have compared him to some of nineteenth-century Russia's luminaries such as the painter Ilya Repin, the baritone Chaliapin, and the novelist Tolstoy. For three decades, thousands of auditors attended Klyuchevsky's lectures that he polished and upgraded continually. These lectures were compiled as the first four volumes of his celebrated *Course of Russian History* that this chapter is based on. Four volumes of his lectures were printed in 1902 and the fifth volume based on his lecture notes appeared after his death in 1913. They have been reprinted many times during the twentieth century.

In one of his public lectures, Klyuchevsky said that "national self-glorification as well as nation self-abasement, are only unhealthy makeshifts for national self-understanding."[37] This was his public declaration against irresponsible intellectuals and molders of public opinion who expressed extreme opinions without basing them on a careful analysis of facts. Instead, Klyuchevsky, even as he was critical of the Russian state, built intellectual bridges not only between the past and the present but also among the communities of educated Russians who were approaching extreme polarization in the decades before the revolution of 1917. Klyuchevsky realized that public speech involved both rights and responsibilities, and he was critical of intellectuals who did not understand the corrosive impact of their ideas on institutions, social organizations, and the state. He famously referred to Tolstoy as a late parody of the Holy Russian Fool, a malicious charge that was unfortunately true.[38] Tolstoy, with his brilliant, logical, and lacerating mind, stripped naked organizations such as the church, the state, society, the army, the empire, and even the institution of marriage. Klyuchevsky, who slowly rose through the social ranks, dedicated his life to shoring up the Russian nation that he hoped would persist despite the vicissitudes of history.

As a historian par excellence, Klyuchevsky, unlike Tolstoy, understood the contingency and the fragility of Russian civilization. He knew well that the nation had been wrested in endless battles with an unforgiving nature and built in the face of formidable external enemies in every direction. Since the continued existence of the Russian nation was of utmost importance to him, Klyuchevsky could not afford to indulge in the sort of intellectual and incendiary anarchism that so many of his political and artistic contemporaries espoused. At the same time, intellectual honesty prevented him from indulging in any kind of unhistorical glorification of the national past to please the autocratic state. Klyuchevsky sought to create and inculcate a sense of civic and dispassionate patriotism among his audience and to turn critical knowledge of the past into a source of strength and identity. His lectures on Russian history became a powerful intellectual and spiritual resource to knit together the sociopolitical body and provide a lodestar for the cultural imagination.

Unlike Trevelyan who was at a loss to understand why consciousness of the British Empire lagged behind the reality of its worldwide manifestation, Klyuchevsky placed imperial expansion at the center of the definition of the Russian nation. Following Soloviev, he concluded that Russian history could be summarized as successive stages of colonization of space. As they mingled with the northern Scandinavian and Finno-Ugric peoples, the Eastern Slavs created the Russian stock and built a civilization that stretched from the Daube Valley to the Pacific in the northeast, and across the western steppes down to the southern Urals, and subsequently across the Caspian Sea into Central Asia. Just as Trevelyan incorporated the Irish, the Welsh, and the Scots into British identity, Klyuchevsky too argued that the peoples of Ukraine and Belarus were an integral part of the Russian Slavic nation, an interpretation that was the gold standard of late-nineteenth-century Russian politics.[39] However, unlike our understanding of colonization as inherently violent and genocidal, Klyuchevsky did not recount the oppression, displacement, and exploitation of the nameless peoples that the Russians encountered during the waves of colonization. He believed that colonization was a process of migration, settlement, and resettlement that was inherent in the story of any great nation that defeated, displaced, and absorbed other peoples that appeared in its path.

Klyuchevsky argued that the Russian people had developed many strategies to acclimate to their harsh natural surroundings and counter the incursions by hostile and aggressive powers to the south, the east, and the west, and that this was a story well worth recounting. And in the later centuries when Russia became an imperial power itself, Klyuchevsky was simply disinterested in the histories of the non-Russian peoples who happened to be either displaced, exterminated, or incorporated into the empire.[40] For Trevelyan, the British Empire was a footnote to the glorious history of England, while Klyuchevsky believed that the spread of Russian populations into the colonized spaces of Eurasia to be the main driver of Russian history. But in the final analysis, Klyuchevsky was ambiguous about the value of empire as he believed that the development of the Russian nation was not commensurate with its international stature and imperial reach. As a result, Russia lagged behind the advanced countries of Western Europe.[41]

While his famous contemporaries, such as Nicholas Berdiayev, Vladimir Solovev, or even Vyacheslav Ivanov, analyzed the evolution of the "Russian idea," an imprecise and woolly intellectual concept, Klyuchevsky was interested in the evolution of the nation as a sociopolitical entity. He argued that Russia was more than an abstract idea; it was a concrete civilization that arose in the interplay of population movements and their adaptation to the local ecology. As he said, there are many good ideas that exist only in the personal realm, but unless they are developed and find expression in either law, economics, or institutions, they can neither become "historical factors" nor increase social welfare in any meaningful way.[42] As a materialist and steeped in the rigorous analysis of primary source materials, Klyuchevsky did not believe that the answer to Russian identity could be found in either metaphysics, the philosophy of the Orthodox Church, and least of all in the imperial destiny of the Russian state.

Klyuchevsky argued that a Russian national consciousness based on a spatial understanding of a common and united territory had emerged long before its formal representation in the Muscovite state in the fifteenth century and in the Russian Empire that emerged under Peter the Great in the eighteenth century.[43] As early as the eleventh and the twelfth centuries during the era of Kievan Rus, there was a popular conviction that the endless space that stretched to the north, east, and south were all Russian lands (russkaia zem'lia). According to Klyuchevsky, there was no unity of state in Kievan Rus, no conclusions about national characteristics, and hardly any notion of either a common historical destiny or even conceptions of duty to the commonweal. However, there was a growing conviction at many levels of society that the Russian land, the fatherland, was a common territorial cause, one that commanded allegiance.[44]

Penza, a fortress town, where Klyuchevsky was born, lies to the southeast of Moscow and is drained by two rivers. The town was a link in a long line of fortifications that were built in the sixteenth century to facilitate the colonization of the western steppes and to protect against the raids of the Crimean Tartars. It was subsequently settled by Russians and protected by the Ukrainian Cossacks who had been placed there by the Tsars through the centuries. The province of Penza straddles the three important geographical zones of Russia: the forest, the forest-steppe, and the steppe itself with its different subregions. For most historians, before the global spread of the industrial age, it was almost impossible to understand the evolution of human history without reference to the environment, as it visibly constrained the material and moral choices of all societies. The environment was not a category of historical analysis but viewed as the primal context in which human civilizations were created after a prolonged struggle with nature.

Historians such as Jules Michelet, Francois Guizot, Leopold von Ranke, Charles Macaulay, Frederick Turner, and many others argued that the beneficent landscapes of France, Germany, England, and the United States had shaped the providential evolution of these exceptional nations. Furthermore, the landscapes had formed the character of the exceptional people who inhabited these nations. Klyuchevsky was far more balanced in analyzing how the interactions between the community and the environment formed both the strengths and weaknesses of Russians. In contrast to most of his European peers, Klyuchevsky was unimpressed by Hegelian approaches that considered history as the manifestation of either universal laws, destiny, progress, class struggle, or divine intent. His prosaic and socioeconomic approach to history was probably drawn from the straitened circumstances of his birth and upbringing.[45] As a result, Klyuchevsky was much more apt to stress the role of adaptation and accommodation to local conditions when explaining the evolution of historical processes, rather than underline the daring genius of the individual, the race, or even a nation in sculpting a successful civilization out of the wilderness.[46]

Soloviev famously described the Russian environment as a stepmother, or *machekha*, to the nation. Unlike the good mother of Western European geography with its temperate climate and sharply delineated topography that led to the rise of city-based civilizations, the open and endless plains of Russia, or so Soloviev claimed, had an adverse effect on the character of the Russians. The geography created a semi-settled people who instead of building dense West European city-based civilizations colonized the plains that spread to the east. The Slavs spread their minuscule populations thinly over the vast spaces to the detriment of the development of trade and commerce.[47] Klyuchevsky's genius lay in his ability to extract a composite character study and, more importantly, delineate the tenor of daily life from Soloviev's broad generalizations about Russian history and its relationship to the environment.[48] Klyuchevsky argued that while the Russian nation emerged from the conceptions of a pan-territorial unity that emerged during Kievan

Rus, the Russian national character was shaped by the waves of peasant and monastic migrations to the northern forests. As the city-states of Kievan Rus collapsed following the Mongol invasions, populations started drifting toward northern Russia. The Eastern Slavs, even as they rendered inestimable service to Western Europe by absorbing and repelling the repeated military onslaughts of warlike and nomadic Eurasian peoples, unlike their Western cousins in Germany, were too far away to benefit from the legacy of the Roman Empire. As a result, they inherited neither Roman law nor Roman rules of commerce, civilization, and warfare.

The second period of Russian history, the appanage period when the land was regarded as a patrimony of the individual rulers in principalities such as Moscow, Tver, Pskov, Yaroslavl, and Rostov among others, Klyuchevsky argued, marked a decisive turn away from the commercial and city-based civilization of Kievan Rus with its intensive trade links with the Byzantine Empire to the south and Baltic Europe in the north. As the Slavs migrated north, they created an agrarian economy in the forest region between the Volga and the Oka River. During this time the Great Russian stock was formed in the forests from the fusion of Eastern Slavic, Finnish, and other local tribes that had migrated to this region after the sacking of Kievan Rus. While many have challenged Klyuchevsky's ethnography of the Russian mingling of the races, in his exquisite descriptions of the Great Russian peasant mentality that developed in the environment of the northern forests, we find corroboration for his key ideas about the emergence of the Russian nation. Russia was not an ideological, metaphysical, or spiritual concept; it was a product of a particular conjunction of time, place, and people.

In his justly famous seventeenth lecture,[49] Klyuchevsky presents a fine-grained understanding of how life in the forests of northern Russia, a land marked by woods, swamps, and well-drained rivers, created certain characteristics in the Russian personality. The Russian rivers, unlike their fast-flowing European counterparts, were broad, lazy, and easily navigable. As a result, there was little incentive to cluster in dense social formations on isolated banks as it happened in Europe, leading to the rise of grand cities of commerce. The very geography of the Russian rivers, the Dneiper, the Oka, the Volga, and the Dvina, facilitated the movement of peoples across the steppes. Klyuchevsky wrote that while the Great Northern forests offered the peasants their daily bread and shelter,[50] the very thought of the forests also induced a deep fog of depression. To wrest a living from this complex and challenging landscape, one had to expend endless and back-breaking labor. As arable lands were rare and intermittent islands in the endless swamps and waterlogged soil, human settlements were sparse and thinly spread. The clearing of the forest for agriculture involved the horrendous expenditure of labor, and the land that was temporarily enriched by the addition of wood ash from burnt trees was quickly exhausted by repeated harvests. The thin and unproductive soils forced the peasants to move yet again. But the ingenious Russian peasants developed an economy that was based on forest products such as bast (fiber made from bark) and twine, fishing, smelting of iron, the gathering of resin/amber, bee-keeping and the harvesting of honey, and the trapping of wild animals for fur.

This meager landscape[51] not only made the Great Russian resourceful, enterprising, and patient, but also taught him to expect very little in the way of surplus. It taught him to maximize his labor during the few summer months when agriculture was possible, but also rendered him unfit for the long term and systematic toil. The forests gave the Great Russian an extraordinarily rich vocabulary based on close observations of nature, but it was a solitary set of truths that man derived from his lonely war with an ax in the deep northern forests. The raucous urban assemblies composed of "free masses," the *veche* in city-republics like Novgorod, disappeared in the northern forests of Russia, and the urban and commercial scaffolding of Kievan society became a distant memory.[52] The nobles attached themselves to princely rulers rather than try to carve out feudal estates in the poor northern wilderness. Orthodox monks who fled to these forests after the dissolution of Kievan Rus tried to recreate the ideas of Eastern Christianity, an idea that was born of meditative life in the desert. The monks became a part of the immense northward movements of peoples from Kievan Rus. Migrant monks carved "desert monasteries" out of the dense wilderness as far north as the White Sea. Later, as these monasteries attracted peasant settlements and pilgrims, they served in turn as the launching pads for the colonization of the steppe.[53] As a result, Klyuchevsky argued that the Great Russian was instinctively individualistic preferring to think about his problems alone in the forest, rather than in and with a community of fellow beings.[54]

For Russians accustomed to the histories of the conservative court historian Nicholas Karamzin[55] and Sergei Soloviev in which autocracy and the educated elites were seen as the demiurge, bringing order, progress, and reason to the backward and uncivilized Russian masses, this was revolutionary history. Written in elegant and well-honed prose, and without theoretical self-righteousness or jargon, Klyuchevsky demonstrated the startling thesis that the state and the elites did not make the nation. Instead, he offered the provocative idea that the Russian nation was born primarily of migration of the peoples and their interactions with ecosystems that they moved through: the plains, the forests, the rivers, the swamps, and the steppe.[56]

Klyuchevsky, writing and speaking in an unfree and censored Russia, was far more critical than Trevelyan of both the Russian state and the ruling class. In his opinion, the appearance of a strong state was a relatively recent development within the history of Russia. The rise of Moscow in the fifteenth century was related to its geographical location at the confluence of rivers. The union of the different independent principalities in this region was helped by the presence of enemies on every side: the Polish and Lithuanian kingdoms to the west, and the power of the Mongol khanates to the east and the south. But Klyuchevsky regarded the evolution of the Muscovite principality into a Great Russian state during the fifteenth century, and then into the All Russian Empire under Peter the Great and Catherine the Great in the eighteenth century with manifestly mixed feelings. On the one hand, the creation of the Muscovite state and the conquest of the khanates of Kazan and Astrakhan from the Mongols set in motion the second movement of peasants who colonized the rich black soil of the steppe, toward the Lower Volga. But the extreme centralization of power that accompanied the growth of the Russian state and its enormous increase in its warlike capabilities that was served by a military and landowning nobility adversely affected the peasant-colonists. According to Klyuchevsky, the first link of peasant bondage was forged on the noble estates on the rich black earth region of the steppe, where the peasant was bound legally to the master. Instead of becoming a free and independent homesteader, the Russian peasant became an indentured servant, a foot soldier of the Great Russian state.[57]

The intensification of the yoke of serfdom continued under Peter the Great. Unlike the Slavophiles who believed that Peter the Great had distorted Russia's natural organic evolution or the Westernizers who approved of Peter's violent attempts to modernize Russia and make it into a European country, Klyuchevsky emphasized both the elements of the continuity and change during this period. His analysis of Peter's reign is rightly considered to be some of the best that has been written about the brilliant and erratic emperor.[58] In his subtle psychological portrait of Peter, Klyuchevsky presented him not as the consequential driver of history, but as a dynamic individual who was responding to extraordinary times. Much like the peasant in the Northern forests, Peter was shaped by his circumstances even as he impressed his extraordinary will upon his surroundings. According to Klyuchevsky, Peter was interested in technology rather than in scientific principles. He was an artisan who preferred working with his hands, rather than a conceptual architect who could bend and raise space toward a preconceived form. Raised far from the Kremlin court, Peter became adept at using the ax, the lathe, the saw, and the cudgel. But unlike the lonely peasant in the forest, he did not wield the ax with equal dexterity nor did he understand the ecology of the world that he inhabited. When Peter traveled to the West, he was interested in the techniques of metallurgy and shipbuilding, in the workings of factories and foundries, not in the abstract principles of European science, culture, or civilization. When he visited England, Peter did not visit the Parliament as he was disinterested in the political and social attitudes that produced the scientific revolution in the West. Although he desired the fruits of the scientific and technological revolution, Peter did not deem important the systems of knowledge that led to the production of these coveted Western goods.

According to Klyuchevsky, Peter was not an intentional revolutionary with a well-thought-out plan of action. Instead, Peter inadvertently set in motion a violent revolution through his responses to the circumstances Russia found itself in at the time. The endless wars with the powerful Swedish Empire and the Ottoman Empire set the context for Peter's creation of a modern army and navy, many elements of which he borrowed from the West. Peter also created a state-based economic order and a system of civil administration that maximized the extraction of labor and revenues from the people. Peter did not want to create a European Russia; instead, he wanted to use European technology to create a Russia that could assume a position of strength in Western Europe. Peter created a slave state through the use of force, but unaccountably he wanted the slave to act consciously and freely. Till the end, Peter was unable to realize that slavery and despotism were inimical to the social, economic, and political development that he desired for Russia.[59]

Klyuchevsky somberly counted the costs of a waxing state amid an impoverished and oppressed people. While he believed that serfdom had originated from peasant indebtedness rather than state-imposed obligations, he agreed that Peter's imposition of a universal poll tax on the peasantry further compounded their misfortune. Later, under Catherine the Great the history of Russia became the history of serfdom. If serfdom crippled the peasant and destroyed his initiative to either increase agricultural surplus or accumulate capital for trade and commerce, its impact on the serf-owning noble class, freed by Catherine from state service, was even worse. Servile, slothful, prone to luxurious and effete living, they failed to provide moral and intellectual leadership when the Russian nation needed it the most. Part of the reason for noble degeneration was the fact that they were a hothouse growth of Peter and Catherine's ill-conceived attempts to import Western technology and culture in Russia, without first preparing the country adequately for the reception of these new ideas and practices. Poorly acclimated to the actual conditions of Russia, these Westernized Russians, in Kluchevsky's words, were in transit through Russia to another world: in transit through their native land, whose habits and customs were a source of mere inconvenience to them.[60]

In his brilliant lecture on Pushkin's famous poem "Evgeny Onegin," Klyuchevsky analyzes Onegin's ancestors and peers whose superficial adoption of Western culture made them strangers in their own land. These noblemen handed over the agricultural estates to their stewards instead of working to make their land productive and fruitful. They read French tracts about the political economy and the rights of individuals even as they sexually abused serf women and physically chastised peasant men. Instead of participating in local self-government, they delegated their political responsibilities to local marshals. Onegin, the bored, dissolute, and irresolute nobleman, with a "French book in his hand," wreaks havoc through his inability to understand the reality of the Russian countryside. He is the poetic embodiment of generations of disillusioned, Westernized, and alienated noblemen. Klyuchevsky was as scornful of revolutionaries as he was of these "superfluous men" whose book learning and cultural refinement prevented them from working for the general well-being and the good of the nation. When these French-educated men tried to reclaim their Russianness and Russian patriotism during the Decembrist Movement of 1025, their attempts were poorly thought out and impractical. "They discovered that one cannot extricate oneself from all difficulties by means of foreign minds and experience, that it is stupid to reinvent a machine that has already been invented . . . that one must adapt to one's environment—and to do so one must study it, and only then proceed to reform it if it becomes inconvenient."[61]

In Klyuchevsky's work, the elites were a semi-colonized and inauthentic ruling class who themselves were in thrall to Western ideas and technologies. They understood these imported ideas poorly and tried to clumsily put them in a soil that was inadequately prepared for the great transplanting. The greater tragedy of unfree Russia in Klyuchevsky's eyes eclipsed the minor tragedies of the many non-Russian peoples that were colonized, displaced, resettled, and even killed to create the Great Russian Empire.[62] Klyuchevsky failed to elucidate when the former warlike peoples of the steppes who menaced the Russian nation—the Nogai, the Tartars, the Bashkirs, the Kirghiz, the Kalmyks among others—became the targets of Russian imperialism and were subdued, forcibly sedentarized, and moved from their land, losing their identity and their homelands. He was silent about the enormous violence that was expended in the conquest of the Northern Caucasus. The massive colonization of Siberia and Central Asia that was ongoing during his lifetime in the late nineteenth century merited only a few lines in his lectures.[63] And since the White Russians and the Ukrainians were a core part of the Russian nation whose common origins were in Kievan Rus, the mother of all Russia, Klyuchevsky would have been utterly baffled by their claims to nationalism and their demands for a separate homeland.

Conclusion

Ironically, despite Trevelyan and Klyuchevsky's documentation of and attention to the activities of the common people in their scholarship, their renown and reputation were undone at the hands of Marxist intellectuals. Klyuchevsky's student M. N. Pokrovsky, who created Marxist historiography during the 1920s and in the early 1930s, had accused Klyuchevsky of shoddy bourgeois thinking and for doing insufficient research in primary sources even before the revolution of 1917.[64] Pokrovsky, who like Lenin called Russia a "prison house of nations," was deeply critical of pre-Soviet historiography that downplayed the history of Russian imperialism.[65] With the Soviet turn to Great Russian nationalism and Empire building under Stalin,[66] Pokrovsky's proletarian internationalism was repudiated and Klyuchevsky's histories were slowly rehabilitated. However, Klyuchevsky was accused of bourgeois economism and for paying insufficient attention to the role of the revolutionary masses in history even after his partial rehabilitation. This serious charge was also echoed by his sympathetic biographer M. V. Nechkina, who did more than anyone in resurrecting Klyuchevsky's work during Soviet times.[67]

In the United Kingdom, Marxist historiography was created both by homegrown socialists and anarchists and by scholars trained in the Soviet Union such as Christopher Hill. Eminent left-wing historians such as E. P. Thompson, Eric Hobsbawm, and Christopher Hill eviscerated Whig historians such as Trevelyan for ignoring the role of the lower classes in the writing of British history. He was roundly criticized for suppressing the moments of revolutionary insurrection and class struggle in English history that became the central story in the writings of Hill, Thompson, and Hobsbawm.[68] Trevelyan also became the favorite whipping boy of liberal historians such as J. B. Bury, Herbert Butterfield, and Geoffrey Elton, who accused him of conducting insufficient research in the archives. Trevelyan was criticized for producing saccharine nationalism instead of critical history.[69]

Klyuchevsky and Trevelyan believed that they had a dual responsibility. As professional scholars, their task was to uncover important historical processes that had hitherto been unknown or suppressed. They reinterpreted the roles that subjects, both elite and ordinary, had played in the creation of the national past. They were interested in the questions of historical periodization and contributed original ideas to this area of inquiry. As scholars of their respective nations, however, they believed that they had a second and more important task. Writing intelligently, and above all empathetically about a shared past was one way of creating a living national history that elicited critical inquiry and inculcated a sense of belonging. Trevelyan and Klyuchevsky also hoped that their histories would lead to the development of nationalism and that their works would inspire an emotional and physical attachment to the land and its peoples.

Klyuchevsky and Trevelyan chose to write for a general public, who they were assiduous in building and cultivating. Rather than converse exclusively in a specialized language with fellow academics, they took upon themselves the immense responsibility of incubating a national self-consciousness among their students and fellow citizens. Klyuchevsky and Trevelyan argued that the main task of the historian should be the creation of civic citizenship through the use of affect and reason and that an understanding of the past should strengthen the social relationships that form the national fabric.[70] It is important to remember that they believed in cultivating a civil nationalism of assimilation and social belonging, rather than the illiberal nationalism of murderous hatred against an enemy. And finally, their studied indifference to imperial adventures and misadventures served to reinforce the trope of the good nation and civic nationalism that became enormously useful in post-imperial Russia and the United Kingdom.[71]

Verified facts and historical research are inimical to the strength of both the nation and the empire. The nation and the empire thrive in the absence of history, as nationalists and imperialists derive their self-confidence from a preferred self-image rather than from an accurate body of historical information that has the power to destroy these carefully constructed narratives. The historian's craft gathers political purpose and historically informed self-knowledge emerges only during the twilight of the nation and in the fading of the empire. What Hegel said about the discipline of philosophy that "the owl of Minerva spreads its wings only with the falling of the dusk" is much more appropriate when applied to the discipline of history. Klyuchevsky and Trevelyan were excellent scholars but also ardent nationalists who understood well the enormous powers of creation and destruction that they commanded through the discipline of history. Historians are usually a cosmopolitan lot trained to be indifferent to the siren song of nationalism when they dig for the truth in the archives, but these men put the nation ahead of their obligations to Clio and members of her rootless tribe.

4

Alone and against Systems Thinking

Emma Goldman and M. N. Roy

The story of the twentieth century has been narrated for the most part as a titanic struggle between Soviet communism (China and East bloc) and Western liberalism (the United States and Western Europe), ending with the decisive victory of the latter in 1991 when the Soviet Union imploded. While recent scholarship has expanded our understanding of modern world history by including the narratives of decolonization in Asia, Africa, and Latin America (and the rise of new nations on the ruins of European Empires), our image of the Left continues to be dominated by Soviet socialism, and state-based socialist systems in Eastern Europe, China, Vietnam, Cuba, Tanzania, North Korea, Cuba, and others. The Leninist-Stalinist-Maoist model of one-party rule, authoritarian male leadership, state-sponsored development, and gigantic bureaucratic welfare systems has effectively subsumed the alternative intellectual genealogies and political visions within the global left.[1]

We have thousands of biographies of Lenin, Stalin, Mao, and to a lesser extent of Che Guevara, Ho Chi Minh, Erich Honecker, Tito, Julius Nyerere, Pol Pot, and others, and many, many volumes on the activities of state-centered communist parties and social-democratic parties. This is particularly true about the field of Soviet Studies that has been concerned for the most part with the Bolsheviks led by Lenin, the Communist Party of the Soviet Union (CPSU), and the activities of the Communist International (Comintern).[2] However, we still know very little about the global non-Soviet left, a comprehensive if inelegant description of a cohort of mostly unknown members whose ideas and journeys crisscrossed the globe. Our knowledge gap about anarchists, Russia-centric anarchist moments, and the impact of anarchist thought on economics and philosophy is particularly profound.[3] This is unfortunate as these traditions of counter-modern thought and politics can help us reevaluate our ideas about modernity, selfhood, and state formation in the twenty-first century.

In this chapter, I provide a brief overview of Emma Goldman's and M. N. Roy's political careers, and consider how their experiences in the Soviet Union led them to resist the state-centric communism that was pioneered in the Soviet Union. But surprisingly, their "disillusionment in Russia" did not translate into uncritical support for systems of parliamentary democracy and capitalism. Instead, they devised horizontal models of community that were built around the rights and duties of the individual. In the second part, I examine the political alternatives that Goldman and Roy offered to illiberal and liberal modernity in the twentieth century. Although Goldman and Roy were both in Moscow during the years 1920 to 1923 when they were learning about the Soviet revolution, I have no proof that they either met or knew about each other's politics. Goldman had built a global reputation at that time, while Roy was relatively unknown. But they had a common acquaintance in Angelica Balabanoff, the secretary of the Comintern, who, like Goldman, was also an early critic of Bolshevik authoritarianism. Despite being located in separate hemispheres, one in the West and the other in Asia, Goldman and Roy came to astonishingly similar conclusions about the Soviet Union. Goldman, a lifelong anarchist, realized very early the limitations of the Soviet attempts to transform a decentralized socialist ideology into a system of state-sponsored and technocratic modernization that was directed from above. Roy's doubts about the Soviet experiment developed more slowly during the interwar decades and his ideas only appeared in print as a fully elaborate humanist critique of Soviet socialism in the 1940s.

Until the Twentieth Party Congress of 1956 and the onset of an officially sanctioned policy of de-Stalinization, intellectuals, progressives, and left-wing activists throughout the world were forced to choose between one of two options. Some supported the CPSU publicly while stifling their private misgivings about the lack of intra-party democracy and the widespread use of terror. Others publicly denounced the Soviet Union in acts of "liberal repentance," and went on to have successful careers as influential Cold Warriors. Goldman and Roy, risking ostracism and oblivion, avoided these two binary choices. Instead, they developed highly original critiques of liberal capitalism and state socialism that are worthy of our consideration. Goldman, famed anarchist and feminist, was forcibly deported from the United States to the Soviet Union in 1919 during the infamous Red Scare. But instead of finding a sinecure with the Bolshevik government as so many of her deported compatriots did, Goldman was one of the first left-wing intellectuals (along with Karl Kautsky, Rosa Luxembourg, and Angelica Balabanoff) to publicly criticize the Leninist model of revolution in her influential book *My Disillusionment in Russia*. Roy, an Indian nationalist, communist, and subsequently a self-styled radical humanist, fled to Berlin from the Soviet Union in 1928 during Stalin's bid for party leadership, and worked with the Communist Party Opposition in Berlin. Later, after a long period of incarceration in British India, Roy published his philosophy of "radical humanism" in his seminal two-volume, *Reason, Romanticism and Revolution*. Unlike most state and party-centered thinkers who were prominent during the interwar period, Goldman and Roy created a compelling vision of a sovereign individual, who would neither rule nor consent to be ruled, and who aspired to build a society based on a framework of radical equality. Goldman's and Roy's writings about selfhood and political power serve as an unacknowledged bridge to the New Left in the 1960s and help us understand how we, as individuals, bear responsibility for the creation of authoritarianism in both liberal and socialist societies.

Goldman and Roy were important members of the global non-Soviet left who are often left out of the history books of this period. This vast patchwork of ideas and individuals lacks an intellectual genealogy, an organizational category, an easily accessible body of theory, a catchy label, and, most importantly, a library descriptor.[4] Too often these independent thinkers have been reduced to bit parts in national histories as unruly individuals who cannot be grouped satisfactorily within political parties, intellectual canons, or even be ascribed a convenient label. They have been dismissed by both the communists and the liberals as "impractical" utopians whose ideas have little relevance to the stern ideologies of state-sponsored industrialization, modernization, and system-based theories that have dominated the twentieth century. Roy and Goldman theorized the renunciation of political power as the cornerstone of their political system and dreamed about the disaggregation of the vertical systems of one-party rule and parliamentary democracy. They believed that communities should be built around the principles of mutual aid and that relationships of reciprocity could only exist between strong and empowered individuals. They understood history in terms of actions that thinking individuals undertook, rather than attribute causality to the inscrutable workings of structures, classes, parties, and leaders. Since Goldman and Roy refused to theorize individual moral actions as an aggregate sociological phenomenon, they found little traction in an academy that has prized the role of the state over the actions of the individual.

Emma Goldman's Disillusionment in Russia

Emma Goldman died on May 14, 1940, in Toronto after a series of debilitating strokes, at the age of seventy. At the time of her death, Goldman had become a relatively marginalized figure in international politics and had suffered many political and personal disappointments.[5] After two decades of intense labor militancy in the United States, in which Goldman had played a major role, American capitalism emerged vastly strengthened after the First World War with the concerted help of the federal government. On the other side of the world the long-awaited Russian Revolution, a series of unstoppable popular movements that broke out at every level of the society, had been hijacked by the Bolshevik Party led by Lenin.[6] Popular demands for equality, international peace, cooperative labor, and the communal ownership of resources in Russia had been replaced by a highly inefficient system of coerced modernization. Finally, the Spanish Revolution of the 1930s, during which Goldman had worked very hard to advance the cause of grassroots community building, had ended with the victory of fascism and Stalinist communism. The enormous strengthening of authoritarian and liberal states in the twentieth century seemed to be an unnatural apotheosis after almost a century of anarchist politics at the local and the transnational level.

Goldman's tragedy was not hers alone, but of the many who had dared to dream of democratic self-governance and of a commonwealth formed of and by "sovereign individuals." Such dreamers were legion in the late nineteenth and the early part of the twentieth century, but many of them came to reluctantly acknowledge the power of historical reality and adopt the politics of "practicality." Overcoming their initial reservations, progressives, labor activists, intellectuals, artists, religious leaders, journalists, and students chose sides in the Cold War that enveloped the globe, affiliating themselves either with the United States or the Soviet Union. In the process, they pledged allegiance to abstract entities such as national political parties, the state, and the market. These entities were to efficiently organize the entirety of human existence without any input from individuals. Goldman refused to acquiesce to the new systems and proudly held fast to her principles: all the way to political oblivion. Her continued search for radical equality, and her refusal to consider either authoritarian dictatorship or parliamentary democracy as the only two political options in the world, set Goldman apart from those on the Left, the liberal center, and the Right. Till the very end of her life, Goldman was un-persuaded by arguments generated by "common sense" and "pragmatism": intellectual positions that convince us that the present is the best of all possible worlds. She died as she had lived: certain that the journey was more important than the destination; and that her ideal of a self-governing individual in a self-governing society was worth fighting for.[7]

Emma Goldman was born in Kovno (Kaunas, Lithuania) to a Jewish family in the Russian Empire in 1869. Goldman spent three years in a ghetto in St. Petersburg from 1882 to 1885 (important years of nihilist activity in Russia) as a teenager, during which she became enamored with the life of revolutionary politics. Goldman immigrated to the United States in 1885 at the age of seventeen to escape from her autocratic father and messy family politics that impaired her desire for freedom and independence. She learned about anarchist philosophy through immersion in factory work, intensive reading, and conversations with working-class intellectuals.[8] Thirty-four years later, federal authorities forcibly deported Goldman to the Soviet Union in 1919 along with 249 other radicals.[9] Deportation was among the many repressive tactics that the government used to contain the American labor movement during the infamous period dubbed the Red Scare. Despite her initial jubilation about the revolutionary events in Russia in 1917, Goldman was apprehensive about going back to the country of her origin—of relearning a language that she barely spoke. To the end of her days, and despite penning volumes of criticisms about the inequities of American capitalism, Goldman longed to go back home to the United States after being forcibly sent into exile.

Goldman was arrested countless times and served three stints in American prisons. For decades she had been constantly vilified by the mainstream press and had been brutally manhandled at rallies by policemen and vigilantes. But she gloried in the unbounded give and take of a raucous American popular culture that emerged in the early twentieth century when Progressive ideas were being fiercely contested in public places. It was far removed from the genteel, erudite, and secretive culture of the Russian intelligentsia that Goldman knew of secondhand, but revered greatly as an ideal throughout her life. A charismatic and commanding speaker, Red Emma blazed across the American continent for more than two decades lecturing in public about an eclectic array of topics that included individual freedom, labor rights, contraception, women's emancipation, homosexuality, politically inspired theater, and prison reform. She found fame and notoriety in equal measure, but always eschewed financial security even when it seemed to be within her reach. Goldman became a permanent fixture on the American left-wing intellectual circuits that developed before the First World War and was partially responsible for bringing the ideas of European intellectuals such as Pierre Joseph Proudhon, Friedrich Nietzsche, Peter Kropotkin, Nikolai Chernyshevsky, Max Stirner, Anton Chekhov, and George Bernard Shaw to the United States.

As the state was increasingly seen as the locus of all progressive politics in the twentieth century, Goldman's anarchist ideology of extreme individualism lost its luster. Instead, in an ironic turn, Goldman, who had famously scorned the demand for suffrage in her lifetime, became an icon of the feminist movement in the United States during the 1960s. Since then, her life, her work, and her gender politics have been subject to exhaustive scholarly investigation. Biographies abound, as do dissertations and edited volumes on Goldman's life and politics.[10] The Emma Goldman Papers, a project founded by Candace Falk at Berkeley, has made the bulk of her voluminous writings available to scholars.[11] Given Goldman's popularity as a historical subject in the United States, it is therefore surprising that her anti-Bolshevik memoir, *My Disillusionment in Russia*, has received little attention either in the field of Russian history or Russian-American relations.[12] Perhaps Goldman's anarchist critique of Bolshevik centralization of power was unpalatable to members of the Left in Europe and the United States, whose members were deeply supportive of the Soviet ideal of the all-encompassing welfare state that would provide for all human needs. Her vision of a self-regulating and cooperative society composed of self-reliant and self-made individuals fell by the wayside. Instead, the long and enduring romance with the interventionist welfare state that emerged in the last century continues into the present as the political paradigm of choice in influential political circles.[13]

During the twentieth century, many progressive intellectuals argued that only the state could alleviate poverty, distribute resources equitably, and bring about industrialization and modernization effectively in a way that ensured progress for all strata of society. Anarchists such as Goldman, drawing on the ideas of Leo Tolstoy, Peter Kropotkin, Mikhail Bakunin, Max Stirner, Joseph Proudhon,[14] and others, argued that the state was the original realm of unfreedom that created private property, unequal taxation, conscription, and war-mongering. The state used a punitive moral code and religion to uphold the rights of the few at the expense of the many. Most importantly, anarchists claimed that the growing power of the state destroyed popular initiatives, disrupted models of cooperative living and community organizing, and killed ideas related to individualism and self-development.[15] Rather than use the state to democratize and modernize society, Goldman argued that society should facilitate the growth of strong and free individuals who would neither rule nor consent to be ruled. Goldman's contention that the state, whether in its authoritarian or liberal incarnation, was an instrument of uniformity and inequality that deformed individuals in its path found little support. During the interwar years in the United States and Europe, the state became the locus of all progressive politics.

Goldman criticized the inability of liberals and Marxists alike to trust in human ingenuity, mutual aid, and individual endeavor. She believed that that the basic intent of politics should be to liberate the individual from the pernicious belief that we can only be saved from above: by leaders, by parties, by the state, and by authority figures. Goldman was an impoverished, working-class immigrant, with few social connections. She possessed little in the way of formal education. A persistent autodidact, Goldman transformed herself into a formidable public intellectual. Her inquiring mind, her ability to engage in discourse, and her habit of reading extensively helped her stay current with developments in politics and philosophy. An avid and intelligent reader,

Goldman took to heart Nietzsche's message of self-transformation through the application of will and energy. Like many working-class Russians during this period, Goldman saw knowledge and culture as a means of freedom and as a ladder that allowed her to join a transnational class of progressive intellectuals.[16] She had freed herself from her attachment to the patriarchal family and abhorred the social and religious conventions that accorded women a second-class and subservient status. Goldman wanted to build a society where everyone had the same opportunities, and did not want to be a recipient of philanthropy from her so-called social superiors. She scorned the well-intentioned paternalism of twentieth-century liberals that expressed itself through a preference for mammoth state projects, and close regulation by impersonal and, presumably, well-intentioned bureaucrats.

Goldman in Russia 1919

Goldman arrived in Russia in 1919, to a country that had been torn apart and devastated by years of war, revolution, and civil war. Her command of the Russian language was inadequate, and Goldman found it unnerving to be completely at the mercy of the Party. She found it distasteful to be forced to ask for food, shelter, and employment after decades of feisty self-reliance. The hardships of everyday life seemed to be overwhelming and in her private correspondence, Goldman begged her friends and family to send her mundane things such as aspirin, crackers, needle and thread, and warm clothes: things that were simply unavailable in war-torn Russia.[17]

Goldman's understanding of the Russian Revolution had been greatly influenced by her mentor, famed political thinker, and scientist, Peter Kropotkin. Kropotkin had returned to Russia after many years of exile in the West to participate in the Soviet experiment.[18] Like Kropotkin, Goldman believed that the revolutionary events of 1917 were powered by extensive and unregulated social movements from below that represented the democratic and community-based aspirations of millions of peasants, workers, soldiers, and members of the intelligentsia. Peasants, workers, students, anarchists, liberals, Tolstoyans, Socialist Revolutionaries, and many other participants argued that the real meaning of the Russian Revolution lay not in the published works of Lenin, nor in the political actions of a Trotsky or a Stalin. The Russian Revolution of 1917 was the culmination of countless acts of resistance by unnamed revolutionaries in the Russian Empire for several centuries.[19] The Bolsheviks had hijacked a social upheaval of gargantuan proportions and falsely imprinted their exclusive rights to a political volcano that had erupted through multiple craters during this revolutionary period of history.

Kropotkin was in a quandary that many left-wing activists faced with the Bolshevik ascent to power after the October Revolution. On the one hand, he refrained from overt criticism of the Bolsheviks, as he did not want to provide ammunition to the White Army or to Western powers such as Germany, Great Britain, France, Japan, and the United States that were intent on destroying the Russian Revolution and bringing back the rule of the propertied classes. Kropotkin found the politics of Western intervention and of the White groups that backed the restorations of monarchy and feudalism to be utterly abhorrent. At the same time, Kropotkin realized that the Bolsheviks were perverting the basic tenets of socialist democracy in their quest for undiluted power. This was a dilemma that many faced during this pivotal moment of history. Kropotkin, aged and infirm, chose to take the path of dignified silence, soothing his conscience about Bolshevist excesses with his labors in his garden at Dmitrov, at some distance from Moscow. Kropotkin, during this last period of his life, worked on a major manuscript on ethics that he was unable to publish before his death.[20]

Goldman, along with a few others such as Rosa Luxembourg, Ekaterina Breshko-Breshkokovskaia, Angelica Balabanoff, Alexander Berkman, Voline, Nestor Makhno, and M. N. Roy, to name only a few, came to the opposite conclusion that Kropotkin had reached. They believed that it was their political and moral duty to publicly criticize Bolshevism and keep alive the many philosophies of the global left that had existed long before the advent of Leninism. These individuals refused to embellish the Bolshevik myth that only a revolutionary avant-garde could save the masses and lead them to a modern and egalitarian future. Like Goldman, they freed themselves from a misplaced sense of duty to the Soviet cause that many on the Left continued to cherish up until the revelations of Stalinist excesses at the Twentieth Party Congress of the Communist Party of the Soviet Union in 1956, and beyond.

Goldman's time in the Soviet Union was marked by many tragedies. She saw the potential of cooperative labor repeatedly undermined by state dicta. Instead of encouraging workers' ownership of the labor process, party control was implemented in the new institutions that were being created in the fields and factories. She witnessed the unequal living standards that were beginning to divide the Party members from ordinary men and women. She learned of the repression of anarchists and Socialist Revolutionaries such as the famous Maria Spiridonova, and the savage wars that were waged against the legions of peasant anarchists in the countryside including those led by Nestor Makhno in Ukraine.[21] But as the book unfolds, it is clear that the death of Kropotkin and that of her friend and colleague John Reed, author of the famous work, *Ten Days that Shook the World*, really shook Goldman to the core. Goldman was puzzled by Kropotkin's and Reed's refusal to communicate their legitimate fears about the authoritarian degeneration of the Russian Revolution to a larger public. She simply did not understand the reasons for their political silence and adherence to a revolutionary dream that was quickly becoming a nightmare of authoritarianism.[22] But Goldman's grief caused by the untimely deaths of Kropotkin and Reed slowly hardened her decision to go public about her "disillusionment in Russia."

Reed, perhaps the most devoted of the legions of fellow travelers, died an early and unfortunate death, possibly because of the indifference of Bolshevik authorities to his ill health. Instead of providing adequate medical treatment, Grigori Zinoviev, head of the Communist International, forced Reed to go to Baku to speak at the Congress of the Toilers of the East where typhus was rampant.[23] Reed died of typhus two months later in October of 1920. According to Louise Bryant, Reed's wife and fellow journalist, Reed died believing that he was caught in a trap from which there was no exit.[24] Goldman's decision to break out of the leftist trap of silence, inaction, and tacit support for the Bolsheviks was solidified in the aftermath of the Kronstadt Rebellion of 1921.[25] When the Bolsheviks used armed repression to put down an uprising of soldiers, sailors, and workers calling for freedom of speech, assembly, and democratic self-governance, Goldman was heartbroken. She, along with Alexander Berkman, realized that they had to break with the Bolshevik regime no matter the consequences. Goldman's decision to leave the Soviet Union after the Kronstadt Rebellion probably saved her life, as many of her friends including William Shatov and Maria Spiridonova perished in the Stalinist purges of the 1930s.

Goldman's memoir has been read mostly as an indictment of the Bolshevik system and its mania for centralization, political control, and repression. Goldman argued that instead of trusting the people, Bolsheviks used them for political ends and in the process destroyed independence, rational thinking, and creativity. Goldman was unimpressed with the state-sponsored system of arts and culture in the Soviet Union. In her opinion, the Bolsheviks had failed to produce strong and fearless intellectuals such as Tolstoy and Chekhov because they neither understood nor valued the freedom of expression and thought. According to Alice Wexler, Goldman was responsible for perpetuating a totalitarian version of Bolshevik history that drew a straight line between the Bolshevik revolution of 1917 and Stalinism, and of ignoring the social-democratic potential of the NEP era.[26]

In *My Disillusionment in Russia,* along with an analysis of the Bolshevik system and its proto-totalitarian tendencies, Goldman also provides masterly portraits of individuals living in the Soviet Union. As a result, her book contains a sociological analysis of the ways in which people adapt to or resist political systems, especially authoritarian ones. Both reviewers and academics have ignored Goldman's examination of the ways in which ordinary men and women responded to Bolshevik rule and how they shaped the Soviet system. The more famous philosopher Hannah Arendt understood the rise of totalitarianism as a political phenomenon that evolved in Europe during the transition from a society dominated by the high bourgeoisie to the age of mass politics. Eschewing a structural analysis, Goldman described authoritarianism as the cumulative product of an individual's decision to abandon the tools of critical and independent thought, the lack of moral courage, and the inability to offer physical resistance to state pressure. Goldman argued that Homo Sovieticus was not just the inevitable product of a repressive Soviet system created from above as scholars of the totalitarian school were to argue in the following decades. Instead, she proposed that since the early days of Bolshevik rule, individuals had the choice to conform, collaborate, submit unthinkingly, and even profit from the Soviet system as it evolved. Some submitted unwillingly, engaging in slow sabotage and foot-dragging. Others, like Goldman, argued and protested vocally. And some like Nestor Makhno and other anarchists engaged in armed resistance. Goldman suggests that instead of the Soviet system shaping its citizenry in predetermined molds, the range of responses and actions by individuals led to the creation of a flexible Bolshevik system. And the evolution of the Soviet system could be traced through the range of interactions between the individual and the state. Furthermore, this allowed the state to hone its techniques of repression and character formation.

Goldman's literary portraits of friends and colleagues in *My Disillusionment in Russia* offer a fine case study in the historical analysis of revolution. William (Vladimir) Shatov, an influential labor organizer in the United States and a Russian-American émigré who returned to the Soviet Union, buried his anarchist misgivings and rose to become the Minister of Transport in the Far Eastern Republic. Shatov tried to convince Goldman that the Bolshevik system, despite its flaws, was the only socialist system in the world and thus it deserved their uncritical support. Goldman's political host, Sergei Zorin, secretary of the Petrograd Communist Party, started as a hardcore revolutionary but changed before Goldman's eyes into a careerist who regarded the right to free speech as a mere "bourgeois superstition."[27] Zorin, like Shatov, increasingly enjoyed the material perks of his office and, as Goldman observed, his devotion to bureaucratic duties dulled his revolutionary sensibilities.

Maria Spiridonova, a famous Socialist Revolutionary who had suffered many years in the tsarist prison system, took up active politics after the February Revolution when she was released. Spiridonova was punished severely for her political opposition by the Bolshevik government. She was repeatedly incarcerated and was even confined to a mental asylum for a period of time. Spiridonova, aged and infirm, finally chose silence as her political response. Spiridonova's pacifist response of noncompliance was different from the careerist embrace of the Bolshevik state by a Shatov or a Zorin. And according to Goldman, Spiridonova's revolutionary integrity, like that of Kropotkin and

Reed, remained unimpaired. Angelica Balabanoff, secretary of the Third Communist International, shared Goldman's doubts with the anti-democratic and anti-egalitarian tendencies of Bolsheviks, and like Goldman left the Soviet Union in 1922. Young Fanya Baron, another anarchist émigré from the United States, chose to ally with the anarchist organization Nabat and was executed by the Cheka for her opposition to the regime.

Goldman's decision to include lengthy vignettes about individuals in her book is both a political and a literary strategy. She effectively conveys that a political system is not simply the creation of a ruling class or a party, but the sum total of individual actions performed by those living within it. Political systems are not only extraneously imposed on oppressed populations but are the product of human fear and conformism, as well as the desire for power, material success, and upward mobility. They are born out of individual acts of courage and moral turpitude and nourished by the irrational and misplaced loyalty on the part of those who should have known better. For a revolution to be truly successful, it has to destroy not just the physical representation of authority in state and economic systems but the human fear of and belief in authoritarian systems. These systems persist because they suppress our basic human desire for freedom and destroy our faith in our ability to defy and resist. But in the long run, these systems collapse because, as Goldman said, "the craving for liberty and self-expression is a very fundamental and dominant trait."[28]

With the publication of *My Disillusionment in Russia*, Goldman became a persona non grata in the progressive circles of Western Europe and the United States. Her erstwhile American colleagues such as Lincoln Steffens, Rose Pastor Stokes, Ella Reeve Bloor, and others publicly attacked Goldman for betraying the Left.[29] And her crusade to demolish the Bolshevik myth of the equalizing and modernizing state, for the most part, fell on deaf ears. During this period, many progressive intellectuals became fellow travelers as they were deeply impressed by the potential of state planning, regulated welfare systems, and centralized support for art and culture.[30] As leftist intellectuals tried to justify Bolshevik methods to further the socialist cause worldwide, they were shocked and angered by Goldman's impolitic revelations and untimely candor about the deficiencies of the Soviet Union. Goldman even tried hard to recruit eminent British intellectuals such as Bertrand Russell and Harold Laski to speak on behalf of the imprisoned anarchists in the Soviet Union, with little success. Ultimately, she failed to find support for her unique brand of anarchist politics and to create a broad-based resistance to well-meaning but authoritarian state systems.[31]

Across the ideological divide, even as they loathed Goldman for her anarchist and feminist beliefs, *My Disillusionment in Russia* provided much ammunition to American conservatives in their crusade against Soviet politics and economics. Anti-Soviet publications such as the *New York Times, The Times* (London), and *The Chicago Tribune* reviewed her work favorably.[32] But Goldman did not fit the mold of the repentant ex-Leftist or the disillusioned Cold Warrior: two political positions that gained enormous importance in the mid-twentieth century. Erstwhile leftists such as Andre Gide, Louis Fischer, Arthur Koestler, Richard Wright, George Orwell, Irving Kristol, and many others publicly recanted their adherence to socialism during the Stalinist oppression of the 1930s and 1940s and proclaimed their allegiance to the liberal order by participating in anti-communist politics.[33] Goldman, on the other hand, continued to air her trenchant criticisms of the liberal state and capitalism, even as she dismissed the pretensions of state socialism. As Goldman wrote perceptively in 1940, "it is power that degrades and corrupts both master and slave and it makes no difference whether the power is wielded by an autocrat, by Parliament, or Soviets."[34] As a self-avowed anarchist, Goldman proved to be simply unusable as an intellectual battering ram on either side of the political spectrum during the Cold War. Till the very end of her life, Goldman was unmoved by the blandishments of political power and of material privilege. She refused to find a sinecure as a spokesman for either the Bolshevik political system or serve as an anti-Soviet spokeswoman in the West. Life is hard for those who refuse to obey and conform to the prevailing wisdom!

M. N. Roy's Disillusionment in Russia

M. N. Roy was a consummate revolutionary, who believed that only armed struggle would rid India of British rule. Vinayak Savarkar was an early inspiration as was the romantic Indian novelist, Bankim Chandra Chattopadhyay. Their firmly held beliefs that one's love for the nation should express itself as social and political service, as well as self-sacrifice, greatly appealed to the young Roy who flung himself into the radical arm of the Indian independence movement in Bengal. Roy knew very little about communism as he had been trained as an impassioned nationalist by important Indian leaders such as Jatin Mukherjee and Aurobindo Ghosh. Roy was sent abroad by Indian nationalists to procure weapons from the German government during the First World War. After his travels throughout China, Japan, Batavia, and other parts of East Asia in search of arms and material support, he landed on the West Coast of the United States. Roy met many left-wing American intellectuals at Stanford and Berkeley, and they shaped his politics and evolving worldview. Roy's coterie of friends included the young radical Evelyn Trent, a student at Stanford and his future wife and political companion in the Soviet Union. Roy was introduced to socialism in the United States where he exchanged his nationalist fervor for the cosmopolitan and universal ideas of socialism.[35] When the American authorities cracked down on Indian revolutionaries at the behest of the British authorities,[36] Roy fled to Mexico carrying a letter of introduction from David Starr Jordan, the pacifist president of Stanford University. He befriended Mikhail Borodin, a former Russian émigré to the United States, and helped found the Communist Party of Mexico. In Mexico, Roy utilized the generous subsidies of the German government and Borodin's intellectual tutelage to learn the socialist canon.[37]

Roy quickly rose in the transnational world of communism on account of his oratorical brilliance, theoretical abilities, and unshakable self-confidence even as he rapidly changed his political views according to the changing political contexts. However, Roy's ability to change his mind based on evidence and reason proved anathema to many who believed that ideological consistency alone was the hallmark of a true revolutionary. He was invited to the Soviet Union at the behest of Borodin and famously challenged Lenin when his colonial theses were presented at the Second Congress of the Comintern (Communist International) held in Moscow in 1920.[38] Lenin and other Soviet leaders wanted to support the national wars of independence in the colonies of Asia and Africa as a way to weaken European Empires and ultimately bring about the proletarian revolution in the heart of Europe. Roy, on the other hand, argued that British rule in India had created a powerful native bourgeoisie that was becoming increasingly influential in the Indian independence movement through its affiliation with the Indian National Congress. In both India and China, Roy advocated that the Soviet Union support and subsidize decentralized workers and peasant movements rather than promote nationalist movements per se. Mere freedom from British rule rather than a social and economic revolution in India, Roy argued repeatedly throughout his life, would strengthen the Indian bourgeoisie and hasten the spread of transnational capitalism.[39]

Roy proved to be persuasive and at the Second Comintern Congress of 1920, both Lenin's and Roy's theses were presented to the delegates. Roy recreated himself as a highly authoritarian leader in the mold of the tough Bolsheviks that surrounded him. He became a member of the Central Asian Bureau of the Comintern, and operating from Tashkent, he used revolutionary networks to help destabilize the western borders of British India in Afghanistan and the Northwest Frontier Provinces. This was a replay of the Russian and British Great Game of the nineteenth century.[40] Roy contributed to the formation of the Communist Party of India through his theoretical publications on the applicability of communist theory to colonial conditions. He was a member of the Presidium of the Comintern for eight years during which time he was active in the revolutionary movements of Western Europe, especially in Berlin, a city that he truly loved.[41] Perhaps because of Roy's uncompromisingly hard and Bolshevik attitude, he was chosen to accompany his erstwhile mentor,

Mikhail Borodin, to bring about a socialist revolution in China. However, Chiang Kai-shek, the leader of the Kuomintang, upset the poorly conceived Soviet plans for a proletarian revolution in his country by refusing to cooperate with Soviet plans. The Chinese debacle of 1927 helped Stalin popularize the idea of revolution in one country. Socialism in one country also became an internal blueprint for reorganizing the economy under the Soviet Five-Year Plans.[42]

This marked a major foreign policy shift against Trotsky's ideas about a permanent and worldwide proletarian revolution. International communist parties were explicitly instructed that the social democrats and all those who resisted Moscow's line were the real enemies. Fascism was to be regarded as nothing more than the most extreme form of capitalism and considered to be relatively harmless. Roy, who had initially sided with Stalin in his fight against Trotsky and had even voted for his expulsion from the CPSU, eventually came to disagree with Stalin's monumentally obtuse understanding of fascism. He managed to leave Moscow for Berlin with the help of the German communist Louise Gessler and Nikolai Bukharin in 1928. Roy was formally expelled from the Comintern in 1929. Subsequently, Roy declared his open support for the Communist Party Opposition in Berlin and worked with prominent members such as Jay Lovestone, August Thalheimer, and Heinrich Brandler, the latter two being his former mentors and comrades. This group was composed of disciples of Rosa Luxembourg, one of the most original critics of Leninist ideas about party centralization and dictatorship.[43] In a series of articles published in *Gegen Den Strom*, a communist opposition journal, Roy warned that the undemocratic centralization in the communist movement under Russian, rather than international, leadership, would inevitably lead to state terror.[44]

Roy returned to British India against all advice to the contrary in 1930 and played a significant role in organizing the Indian trade union movement. After an extensive manhunt, the British authorities in India arrested Roy in 1931, and accused him of "conspiring to deprive the King Emperor of his sovereignty in India." He was sentenced without a trial to a twelve-year term of imprisonment. He served five and a half years in various British prisons in India under circumstances so terrible that it drew protests from many Western intellectuals. Notably, Albert Einstein participated in a campaign orchestrated by Roy's companion and future wife, Ellen Gottschalk, to free Roy from his incarceration.[45] Roy came out of prison in poor and broken health but armed with nine volumes of his *Prison Writings* that ranged from texts on material philosophy, history, feminism, and even a beautifully written memoir of a cat.

At the express invitation of Jawaharlal Nehru, Roy joined the Indian National Congress (INC) hoping to turn the struggle for independence into a simultaneous struggle against Indian capitalists and landowners. Nehru was well aware of Roy's international reputation and hoped that he would boost the fortunes of the INC and attract more politically active sections of workers and peasants to the party. But Roy's hopes of radicalizing the INC soon faded in the face of Gandhi's political vision for a peaceful Indian independence movement. Roy's vision of a decentralized movement of peasants and workers, led from below, was strangely similar to that of Gandhi, but they disagreed fundamentally on tactics and means. Roy seemed to have also fundamentally misunderstood Gandhi as a man and as a leader and did not delve deep into Gandhi's writing on the development of the Indian village as a prototype for India.[46] Roy compared Gandhi's iron control over the INC to Stalin's hold over the CPSU and refused to treat him as a saint or a prophet as was becoming customary in Indian politics. Finally, Roy was appalled that the INC, under Gandhi's leadership, chose to launch the Quit India movement in 1942, at the height of the Second World War. Roy believed that fascism was the greatest evil of the age and argued that India could not become independent in an unfree and totalitarian world.[47] Roy's proposal that Indians postpone the struggle for independence until after the defeat of fascism was poorly received. Indian communists for their part, instructed by Moscow, accused Roy of deviationism and of being a renegade from Moscow's path.

Roy's inability to follow orders and his independence of thought led him to what some considered to be political wilderness and irrelevance in India during the 1940s, especially after he disbanded his Radical Democratic Party. But during this period leading to his death in 1954, Roy produced some of his most original and compelling political writing that has been little analyzed. Roy had initially published his magnum opus, *The Russian Revolution*, as a series of articles in 1937 after he was freed from prison by the British authorities in India. But he updated this work substantially when he reissued it in 1949. Anticipating that his work would be compared to Trotsky's infinitely better known *History of the Russian Revolution*, Roy critiqued Trotsky's work as "a masterpiece of imaginative literature; but as a work of history, it is of doubtful value."[48] A gifted and prolific writer, Roy in many ways resembled Trotsky, which makes his animosity toward the latter hard to understand. He wrote rather uncharitably that "Trotsky was a great man, and was very eager that he be recognized as such."[49] Roy alleged that Trotsky's egotism came in the way of his political achievements and that Trotsky only achieved greatness when his actions were tempered by Lenin's philosophical guidance and advice on revolutionary strategy. Roy went so far as to hint that but for Trotsky's intransigent opposition to the New Economic Policy, the history of the Soviet Union would have been less ruthless, less terrifying.[50]

Roy's antipathy to Trotsky was strange given that he had become a cosmopolitan internationalist from his early days in the United States and subsequently in Mexico. Roy, like Trotsky, believed in the concept of a global revolution till the end of his life. But whereas Trotsky argued that the Russian Revolution should move to Western Europe for support and sustenance from the working class, Roy believed that the revolutionary ideas of communism would work best among the European colonies in Asia and Africa. Finally, if Trotsky claimed that Stalin and his iron bureaucracy had betrayed the revolutionary promise of October, Roy never quite managed to repudiate his admiration of Stalin. Despite Roy's criticism of the various aspects of Stalinist policies, one can detect an undercurrent of approbation of Stalin the man in his writings.[51]

Roy predicted that Stalin would be remembered as a great leader in world history and extolled his historic military victory over the armies of fascism. But after the Second World War when the Soviet Union colonized much of Eastern Europe, Roy argued that the principles of Soviet communism could not be applied indiscriminately to the democratic and liberal traditions of Western Europe. He was deeply critical of the Soviet turn toward national chauvinism and rightly believed that Stalin's postwar foreign policy represented a resurgence of Russian Pan-Slavism. Roy wrote, "Stalin dropping the long coat and cap of the ordinary Red Army man, the simplicity which made him loved, to don the Marshal's regalia—there is tragedy in that picture. How awkward he looked in that ridiculous outfit, sitting between Roosevelt and Churchill at Tehran."[52] The Soviet imperialistic attack on Eastern Europe was a bitter blow for many colonial Marxists, especially since their attraction to the Soviet Union was based on Lenin's anti-colonial ideology. This was an important "God That Failed" moment for Roy. But as we will see, unlike the ex-communists from the West, Roy like Goldman never replaced the God of liberalism in the place of Marxism. He continued in his quest for a polytheistic and heterodox political ideology based on reason, individualism, and a commitment to social justice. An independent thinker, Roy looked for political freedom that lay beyond the binary intellectual positions of the Cold War and, like Goldman, refused to validate a bourgeois template of liberal politics even as he criticized Soviet socialism.

If communism had degenerated into a one-party dictatorship in the Soviet Union where all original thought and criticism had been stifled, and an expansive universalist vision had been replaced by a chauvinistic nationalism, then Roy argued that parliamentary democracy, although a great improvement on the former, was becoming unresponsive to the needs and desires of the populace in both Western Europe and in an independent India. Parliamentary democracy was a powerful fiction that could disguise class interests only temporarily, and, as a system, it needed to be fundamentally rethought, updated, and recreated to suit the circumstances of each age. Roy argued that his Marxist training had led him to reject all dogma, whether on the right or the left, and had led him to understand that no political system was sacred. He believed that all political systems evolved and changed, and that even the best ones should be continually improved to enlarge and ensure the widest possible democratic participation. Roy believed that the mere existence of more than one political party and the periodic holding of elections could not guarantee that a political system was either democratic or indeed representative of the popular will. He used the example of the dominant role of the Indian National Congress in Indian politics to explain that the adoption of formal parliamentary democracy in India had not created a mechanism for participatory and truly democratic politics. Postcolonial India had not created a truly inclusive and a representative political system.

Disillusioned with the two modern political alternatives of liberalism and Stalinism, Roy proposed a new philosophy one that he called Radical Humanism.[53] Roy combined the intellectual traditions of rational inquiry, scientific method, and the emphasis on individuality and individualism (drawn from Classical Greek, Indic, Islamic, and modern European intellectual thought) with the democratic ideas of community organization at the local level. He drew from anarchist, syndicalist, religious, trade union, and local movements of the global non-Soviet left, a tradition that was exemplified by thinkers and activists such as Leo Tolstoy, Emma Goldman, Rosa Luxembourg, and others. Roy, a passionate believer in individual freedom, argued that the anarchist left of the pre-Soviet era had been too quick to dismiss the claims of individual liberty in favor of the so-called collective. An idealized, utterly ahistorical, and spurious vision of the collective will found its most violent and anti-democratic expression in the deification of the national state in fascist countries and the proletariat in the communist ones. The adherents of both fascism and communism fell into the fallacy that "great men, heroes and supermen" could and should represent the will of the people.[54] They forgot to ascertain the real needs of the people and automatically assumed that the activities of the "great men, heroes and supermen" were always undertaken in the best interests of the former.

But Roy argued that classical liberalism was equally flawed, as in the name of economic freedom and popular sovereignty its followers had created parliamentary democracy: a system that was dominated and controlled by political parties that represented the interests of their donors, rather than the people that they claimed to serve. He said that the periodic elections of party representatives did not exemplify democratic self-expression, but instead signified the surrender of individual political rights to political parties that were themselves utterly undemocratic institutions. In a parliamentary system, popular sovereignty was vested in political parties rather than in the people themselves. Roy described elections thus: "With music, brass bands, flags, and shouting, the judgment of the people is dulled and benumbed; they are placed under some spell, and in that condition, they are asked to decide their fate. This is naturally more so in backward countries, but on principle, it is the same everywhere."[55]

Roy returned to a consideration of grassroots democracy as a possible solution to modern politics during the last years of his life.[56] He used the Russian model of the Soviets or workers' councils that was developed during the Russian Revolution of 1905 (when Trotsky played a significant role) to unearth the concept of multi-class and democratic councils that would represent local populations.[57] Roy argued repeatedly that the state had to be coterminous with society, not stand apart as an alien or occupying force, however benevolent or well-intentioned. Political representatives, drawn from local councils, would represent their local electorates and their needs at the next level of government, rather than work at the behest of political parties who for the most part formed around national or elite interests. These representatives had little relevance as they had little understanding of local politics. Roy believed, like Mikhail Bakunin and Peter Kropotkin before him, that a global society could be built on self-governing local councils or peoples' republics. He further advocated that these people's committees should have a designated constitutional status to prevent their assimilation into the structure of the formal party system.

It was not mere happenstance that Trotsky, the architect of the concept of the militarization of labor during the Civil War and the person who helped crush the Workers' Opposition Movement led by Alexander Shlyapnikov and Alexander Kollontai after the Civil War,[58] also returned to the idea of workers' councils in the final pages of his magnum opus, *Revolution Betrayed* (1937). Perhaps revolutionaries only return to ideas of democracy when they lose political power! But even at the end of his life Trotsky was unable to think beyond the Leninist paradigm of the charismatic revolutionary leader leading the masses to political victory. In the final pages of his brilliant and incendiary text *Revolution Betrayed*, Trotsky called for a violent overthrow of the Stalinist system, presumably led by Trotsky.[59]

Lenin had famously updated Marxist thought by arguing that a small disciplined party led by an indomitable leader could lead the proletarian class to power during periods of international crisis.[60] Having little faith in the working class, who by themselves could only produce trade union politics, or so Lenin argued, he put his faith in the revolutionary leader and the party to lead a successful revolution. Trotsky created the Fourth International as an alternative to the Soviet Third International, and he further propagated the Leninist line that only a brilliant leader and his party could successfully mount a working-class revolution. Roy, however, came to the opposite conclusion. He argued that the existence of political parties and power-hungry leaders created conditions of unfreedom in the first place and that even the most qualified leader with the best of intentions could not serve as a cure for political authoritarianism. Roy had admired Lenin his entire life and considered him to be the greatest political leader of the twentieth century. But in 1946,

Roy broke with Lenin's dicta on revolutionary politics and disbanded his party of Radical Democrats as a radical gesture of anti-politics. Roy, contra Lenin, who had brilliantly theorized the road to power, argued that the desire for power and the capture of political power, whether through revolutionary or parliamentary means, created the original problem of modern politics: that is, the loss of individual freedom. This condition of unfreedom was further exacerbated by the concentration of power in the hands of the few, whether in the form of the dictator or a democratically elected political party.

Roy, like Goldman believed that the capacity for free thought and action was one of the essential characteristics of the human condition. He argued that ultimately human beings would rebel against any political institution that was designed to frustrate their innate desire for freedom and equality.[61] The role of a leader was not to capture power either through the ballot box or through revolutionary methods and lead the masses to victory. Instead, the true leader should awaken the desire for freedom, reason, and radical self-government among their fellow human beings. And through that process of democratic awakening, the political leader would be made irrelevant and even redundant. According to Roy, the best leader should dedicate himself to becoming the last among equals. At the end of his life Roy found in education, and in rational and critical thought, the most potent tool of political emancipation and independence. He argued repeatedly that democracy could not function in the absence of an educated and informed electorate, and that aspiring politicians should be educators and facilitators, rather than revolutionary leaders.

Conclusion

Goldman and Roy were lonely voices in the 1920s, 1930s, 1940s, and 1950s, arguing that a strong collective could only be based on the ideas and activities of free individuals. In the interwar period mass politics took many forms: fascism, Stalinism, hyper-nationalism in the European colonies of Asia and Africa, and the consumer societies of advanced capitalism. Influential and seductive authoritarian voices called for the effacement of the individual for the sake of the leader, the state, the nation, the race, the class, and the market. Goldman's anarchist and libertarian self-fashioning seemed strangely out of sync with the times. Her important ideas about "individuality" as opposed to manufactured templates of "individualism" fostered by the state, religious authorities, educational institutions, and private property went largely unexplored. It was not until the emergence of the New Left in the 1960s that philosophers such as Herbert Marcuse published critiques of capitalism and communism as state-centric systems that effaced human individuality. But they failed to acknowledge their intellectual debt to thinkers such as Goldman, Roy, and other members of the global non-Soviet left that included oddballs, cranks, pacifists, homesteaders, agriculturalists, tree-huggers, advocates of vegetarianism, promoters of peasant and indigenous societies, environmentalists, anarchists, anarcho-syndicalists, union workers, associations of artisans and small producers, and many, many, feminists. These marginalized thinkers called for decentralized societies built by sovereign individuals and extolled the importance of bread labor, local production, and mutual aid. They called for the strengthening of local networks through which goods and services would be exchanged, rather than outsourcing them to the state, national parties, and corporations. They were suspicious of grand terms such as modernization, progress, the nation, and refused to sacrifice the present for the sake of a better future. Obstinate, insubordinate, and disrespectful to a fault, they refused to validate the existence of any hierarchy: be it political, social, economic, or even academic. Goldman and Roy dreamed of a post-capitalist and post-state world order: where the individual could flourish in concert with a just, equitable, and cooperative society. The basic tenets of anarchism summarized so brilliantly by George Woodcock as "faith in the essential decency of man, a desire for individual freedom, and an intolerance of domination" seem particularly important in the twenty-first century.[62]

5

Socialism and Capitalism on the Farm

Mukhamet Shayakhmetov and Wangari Maathai

In 1928 the Soviet Union embarked on one of the most controversial programs of its short-lived existence: the collectivization of agricultural lands. The process was poorly planned, hastily executed, and set into motion without consulting the peasantry who constituted over 80 percent of the Soviet population. Collectivization was also implemented against the advice of the Soviet Ministry of Agriculture, whose members were overwhelmingly in favor of a gradual transition to socialized and cooperative agriculture. The massive outpouring of violent resistance in many parts of the Soviet Union as peasants defended their land, livestock, and culture with farm implements and tools forced the government to initially retreat for a brief period. Stalin even gave a speech on March 2, 1930, blaming the local officials for the problems associated with the massive and forceful conversion of peasant landholdings into kolkhoz (farms that were owned collectively by peasants) and sovkhoz (state-owned industrial farms that hired labor). But collectivization soon resumed with great ferocity as the government essentially declared war on its citizens during this pivotal decade that fatally marked the subsequent history of the Soviet system.[1]

The results were catastrophic, and soon parts of the Soviet Union, including parts of the Central Black Soils region, Ukraine, the middle Volga region, the Northern Caucasus, and Kazakhstan, were in the grip of severe famine. Estimates of the casualties range from 5 to 9 million, but after all the counting experts agree that too many people died as a result of collectivization.[2] Millions of peasants were forcibly shipped to work on the newly created giant factory sites such as Magnitostroi and Dneiprostroi. And many recalcitrant peasants labeled as kulaks, or rich peasants, expanded the ranks of coerced labor in the hastily created gulag settlements across the Soviet Union, including the Soviet republic of Kazakhstan.[3] Even if the process of collectivization was a failure and turned the Soviet Union into a net importer of food in a little more than two decades, the state had secured its precarious existence in the short term by defeating the internal enemy: an independent peasantry and its visceral attachment to subsistence farming.

The Soviet Union had also established complete control over its agricultural resources, the main source of revenue for its ambitious plans of turning the Soviet Union into an industrial superpower, one that could rival the United States. It could now mechanize the process of agricultural production, significantly expand sown acreage by consolidating small agricultural strips and eliminate the practice of fallowing under which vast acreage of land lay untilled. Even though diets were impoverished across the empire, collective farms were forced to increase the production of flax, sugar beets, cotton, and oilseeds to aid the Soviet rapid industrialization program. Finally, collectivization transformed the settled peasantry and a population of former nomads in Siberia and Central Asia, who had acquired considerable independence in the tumultuous decade after the Bolshevik Revolution, into a semi-docile labor force. The Soviet Union could rapidly deploy this newly minted labor force in many sectors of the rapidly expanding economy at political will.

In his speech to the 17th Party Congress, also known as the "Victor's Congress," Stalin claimed:

> During this period, the U.S.S.R. has become radically transformed and has cast off the aspect of backwardness and medievalism. From an agrarian country, it has become an industrial country. From a country of small individual agriculture, it has become a country of collective, large-scale mechanized agriculture. From an ignorant, illiterate and uncultured country it has become—or rather it is becoming—a literate and cultured country covered by a vast network of higher, secondary and elementary schools functioning in the languages of the nationalities of the U.S.S.R.[4]

The speech was a fantastical projection of a future that the Soviet Union aspired to, and like the many socialist realist paintings of the period, a terrible distortion of the reality of a famine-stricken countryside that was bedeviled by violence. But in a supreme act of irony, Stalin's sanitized vision of the process of collectivization found a sympathetic audience, and the proponents of modernity broadcast it worldwide.

According to David Engerman, American journalists and experts were enthralled by the "romance of economic modernization" and because of their racialized understanding of "Asiatic Russians," they became inadvertent proponents of forced modernization in the Soviet Union. The Soviet desire to modernize the agricultural economy root and branch and to transform subsistence farmers into wage labor also found special resonance among intellectuals and scholars in the British Empire. While the American responses to the Bolshevik revolution and the Soviet Five-Year Plans have been highlighted in the scholarly literature, the British understanding of collectivization was even more important as they broadcast their views throughout their colonies in much of the developing world.[5] At that time, however, noted British Sovietologists such as Sir John Maynard and Maurice Dobbs, pioneers in writing the economic history of the Soviet Union, considered Soviet collectivization to be a long-overdue step in the right direction, toward a much-desired modernity. In this chapter, I will argue that British experts, native and colonial, viewed Soviet collectivization through the prism of the highly successful British Agricultural Revolution and its conjoined twin, the British plantation economy, that stretched in its colonies from the New World to Africa, and from Asia to Australasia. The British Agricultural Revolution marked the passage of the British economy from feudalism to a phenomenally successful capitalism. The model of the plantation economy undergirded British global dominance. As such, it served the world and the Russian Empire as an important model of agricultural development and economic modernization.

In the second part of the chapter, I will compare Soviet collectivization policies in Kazakhstan with the enormous expansion of the British plantation economy in Kenya that also took place in the 1930s. Few at that time or since then have remarked on the parallel process of land dispossession that occurred in both locations, or compared the scale of violence that was expended toward subsistence farmers and nomads in Kazakhstan and Kenya. This chapter will help illuminate the comparative processes of colonial and socialist modernity in the agricultural sectors of the two empires. Kenya marked the last iteration of an incredibly profitable British colonial system that had been tested worldwide in the last three centuries. The British plantation economy that was developed in the New World in the seventeenth and eighteenth centuries was subsequently deployed to India, Burma, Ceylon, Malaysia, Australia, and New Zealand in the eighteenth and nineteenth centuries. This system finally reached its apogee in parts of South and East Africa in the twentieth century. Plantations were an important source of imperial revenue and the profits that were repatriated to the mother country hastened the processes of British industrialization and modernization. Kazakhstan and Kenya were colonial states, where a predominantly subsistence land-based economy was transformed into a system of industrialized agriculture. Indigenous subsistence farmers and nomads were drawn into the mesh of modern waged labor systems through the process of coercion and the lavish application of violence. In the Soviet Union, monetary profits from collective agriculture failed to materialize and soon the sector became a drag on the Soviet economy. But in Kenya, the plantation economy created a very wealthy class of capitalist farmers as well as an affluent class of native smallholders.

Finally, in the last part of the chapter, I will compare the complex self-understanding that we find in the memoirs of Wangari Maathai, Noble Laureate, and Minister for the Environment in postcolonial Kenya, who grew up on a British plantation in Nigeria, and in Mukhamet Shayakhmetov's two-volume autobiography that was published after the collapse of the Soviet Union. An educator who grew up in Soviet Kazakhstan, Shayakhmetov chronicled the violent sedentarization of the Kazakh herdsman in his native land. Maathai's and Shayakhmetov's writings throw into stark relief one of the most important life processes of modernity: the transition of an individual from subsistence farming to living the life of a professional worker in the modern knowledge economy. Their lives and complex identities demonstrate the irreversibility of modernity and the ways in which colonial subjects themselves became the biggest advocates of modernization.

British Experts and Soviet Collectivization

Walter Duranty, the British-born reporter for the *New York Times*, has been widely criticized for downplaying the extent of the famine caused by Soviet collectivization. According to many, Duranty did so in order to maintain his position as an important Western reporter in the Soviet Union with unusual access to high-ranking Bolsheviks. On August 23, 1933, at the height of the famine Duranty wrote the following inexplicable and convoluted sentences: "The excellent harvest about to be gathered shows that any report of a famine in Russia is today an exaggeration or malignant propaganda. The food shortage which has affected almost the whole population in the last year, and particularly the grain-producing provinces—that is, the Ukraine, North Caucasus, the Lower Volga region—has, however, caused heavy loss of life."[6] Duranty's reluctant acknowledgment of the ill-effects of collectivization was in marked contrast to the full-bodied appreciation expressed by the Nobel Laureate Rabindranath Tagore. Visiting from British India in 1930, Tagore was extremely impressed by the confident and articulate Soviet collective farmers whom he met among audiences that were specially composed for the visiting dignitary. Tagore was struck by the way that former peoples from "backward" Central Asia were transformed by Soviet modernity, and contrasted them unfavorably with the timid and beaten down mien of the Indian farmers oppressed by centuries of British rule.[7]

Russian expert Sir John Maynard, who had served in the Indian Civil Service for over two decades, wrote,

> with a stranglehold on the food supply, for more than a dozen years after the Bolshevik coup d'état the peasants represented, even in their inchoate and spontaneous fashion, a distinct and independent nucleus of power, able to exercise leverage on all other aspects of policy. . . . While a heavy price was paid in human suffering, the main Bolshevik objective was achieved. The economic independence of the peasant was destroyed and a method created for getting grain to supply the cities and industry. A secondary gain was the release of manpower from the rural areas to the cities.[8]

Maynard, who had visited the Soviet Union during the years of collectivization and had even traveled to Ukraine and North Caucasus, the sites of terrible famine,[9] believed that collectivization was well-intentioned and even unavoidable. Modernization of agriculture gave Soviet peasants access to education, science, and technology, and allowed them to leave behind their former life of poverty and ignorance.[10]

Maurice Dobb, the pre-eminent Marxist economist at Cambridge University and author of the classic work on socialist development *Soviet Economic Development since 1917* that proved to be enormously influential in many postcolonial countries in the twentieth century, agreed with this verdict. He wrote, "the cornerstone of the First Five-Year Plan was precisely its combination of bold plans for industrial construction with a yet bolder transformation of the property relations of the village and the traditional forms of rural economy."[11] He praised the Five-Year Plans in terms very similar to those used by Stalin: that collectivization raised agricultural productivity, gave the state control over agricultural surplus, and moved millions of peasants from the fields to the factories. Dobb even recommended that the Soviet model of development be used in independent India in his 1948 reprint version of the book.

What accounted for this similarity of opinions about Soviet collectivization expressed by people who otherwise differed greatly in their ideological affiliations? Neither Duranty nor Tagore was an advocate of socialism, and Tagore was very critical of the Soviet censorship of culture and politics that he witnessed during his visit to the country. Maynard was a member of the Fabian Society and the British Labour Party, while Dobb was a lifelong communist and an ardent supporter of the Soviet Union. Were they simply in thrall to visions of modernity as so many were during this period? Or, as I will argue, did their understanding of the British Agricultural Revolution and the enormous success of the British plantation economy throughout the world shape their understanding of Soviet collectivization? Duranty was born in Liverpool, a British city that was enriched immeasurably by the lucrative transatlantic slave trade.[12] His grandfather was a merchant in the West Indies, a British colony that was an early pioneer of the immensely profitable sugarcane plantations that made their English owners some of the wealthiest people in Europe.[13] Part of the Tagore family fortune came from the shrewd investments that his grandfather, Dwarakanath Tagore, had made in opium, tea, and indigo plantations. Once the East India Company lost its trade monopoly in the rich province of Bengal in British India, aspiring capitalists such as Tagore were quick to avail themselves of these commercial opportunities that came in the wake of British imperialism.[14]

Maynard, while serving in Western Punjab, a province of British India as a civil servant, had witnessed the commercial success of the British colonial economy. Punjab was a model agricultural province that had been created by British engineering, both social and mechanical, in the late nineteenth century.[15] The construction of an extensive system of canals in the late nineteenth century transformed 6 million acres of former wasteland in North-Western India into an agricultural powerhouse that continues to dominate the Indian subcontinent today. Punjab became a province of vast commercial agricultural estates that produced huge quantities of wheat, cotton, and sugarcane for export that was transported by the newly built railway lines in British India.[16] Finally, Maurice Dobb, as an economist, had been deeply influenced by his colleague R. W. Tawney's path-breaking work that linked the successful agrarian revolution with the emergence of capitalism in England.[17]

The late nineteenth and early twentieth century witnessed its fair share of intellectual divisions, fault lines, and partisanship, but experts across the spectrum were curiously united in their attitude toward the peasantry.[18] Peasants, who composed the vast majority of the inhabitants on the globe, and whose labor enabled the very process of modernization, were assailed and vilified by economists on the left and the right with few exceptions. Their very presence was interpreted as a sign of economic backwardness and the persistence of feudalism in a country. Lenin celebrated the rapid growth of a landless agrarian proletariat in Russia in the late nineteenth century as according to him it marked the decline of feudalism in the Russian Empire.[19] As Esther Kingston-Mann's research demonstrates, many Russian economists, including Lenin and Plekhanov, promoted the English model of the Agricultural Revolution as the only path out of Russian poverty and backwardness. According to them, feudal agricultural estates were inherently backward and the empire would be better served if these estates moved toward commercial production. Similarly, the unproductive subsistence farmers who lived on the edge of poverty could serve as a wage labor force for the modernized farms.[20]

The modernity of a country was judged by the percentage of the population that was engaged in agricultural labor and as such the race was on to move peasants engaged in what were considered to be unproductive subsistence labor, to work either in factories or, more commonly, in industrial farms that were engaged in specialized agricultural production for the market. The profitable plantation economy that was developed in the European colonies in the Americas, Asia, and Africa since the fifteenth century offered a model of how to transform former subsistence farmers, foragers, and nomads into efficient but unfree agricultural workers. The plantation economy also proved that it was possible to turn cash crops such as sugarcane, tobacco, coffee, rubber, and chocolate into sources of incredible wealth for those who owned the plantations, especially if the labor costs were kept low through the liberal use of slavery and coercive practices. Punitive taxation policies were also used to extract surplus from subsistence farmers and force them to move from their "unproductive plots" to work on commercial plantations.[21]

Few worried about the environmental impact of large-scale agriculture at that time, and fewer still were concerned with the property rights of the subsistence farmers, foragers, and nomadic populations. Even the diehard populists and neo-populists in Russia, who were passionately devoted to the preservation of the peasant commune, were anxious to bring rationality, science, and modern techniques to the small peasant farm. They believed that it was possible to move peasants from the realm of mere subsistence to a world of plenty through the institution of scientific cooperative agriculture and communal landholding.[22] Marx famously called the peasantry "a sack of potatoes," whose members were incapable of either constituting a true class or developing the requisite class consciousness that would allow for class formation. The peasant's independent vision made it hard for inchoate individuals to coalesce as a class and press for their political goals. In 1851 Marx wrote that

> the small-holding peasants form an enormous mass whose members live in similar conditions but without entering into manifold relations with each other. Their mode of production isolates them from one another instead of bringing them into mutual intercourse. . . . Their field of production, the small-holding, permits no division of labor in its cultivation, no application of science, and therefore no multifariousness of development, no diversity of talent, no wealth of social relationships. Each individual peasant family is almost self-sufficient, directly produces most of its consumer needs, and thus acquires its means of life more through an exchange with nature than in intercourse with society. . . . Their representative must at the same time appear as their master, as an authority over them, an unlimited governmental power that protects them from the other classes and sends them rain and sunshine from above.[23]

Marx's ideas about the innate backwardness of the peasantry and feudalism as an economic system were drawn from the work of generations of

English agronomists and influential commentators such as Jethro Tull, Lord Townshend, and Arthur Young. British agricultural innovations proved that to raise agricultural productivity one had to move from the open two- or three-field system of agriculture that was practiced throughout Europe, West Asia, and the Mediterranean to a closed system of continuous production, crop rotation, intensive manuring, and crop specialization. This system was born in the Low Countries but perfected in England in the eighteenth and nineteenth centuries. Peasant agrarian practices were to be replaced by scientific agricultural sciences, and the subsistence farmer was to be directed by a "master" from above and transformed into a productive wage laborer. The series of enclosure movements in England that started in the fifteenth century and which gained speed in the eighteenth century lay at the heart of the British Agricultural Revolution. Between 1700 and 1850 while the population grew exponentially, the number of people engaged in farming dropped precipitously because of the exceptionally high agricultural yields that could feed the country. By enclosing and consolidating scattered farm strips, a class of capitalist farmers, lords, yeomen, and tenant farmers turned agricultural land into a source of profit. Former small subsistence peasants that surrounded the former manorial estates became landless agricultural workers for these new commercial agricultural estates. Later, these dispossessed peasants would provide labor for the English factory system.[24]

Agronomists believed that the small size of the peasant farm and the communal patterns of landholding militated against innovation, profit, and entrepreneurship. New farming practices such as multi-cropping and continuous crop rotation were instituted on these enclosed farms. The elimination of fallowing or letting land lie unused for a period of time greatly expanded the acreage devoted to crops.[25] The growing of animal feed crops such as turnips on fields that were formerly fallowed increased sown acreage by almost 20 percent in England. Increasing feed crops allowed for larger animal stocks, which in turn meant larger supplies of manure for the enterprising farmer, the principal source of nitrogen fertilizer before the discovery of synthetic combinations in the twentieth century. New methods of animal husbandry increased the stock and health of cattle and sheep populations. The plantings of clover and legumes increased the nitrogen content of the soil leading in turn to vast increases in cereal production. Fens, pasture, and woodlands were reclaimed as agricultural lands, and high-yielding wheat and barley replaced the planting of traditional rye. Newly built canals, roads, and railroads connected farmers with urban markets. Finally, it was much easier to introduce high-quality agricultural equipment, seeds, new crops, and techniques to large independent farms than on small peasant farms that hewed to a communal planting schedule. Marx further argued that the Agricultural Revolution in England also allowed for the evolution of a capitalist mentality that perceived land as a source of profit or return on capital. This profit-oriented mentality turned farmers and merchants into capitalists and former peasants into wage workers.[26]

According to R. H. Tawney, one of the key theorists of the emergence of capitalism as a historical phenomenon,

> agrarian changes of the sixteenth century may be regarded as a long step in the commercialising of English life. The growth of the textile industries is closely connected with the development of pasture farming, and it was the export of woolen cloth, that "prodigy of trade," which first brought England conspicuously into world commerce, and was the motive for more than one of those early expeditions to discover new markets, out of which grew plantations, colonies, and empire.[27]

While Tawney, the moralizing Christian socialist, deplored the rise of capitalism, individualism, and profiteering in England, he ultimately tied the founding and the success of the British Empire to the elimination of subsistence farming and the peasantry in England.

Soviet Collectivization and the Famine in Kazakhstan

It is a truism in the field of Slavic Studies that Russian agriculture was backward compared to its Western European counterparts. Peasants, especially in the Central Black Earth provinces, stubbornly held to the common three-field system of agriculture that included one-third acreage planted with cereals such as wheat or rye, another third devoted to oats to feed the cattle, and the third lying fallow for the common grazing of cattle. Peasants in the Russian Empire used the rudimentary sokha (plow) for shallow tilling of the soil, instead of switching to the deep tilling by steel plows that were becoming popular in Western Europe in the nineteenth century. The narrow strips of sown land and the small parcels of peasant land prevented the widespread adoption of mechanization, even though the peasants themselves were deeply interested in improved quality seeds and tools, and modern agronomic knowledge. The demographic revolution in the late nineteenth century led to increasing pressure on the land in the Central Provinces and considerable migration to areas such as Siberia and newly acquired colonies in Central Asia.[28]

Despite its technical backwardness and the lower productivity of workers compared to the countries in Western Europe, Russian agriculture was a force to reckon with in global commodity markets in the late nineteenth century.

Wheat produced in the Baltics and the vast steppe region stretching from the border of Romania through Ukraine, the Central Agricultural Regions, areas of the middle Volga, southwest Urals, and in south-western Siberia was exported to Europe and allowed countries such as England to feed their industrial workers. Cash crops such as sugar beets were cultivated in Northern Ukraine, and there was a huge increase in cotton production in the new colonies of Turkestan or Central Asia. Russian cotton was sent to Western textile mills, especially when production plummeted in the United States in the aftermath of the Civil War. Agriculture accounted for almost 51 percent of the earnings of the Russian Empire in 1913.[29]

The Stolypin reforms instituted between 1905 and 1911 were intended to help wealthy peasant farms leave the communal land tenure system and become a force for political stability and economic modernization in the countryside.[30] The Bolshevik revolution of 1917 however reversed the inexorable progress of industrial agriculture that Lenin had so desired to see in the Russian Empire. Instead of rapidly moving toward large-scale collectivized estates, the Russian peasantry fell into "backward" ways again as wealthy and large estates were broken up and the land was redistributed on a communal basis.[31] Instead of intensifying grain production on socialized land, there was a huge growth in the number of middle peasants and a concomitant fall in the number of rich and poor peasants. The acreage sown with fodder and feed fell as did the cultivation of cash crops such as flax, sugar beet, and cotton. According to Jim Heinzen, though agricultural production reached its prewar levels by 1927, the marketed surplus of meat, grain, potatoes, beets, and other cereals was significantly lower than in the pre-revolutionary era.[32] The peasant refusal to embrace the gospel of market productivity created huge problems for the Soviet Union and almost all left-wing economists across the spectrum believed that agriculture had to be the source of "primitive accumulation," of labor and resources that would fund the modernization of the socialist economy.[33]

In recent decades, our understanding of Soviet collectivization has been expanded by access to archival information that describes the vast sufferings of peasants under the policies of the Five Year Plans. These archives also give us a fuller picture of the peasants' imaginative acts of resistance.[34] Many scholars have interpreted collectivization as a uniquely Russian/Soviet tragedy, as an act of intentional genocide directed by a totalitarian regime and a homicidal Stalin against the subject peoples of the Soviet Union.[35] These new interpretations have transferred our attention away from the story of Soviet agricultural and industrial modernization that was developed by British Sovietologists such as Maurice Dobb, E. H. Carr, and Alexander Nove. Subsequently, R. W. Davies's and Stephen Wheatcroft's prodigious researches in the field of Soviet agriculture have confirmed many of the findings of the early school of British Sovietology. But British scholars did not compare Soviet policies with chapters of their colonial history, treating collectivization for the most part as a sui generis phenomenon. In the next section, I will highlight the uncanny similarities between the modernization and the development of the countryside in Soviet Kazakhstan and British Kenya.

The Kazakh experience of Soviet modernity reached its crescendo in the early 1930s when almost a quarter of its population, or 145,000 people, died in the famines caused by collectivization. The Russian Empire began intruding into what would later be known as Russian Turkestan as early as the eighteenth century although it formalized military control of this vast region in the late nineteenth century. Fearing encroachment from the British Empire in India, after the acquisition of the North-Western Provinces that abutted Afghanistan, the Russian Empire sealed its control over Central Asia. The Great Game of rivalry and military confrontations in Asia was formally interrupted by the signing of the Anglo-Russian Convention of 1907. A million and a half European colonists (German, Ukrainian, and Russian) moved to Kazakhstan during this period, putting considerable pressure on the nomadic steppe peoples and further restricting their movements. The Trans-Aral Railway that was completed by 1906 facilitated further European migration into Central Asia. By the 1920s, European colonists consisted of almost a quarter of the total population of Kazakhstan. They held the best agricultural lands and had managed to secure the most access to water resources. Turkestan was renamed Soviet Central Asia, and in 1936 the Kazakh Soviet Socialist Republic became a formal part of the Soviet Union.

Another 300,000 dekulakized European peasants arrived there between 1930 and 1933 putting additional pressure on environmental resources and limiting the regions where Kazaks could feed and water their extensive herds of camels, sheep, and horses. Kazakh nomads, a Muslim and Turkic-speaking group, were incorporated into the Russian economy by exchanging Kazakh livestock and animal products for grain and cheap manufactured goods. At the time of collectivization, only 23 percent of the population was sedentary. The majority of the Kazakh herdsmen were desperately poor and took care of the animals belonging to rich herdowners or "bais," much like sharecroppers and peasants on feudal estates. Many were nomadic people who migrated to cooler mountainous regions during the brutally hot summers of Kazakhstan. There was little for the cattle to eat in the hot and dusty plains during summer, and transhumance was an economic necessity that created a rich web of culture and human relationships in its wake.

Kazakhs had suffered terribly between 1916 and 1922 from the political depredations of Russian and the Soviet state that tried to conscript their men to serve in the army. Successive administrations had also tried to collect provisions by force from the nomadic and sedentary populations. The violent policies of colonial expropriation came to a head during the terrible famine of 1921–2 when many lives were lost. Periods of intense droughts that occurred periodically in the region also added to the misery of the inhabitants. Most of the Kazakhs were not self-sufficient nomads, and most of them traded their animal resources like meat, milk, and leather goods for grain, which formed the major part of their diet. As Sarah Cameron has argued in her brilliant book, the famine of 1931–4 was the end of a long process of modernization that started under the Russian Empire, rather than a unique phenomenon that exemplified the violence of the Soviet state. The Russian state exerted pressure on Kazakh diets, nomadic travel routes, and the environment, as did the in-migration of colonists from the Russian Empire. The Soviet state in its heavy-handed way completely sedentarized the bulk of the Kazakh population and significantly changed the lives of the remaining livestock herders. They became low-paid workers in Soviet collective farms.[36]

Collectivization in Kazakhstan was intended to achieve three things: to destroy the power of the wealthy herd owners or bais by confiscating their livestock and grain for use in collective farms; to sedentarize the nomadic Kazakhs in collective farms whose produce the state could then control and use for its purposes; and to turn Kazakhs into a source of modern agricultural and industrial labor, and recruits for the Soviet military. Soviet authorities hoped that Kazakhstan would become the center of a giant meat-packing industry, and later, through Khrushchev's Virgin Lands campaign, there was an attempt to increase wheat cultivation in the drought-prone steppes. Both plans ended in failure. The Kazakhs were sedentarized through an enormous expenditure of violence in which almost a third of the ethnic Kazakh population died. Many fled to neighboring states in Siberia, Uzbekistan, and even China to escape the collectivization of their herds. There was a catastrophic drop in livestock holdings as Kazakhs were not given the resources to feed their herds, while others sold and butchered their animals to meet the state quotas for meat and grain. Animals were also sold surreptitiously to ward off death by starvation. The collective farms were poorly equipped, and the labor was so demoralized and unskilled that they failed to produce the grain in amounts the state desired. Without transhumance, it was impossible to feed herds of cattle in the plains during the scorching hot summers without additional sources of feed. Soon food had to be imported to offset the famine that the Soviet state had itself created. Modernization had come to Kazakhstan, but without the infrastructure, the skilled labor force, or the technology that is necessary to produce the high rates of growth. Later, in the Brezhnev period when the vast oil, gas, and minerals industries of Kazakhstan were developed, this area would become an economic power house that persists today.

Since its publication and translation into English, Mukhamet Shayakhmetov's two memoirs have become an important source to understand the utter inhumanity of the Soviet collectivization project.[37] His stark and vivid prose highlights the sufferings of a nine-year-old boy who is forced to become the man of the house because his father, a kulak or a wealthy peasant, was arrested. Shayakhmetov describes solitary journeys over incredible distances to procure food for his starving family. He mourns the loss of their herds of cattle and the loss of the nomadic lifestyle that was rich in social and cultural relationships. Shayakhmetov recounts the brilliant improvisations of his mother, who became the second "man" in her family after her husband's imprisonment. From gleaning for corn in already harvested fields to endless work in labor brigades, the family survived the famine years due to the kindness of family members, especially his elder brother, Aiken. Shayakhmetov presents us word pictures of corrupt local officials who grew rich through confiscations of land and cattle and of kind Russian colonists who traded goods with the starving Kazakhs. The books contain scenes of unimaginable horror and of hunger and starvation that were rampant in the poorly administered collective farms.

As we read deeper into the memoir, we realize that the famine of 1931–4 that Shayakhmetov so brilliantly describes is but a prologue to the first memoir that is written very much in the tradition of the socialist realist novel. Our young hero faces many trials and adversities, but the Soviet project of universality and modernization gives him a prototype for upward mobility. More importantly, Shayakhmetov realizes that living ethically and for the welfare of others is more important than accumulating wealth and power for the clan. Shayakhmetov's father is unable to adjust to the loss of his nomadic herder status and dies in imprisonment, a broken man who aged rapidly in the face of calamitous circumstances. Shayakhmetov, however, literally fleshes out the Soviet dream of civilization and progress as he advances through the educational system. Although the schools initially discriminate against him because of his Kulak origins, Shayakhmetov perseveres and is rewarded with success. At the end of his career, Shayakhmetov is appointed as the head of the education department for one of the largest regions in Kazakhstan.

Shayakhmetov is wounded in the epic battle of Stalingrad during the Second World War and is decorated by the state as a war hero. It would have been relatively easy for him to profit from his medals and rise to the commanding heights of the Soviet system. But Shayakhmetov turns down offers to rise in the Soviet party hierarchy and refuses to be a careerist, beholden to others for his promotions. Instead, he dedicates his life to educating Kazakh children so that they can succeed in the Soviet system like him. One of his role models is a young teacher, Trofim Trofimovich Adamenko, who gives him the best gift of all: a command of Russian, the language of the colonizers.[38] A second mentor, Semion Akimovih Yakovenko, admits Shayakhmetov to school despite his kulak background and helps him with his lessons.[39] His proficiency in Russian helps Shayakhmetov leave behind the life of a nomadic livestock herder and dodge the terrible fate of being condemned to servitude as an agricultural worker on a state collective farm. He fully embraces the life of a modern Soviet citizen who is more at ease in his apartment in the city than in the tents with the nomads. Interestingly, Shayakhmetov retains his affection for those elements of Kazakh culture that are consonant with the tenets of Soviet ideology: a strong work ethic, generosity toward those in need, and reverence for the family. But Shayakhmetov's family values include a firm commitment to gender equality, and he exhibits a special concern with advancing women's education, a central tenet of Soviet feminism. He has made himself the perfect Soviet subject, national in form and socialist in content.

Shayakhmetov's changing attitudes toward nature, which are recorded in the two memoirs, illustrate perfectly his long journey from nomadic living to his identification as a modern subject who can only be at home in the built environment. Nature is transformed from the realm of a meager and hardscrabble subsistence of his childhood to that of aesthetic contemplation, and a place where Shayakhmetov can relive select memories of his childhood. In the first book, the natural landscapes of Kazakhstan are filled with hunger and want, where a young Shayakhmetov struggles hard to fill his belly. He is at war with nature, trying to wring the basic minimum from it to bring a little food home to his starving family. The paths through the valleys are dangerous, and human and animal predators lurk at every turn and corner. In the second volume, when Shayakhmetov has become a successful Soviet citizen, we find lush descriptions of the mountains and valleys teeming with game for the avid hunter. The rivers are full of fish, enough to satisfy the desires of the most ardent angler. But Shayakhmetov leaves the beautiful Ulan district "without a shadow of regret in my heart" because his wife is ill and she needs modern medical care in the city.[40] The transformation is complete, and the modern Shayakhmetov realizes the limitation of the natural world. He happily embraces the conveniences of modern living.

Later, in the second volume, the thoroughly citified Shayakhmetov returns to the mountains in the summer to partake of the kumys cure or "folk medicine" as he calls it. Kumys is a fermented and probiotic drink made from mare's milk that has sustained the peoples of the steppes for many centuries. Despite its humble origins, many upper-class Russians came to the steppes in the last two decades of Tsarist Russia to avail themselves of the miraculous kumys cure for upset and disordered stomachs, ennui, and even emotional suffering. Shayakhmetov is unconscious of the patronizing tone that he uses to describe this folk medicine. It is doubly ironical that he reverts to the remedies of his Kazakh past to treat the modern ailments of acidity and indigestion that are caused by processed foods and other products of industrial agriculture.[41] By the end of the book, Shayakhmetov is just another tourist returning to his roots momentarily, to indulge in his passion for wide-open spaces. He retreats to "the simple life" intermittently from the safety of his modern and ordered existence. For the ex-nomad, the Kazakh steppes have become a series of "dude ranches," or plantations where one can relive a sanitized version of the past that can be seen safely in the rear-view mirror.

The Plantation Economy in Kenya

Two important books were published on the plantation economy during the 1930s and early 1940s, the decade of the infamous Soviet collectivization efforts. But few commentators in the Anglophone world linked the two systems of agricultural production in a single analytical frame. In 1931, Edgar Thompson, himself the son of a plantation owner, defended his dissertation on the form and nature of the plantation at the University of Chicago. He described the plantation primarily as a "race-making institution." Thompson claimed that the plantation system was an instrument of European imperial expansion and that it led to the creation of its colonial settlements in the Atlantic world.[42] He argued that the commercial success of the plantation economy was linked to two important pre-conditions: access to global markets where the products of the plantation economy could be sold to a very large consumer base. Second, Thompson claimed that the plantation economy was dependent on forced labor for the entirety of its production process.

In 1943, Eric Williams, born in Trinidad and educated at St. Catherine's College at Oxford University, published an equally compelling account of the sugar plantation economy in West Indies, but advanced a completely different set of explanations for its success. Unlike Thompson, a white man, who was interested in the race relations of the plantation, Williams was much more interested in how the plantation contributed to the development of British capitalism. Williams, who was of Afro-Caribbean origin, argued that the plantation was not a race-making institution per se, but a profit-seeking system that was agnostic in its exploitation of labor resources and played little attention to the skin color of the slave. According to Williams, "negro slavery" was the third installment of a well-established system of economic servitude that had previously enslaved poor whites and then when they proved to be of little value turned to native Indians. Williams claimed that "negroes" were a superior class of workers, with stronger constitutions, and had an excellent work ethic. The fact that negro slaves could be procured more cheaply than their white or native Indian counterparts also made them indispensable to the plantation economy.

Williams wrote that "as compared with Indian and white labor, negro slavery was eminently superior."[43] But Williams concurred with Thompson that the

British plantation economy was a tremendously profitable system, so much so that its profits underwrote the success of industrial capitalism in Great Britain. Capitalism in turn destroyed the institution of slavery because in the long run wage labor proved to be more profitable. Williams was very critical of non-economic arguments that claimed that slavery ended in the Atlantic world because of the moral indignation of liberal audiences in the British metropole. He was unconvinced that anti-slavery movements alone would have succeeded in dismantling this profitable system. Instead, he provided plenty of counter-evidence to prove the economic superiority of wage labor that ultimately led to the decline of the use of slave labor in the plantations in the Caribbean.

The plantation economy was perhaps the most ubiquitous face of the British Empire, and by the early nineteenth century, the economic value of plantations in the New World along with the African slave trade translated to almost 11 percent of the British economy.[44] Plantations in the British Empire started as the slave-based sugar and cotton plantations of the New World, but they grew increasingly sophisticated and diverse as the system spread across the world. The system also evolved and adapted to prevailing conditions and local circumstances. Plantations grew to encompass the farming of opium, tea, coffee, spices, rubber, indigo, and many other products in the British colonies of India and Southeast Asia in the eighteenth and nineteenth centuries. Instead of relying on slave labor, the plantations in Asia depended on sophisticated systems of debt peonage and bonded labor. The plantation economy found its third iteration in the new colonial possessions that the British Empire acquired in Africa in the late nineteenth and early twentieth centuries, about the same time the Russians were colonizing the immense expanse of Central Asia, including Kazakhstan.[45]

Between 1880 and the early 1900s the enormous continent of Africa was divided between the empires of France, Britain, Germany, Portugal, and Belgium. British imperialism in Africa took several forms depending on the geography, climate, the availability of natural resources, and the proximity to existing trade routes. Thus for example the British deepened their hold over Egypt and Sudan by investing heavily in slave-based cotton plantations that emerged during the collapse of the American cotton markets during the American Civil War. Imports of Egyptian cotton were vital to sustaining the cotton mills of Lancashire that had been devastated by the decline in American cotton imports.[46] In places such as Ghana and Nigeria, the British used the system of indirect rule by propping up local rulers and using them as instruments of British taxation. The Imperial British East Africa Company was formed to exploit the natural resources of this region and safeguard the trade routes to India. The East Africa Company created the East Africa Protectorate, but ultimately it became a British Crown colony in 1895. The creation of Uganda to the west of the Protectorate meant that the British were in control of the headwaters of the Nile River, essential to their control of Egypt and the Suez Canal. The establishment of the Kenya colony, a part of the East Africa Protectorate, was intended to administer a strong rebuff to German colonial aspirations in East Africa. The Colony and Protectorate of Kenya ceased being a commercial possession in 1920 and became a full-fledged British colony that was administered directly by the Crown.

Between 1896 and 1901 the British authorities built a railway system from Mombasa on the East African coast to Lake Victoria in the interior. The railway system was critical for British attempts to solidify their hold over the territory and to facilitate trade and commerce in the region. Skilled laborers were imported from India to help with the construction. The Russian Empire built the Trans-Aral railway that snaked across the Central Asian steppes at roughly the same time.[47] Railways were costly to build and maintain, and in order to recoup the costs of construction, the British treasury was keen to make profits in their colonies. Colonies became useless when revenue was expended on modernization efforts or on welfare projects for the natives. In Uganda, the British developed a robust system of commercial peasant farming, which resulted in a steady source of income from taxes. Kenya, on the other hand, especially the temperate highland areas of the Central Valley and the Rift Valley, was considered appropriate for settlement by Europeans, many of whom came from British South Africa. The European settlers brought capital and management skills, but the inhabitants of the Kenya colony supplied the land, the labor, and the natural resources.

To mark the inception of their direct rule, the British declared that all land in the Kenya colony belonged to the Crown, and as such all native residents were automatically transformed to the status of tenants at will. This had the effect of erasing millennia of land-use rules that had emerged through conflict and cooperation among various tribes and former Arab rulers. It also allowed the authorities to appropriate the best agricultural lands for a small class of European settlers. The settlers created extremely profitable coffee, sisal, or fiber, and, later, corn plantations on the land that was granted to them at a very low cost by the Crown Lands Ordinance of 1902. This land grant was renewed again in 1915. The versatility and portability of the plantation economy were on full display in the central highlands but, over time, this system spread over 25 percent of the total land in Kenya. Through the widespread application of military force nomadic Masai cattle herders and agriculturists, such as the Kikuyu tribesmen, were moved to make space for European-owned plantations. Villages were burned, livestock appropriated, and many people were killed in operations conducted by the British army. But the British colonial authorities, like their Soviet counterparts, also had to guarantee a source of agricultural labor for the plantations, because, without this vital resource, the plantation economy was of little value either to the European settlers or the British treasury.

While the use of force was pervasive during the dark decades of British colonialism in Kenya, the authorities used an ingenious system of taxation and land-use policies to transform native inhabitants into a permanent source of cheap labor. These policies were used widely in British Africa. The Native Hut and Poll Tax in Kenya strangely resembled Peter the Great's infamous poll tax of 1722 that was levied on peasants in the Russian Empire. Each native male in the Kenya colony was required to pay a sizable tax portion yearly, at first in kind, but after the First World War it was collected in the form of cash. Because of the undeveloped cash economy, the only way to pay the taxes was to work for very low wages in the British-owned plantations. Chiefs on the native reserves became procurers of cheap labor and were rewarded lavishly for their services. Kenyan tax defaulters, like the Soviet kulaks, were treated very harshly: they were imprisoned, and their huts burned down. Often they were given compulsory labor assignments of up to sixty days. Furthermore, Kenyans, who were moved to specially demarcated Native Reserves, were forbidden from growing lucrative cash crops such as coffee and sisal. Like Soviet collective farmers who had to carry internal passports that constricted their travels in their own country, the residents of the infamous Native Reserves in Kenya were assigned an identity pass that allowed authorities to regulate their movements.[48] The pass was encased in a piece of metal and had to be hung from a neck collar for all to see. This passport system was harshly enforced when natives visited urban areas.[49] These same principles were used to create Bantustans in South Africa, Maori Land in New Zealand, and Native Land in Fiji.[50]

Kenya erupted in widespread conflict in 1952 with the onset of the Mau Mau uprising. The uprisings were led by the Kikuyu people but sections of the Kamba and the Masai tribesmen provided considerable help and resources. The British treated the widespread and violent movement as an insurgency rather than as an independence movement. Military plans of containment that had been used in the colonies of Northern Ireland and Malay were used in Kenya as well. Aerial bombing, the widespread use of torture, and hastily erected mobile gallows resulted in at least 20,000 to 30,000 deaths. Hundreds of thousands of insurgents were arrested. In addition, through the infamous villagization program, almost a million people were confined in heavily guarded camps ringed by barbed wire to prevent the Mau Mau from getting access to the village food stores. The conditions in the camps were extremely violent, and torture was so widely used that the British authorities themselves likened them to Nazi concentration camps.[51]

Wangari Maathai, the Kenyan Noble Laureate and world-renowned environmental activist, claimed that by 1954 one out of four Kikuyu men were imprisoned. Sexual violence was routinely inflicted on women in the camps to discourage support for the Mau Mau. Land was taken away from the rebels and given to loyalists, the small class of Kikuyu landowners who had prospered under British rule.[52] Maathai's memoir is similar to that of Shayakhmetov in that she is relatively circumspect about the negative impact of British colonialism in Kenya. The major part of the book is devoted to her sufferings in postcolonial Kenya under the authoritarian leadership of Daniel Arap Moi. Maathai begins with descriptions of her near idyllic childhood, and her beautiful descriptions of nature alert the reader that this is an environmentalist in the making. She grew up in a compound of homes that her father built to house his large family that included several wives and many children. Maathai describes the self-sufficiency of the village and the plentiful harvests of greens, gourds, and tubers that her mothers and aunts derived with little effort from the rich, nutritious soil. Later, her father moved to work on a colonial farm in the Rift Valley taking the family along with him. Like Shayakhmetov, Maathai describes her interactions with the colonizers as cordial and says that her father was treated well by the British farm owner who employed him.

At the age of eleven Maathai was enrolled in a Catholic girls' school, a move that dramatically changed her life. As an exceptional student, she was selected to finish high school in another Catholic convent. Similar to Shayakhmetov, Maathai learned the language of the colonizers and proved to be an apt and attentive pupil. She made remarkable progress in the systems of higher education in Kenya, the United States, and, later, Germany. Maathai received her undergraduate and graduate degrees in biological sciences in the United States, completed more graduate work in Germany, and finally received her PhD in veterinary anatomy from the University College of Nairobi. While she acknowledged experiencing some racism during her stay in the United States, Maathai was extremely enthusiastic about the systems of Western education. Just as Shayakhmetov's identity was completely transformed because of the Stalinist revolution, the modernization of Kenya allowed Maathai to lead a life of feminist independence if not of plenty. Although Maathai is extremely admiring of her mother's abilities as a farmer and of her courage and capacity for affection, Maathai shows little desire to follow in her footsteps and make a living as a subsistence farmer.

The bulk of Maathai's memoir is focused on three main themes: her gender oppression in postcolonial Kenya where people resented her forthright manner and criticized her for refusing to submit to customary mores that regulated women's behavior. She fought for the rights of women scientists and academics and describes numerous occasions when she was treated poorly on account of her sex. Maathai's husband was unable to deal with a strong-minded and independent woman who could think for herself, and more importantly provide for herself and her children. Her marriage soon ended in divorce. Maathai's second struggle was for the restoration and expansion of multi-party democracy in modern Kenya. She ran for elections many times, but with little success. She challenged the government of Daniel Arap Moi when they attempted to privatize public lands, parks, and forests for commercial use. Maathai formed a significant grassroots movement that stood for women's rights, democracy, and environmental conservation in Kenya. After much political fighting and stints in jail, when Daniel Arap Moi finally stepped down from power in 2002, Maathai ran for elections again, and finally emerged victorious. In 2003, she was appointed the Assistant Minister in the Ministry for Environment and Natural Resources.

Maathai's most significant contribution for which she received a Nobel Peace Prize in 2004 was the creation of the environmental movement in Kenya that drew global attention. She differed markedly from Shayakhmetov's relative unconcern about the ecology of Kazakhstan that had been deeply affected by modern agriculture and mining. Maathai was the founder of the Greenbelt Movement that subsequently became a worldwide phenomenon. Her organization was responsible for planting almost 20 million trees in Africa to prevent soil degradation and erosion. Maathai realized that the degraded and arid soils that had replaced the lush and green environment of her childhood were the main cause of rural poverty in Kenya. Instead of relying on the panacea of the inaptly named Green Revolution as so many politicians did in postcolonial countries, Maathai came up with a radical solution with far-reaching environmental gains. The Green Revolution was built on a costly system of chemical amendments and inputs that compounded the problems of soil degradation and falling levels of the water table. Instead, Maathai argued that the planting of trees on an epic scale would solve three important problems. First, trees would trap water in their root systems, and restore the water table that was essential for farmers. The leaves would provide organic compost to amend the soil. Second, native stands of local trees could also be a local source of food and fuel for rural women who were forced to walk miles in search of fuel and fencing materials. Finally, Maathai had the most important realization of all, one that fundamentally changed the nature of the environmental movement. Instead of being an elite organization that provided plans and materials from up above, Maathai's Greenbelt Movement worked with groups of local women and paid them small sums of money to raise the seedlings and take care of the trees. Wangari realized that environmental conservation, democracy, and women's rights were interrelated and interlinked and that all three goals had to be pursued simultaneously if they were to be successful.[53]

Conclusion

The simultaneous mapping of Shayakhmetov's and Maathai's lives is more than just an intellectual exercise in a book that traces the comparative imperial history of Russia and Britain. This chapter also has to do with the self-understanding of modernity as a lived system that slowly enmeshed the world, rather than something that was imposed at gun-point from above.

On the face of it, Kenya and Kazakhstan have very little in common in terms of ecology, race, culture, or language. These countries have had few opportunities for either trade or contact in the past. But as imperial sites of occupation and settlement, Kenya and Kazakhstan saw the violent institutionalization of modern agriculture in the form of the plantation economy and the collective farm. The native inhabitants were dispossessed and forced to make place for industrial agricultural systems that then rehired them as cheap and coerced labor. These processes were made possible by the liberal application of violence that was justified in the name of modernization and civilization. Both countries were the site of vast human suffering and environmental degradation.

The plantation economy was instituted for European settlers; it proved to be enormously profitable. The Soviet collective farm system to the contrary became a major drag on the Soviet economy within a short period of time. But without collectivization, the Stalinist revolution would have been politically impossible. A vision of modernity lay at the heart of both systems. This included the transformation of land from an ecosystem that provided subsistence, however meager, to multiple species, into an identifiable source of marketable products. This vision included the transition of errant herders and unproductive peasants into disciplined waged workers. Finally, our understanding of nature as an awe-inspiring, interconnected, and complex landscape where human presence was tenuous, provisional, and interdependent with other species of flora and fauna was replaced by images of linearity. Land was mapped, tamed, and marked by the computation of costs, benefits, and profits. Maathai more than Shayakhmetov understood the ill-effects of modern agriculture, and she devoted her life to environmental conservation and preserving the livelihoods of small farmers. But when we read their memoirs in tandem, we find that they also exhibit an unshakable attachment to the modern systems of Western education and a deep-seated belief in gender equality. Most surprisingly, Shayakhmetov and Maathai, despite the violence that has been wreaked on their culture and traditions, use the master's tools, the building blocks of modernity, to create themselves.

In his perceptive book on Soviet Kyrgyzstan, Ali Igmen has given us an excellent description of a composite and hybrid identity that emerged as a result of colonization and the violent clash of cultures.[54] The title of his book resonated with me greatly as I have spoken English my whole life, but with an Indian accent. Igmen argues that Kyrgyz elites and aspiring members from the lower classes pursued cultural modernity and Soviet education, even when many members of their family perished in Stalinist purges. If we consider Kazakhstan and Kenya after independence, we find that both countries have enlarged on the economies that were created by the colonial authorities.

Kazakhstan's major sources of revenue come from its vast oil, natural gas, and mineral industries that were developed under Soviet occupation and with the help of Soviet scientific expertise. Russian continues to be a semi-official language used at all levels of the state, and ethnic Russians comprise almost 20 percent of the population. Soviet commitment to universal education had created a strong but relatively poor middle class in Kazakhstan, and this has grown substantially in the post-Soviet era due to revenues from oil, gas, and mineral wealth. Kazakhstan is not a democracy by any stretch of the imagination, but while the state safeguards the heritage of nomadism as a cultural system, it is regarded as a relic of the distant past by most. Agriculture has been modernized substantially after independence in 1991 and Kazakhstan is now one of the big exporters of wheat, a crop that the former nomadic peoples were forced to grow by Stalin's government.

While the agricultural sector employs less than 20 percent of Kazakhstan's small population, 75 percent of Kenyans are employed in this sector that includes forestry and fishing. Kenya's principal exports are tea, coffee, horticulture, sisal, wheat, corn, and pyrethrum: colonial products that continue to be farmed decades after independence. Kenya's cut-flower industry is one of the largest in the world and accounts for most of the sales to Europe. Kenya also has a thriving technology sector that is one of the fastest-growing in the African continent. The Masai tribes have been integrated into Kenya's large and growing tourist industry, and their cultural performances are now a key part of the safari experiences created for global tourists. The yurts of the Kazakh herdsmen where one can drink the famous fermented mare's milk, kumys, is now being promoted as a probiotic health drink and an integral part of the eco-tourist experience by the Kazakh government.

6

The Cold War Retold
Zainab Al-Ghazali and Urszula Dudziak

Winston Churchill's Cold War address, delivered on March 5, 1946, at Westminster College in Fulton, Missouri, has stood the test of time as one of the most remarkable political speeches of the twentieth century.[1] The speech not only marked the end of the Grand Alliance against the fascist powers forged during the Second World War, but also signaled the dawn of the Cold War as a new paradigm for geopolitics. Titled misleadingly as the "Sinews of Peace," the talk was to go down in history as the "Iron Curtain" speech, in reference to Churchill's evocative sentence that set the imaginative frame for the Cold War. "From Stettin in the Baltic to Trieste in the Adriatic, an iron curtain has descended across the Continent. Behind that line lie all the capitals of the ancient states of Central and Eastern Europe." Churchill was an unusually gifted writer, a fierce polemicist, and a master orator who relished being in the public eye. The presence of President Truman gave the occasion further political gravitas. Later, Truman in his address to the United States Congress on March 12, 1947, was to substantially echo Churchill's call for the defense of freedom and liberty in the face of totalitarian oppression.[2] However, Truman rejected Churchill's core proposition that the containment of the Soviet Union based on an Anglo-American alliance should work to preserve the full extent of the British Empire.

Although Churchill's speech was published in the Soviet Union only in 1989, a few days later Stalin gave an interview to the Soviet newspaper *Pravda* in which he lambasted Churchill's speech as crude Tory war mongering.[3] For a highly intelligent man, Stalin made a mistake in that he justified the growing popularity of communist parties across Eastern and Western Europe as the genuine result of a heroic wartime alliance against fascism that was led by the Soviet Union. By referring to the many, many losses, both human and material, that the Soviets had incurred at the hands of the vicious Nazis, Stalin was fighting a rhetorical battle of legitimacy that was based in the recent past. Meanwhile, Churchill had created a Cold War Strategy and it took the Soviet Union some time to to craft a credible response. The response to Churchill's speech and the Truman Doctrine came during the founding conference of the Communist Information Bureau in September 1947, better known as the Cominform. The bureau was created to ensure the loyalty of European communist parties to the Soviet Union that was being increasingly threatened by the unveiling of the Marshall Plan in Europe and by the proclamation of the Truman Doctrine.[4] Delegates from the Communist Parties of the Soviet Union—Poland, Italy, France, Yugoslavia, Bulgaria, Romania, Hungary, and Czechoslovakia (many of them from the ancient capitals of Europe that had been recently cut off by the "Iron Curtain")—gathered in the name of peace, democracy, and anti-imperialism in Szklarska Poręba in Poland.

Was the Cold War just the sub-rosa continuation of the Great Game, the famous Anglo-Russian imperial rivalry that had dominated the geopolitics of the late nineteenth and early twentieth centuries?[5] I would argue that from 1918 to 1991, instead of witnessing decolonization, the world saw a renewed onslaught of European imperialism. But this time the European Empires faced determined national resistance across the globe. The unprecedented popularity of the nation-state forced European empires in the Middle East, Africa, and Eastern Europe to create a set of imperial discourses within which the power of nationalism could be safely managed. The British used the form of the Protectorate and the Mandate Territory in the Middle East to prolong their occupation of this crucial area, while the Soviets used the concept of a people's democracy to conceal their imperial project in Eastern Europe. Finally, the emerging nation-state was not entirely a secular project, as it was shaped by the ideas of religious constituencies that have been overlooked in the scholarly literature. In this chapter, I analyze the rise of religious feminism in the Middle East and Eastern Europe as an illiberal response to imperial universalism that was enforced by the British Empire and the Soviet Union.

Andrei Zhdanov, fresh from mismanaging the postwar famine in the Soviet Union when over a million victims perished, now set his signature ideological imprint on the Cold War by elaborating on the concept of a people's democracy as a subset of Soviet imperial policies.[6] With Stalin's approval, Zhdanov had earlier set the standards for ideological purity within the Soviet Union by publicly shaming renowned writers such as Anna Akhmatova and Mikhail Zoshchenko. He accused them of peddling bourgeois individualism and decadent pessimism and thus weakening the nation. While Zhdanov shared what was later to be known as the Zhdanov doctrine with those in attendance at the founding meeting of the Cominform, it was a composite doctrine that reflected the Party leadership's thinking, especially that of Stalin. Zhdanov spent little time in documenting Soviet wartime losses, a task that he left to Georgy Malenkov, his bitter rival for Stalin's attention. He laid out the key elements of Soviet postwar policy that contained surprisingly few references to socialism but presented the Soviet Union as the global champion of anti-imperialism. The strange reconfiguration of the Soviet Union, a colonizer par excellence, into a champion of anti-colonial movements throughout Africa, Asia, and Latin America, a process that started soon after the Bolshevik revolution of 1917, a phenomenon that was documented in Chapter 4, was surely one of the greatest ironies of the twentieth century!

According to Zhdanov, the world after the Second World War was divided into two irreconcilable camps: an "imperialist and anti-democratic camp" led by the United States seeking to forcefully impose capitalism, military bases, and a world government across the globe. Meanwhile, the USSR, an agent of world peace, led the "anti-imperialist and democratic" camp that emphasized equitable modernization, national liberation, and a people's democracy composed of workers, peasants, and progressive members of the intelligentsia. Zhdanov singled out the liberation movements in colonized countries as a key element of the Soviet anti-imperialist bloc.[7] He further charged that the United States wanted to reduce the former imperial powers such as Britain, France, and Holland to the status of vassal states, and gain capitalist hegemony at their expense in their current and former colonial holdings in Asia, the Middle East, Africa, and Latin America. This last accusation of Zhdanov held a great deal of truth.[8]

If the Soviet discursive shift from advocating socialism to national liberation and democracy seemed odd, Churchill's Iron Curtain speech was equally strange in what was not mentioned. Churchill was careful to emphasize the fact that he spoke solely on behalf of the 46 million inhabitants of the United Kingdom, who were ready to fight for freedom and liberty. While he included the commonwealth countries such as Canada that were also committed to the right side of the Cold War, Churchill remained silent about the hundreds of millions of British colonial subjects in Asia and Africa and in the Protectorate and Mandate territories of the Middle East. Perhaps these subjects desired neither freedom nor liberty. More improbably Churchill, the arch imperialist, who deeply regretted the dismantling of the British Empire,[9] in his Fulton speech spoke about the need to "walk forward in sedate and sober strength seeking no one's land or treasure." With the Soviet Union and the British simultaneously disavowing imperialism, the Cold War was beginning to inject an unexpected note of sobriety into European colonial discourses. As the century progressed, it was going to dramatically impact European imperial practices.

While Churchill eloquently brought to global attention the growing strength of an oppressive Soviet Union, Zhdanov unerringly put his finger on the weakest link of the American Cold War containment strategy: the existence of the vast imperial holdings of Britain, France, Portugal, Belgium, and the Netherlands in Asia, Africa, and the Middle East that confounded American claims of fighting a truly just Cold War: a war fought in the name of liberty, freedom, and democracy.[10] George Kennan had alluded to the problem of European colonies in his famous "Long Telegram," that he sent in February of 1946 from Moscow. According to Kennan,

> particularly violent efforts will be made to weaken power and influence of Western Powers of [on] colonial, backward, or dependent peoples. On this level, no holds will be barred. Mistakes and weaknesses of western colonial administration will be mercilessly exposed and exploited. Liberal opinion in Western countries will be mobilized to weaken colonial policies. Resentment among dependent peoples will be stimulated. And while the latter are being encouraged to seek independence of Western Powers, Soviet dominated puppet political machines will be undergoing preparation to take over domestic power in respective colonial areas when independence is achieved.[11]

But Kennan diplomatically omitted any reference to European imperialism in his famous "Sources of Soviet Conduct" that was published in the journal *Foreign Affairs* in 1947.[12]

Recently, scholars have characterized the twentieth century as one of decolonization but it is important to remember that it also witnessed new waves of colonization.[13] In the aftermath of the First World War, the British Empire expanded its territory considerably by acquiring possessions in the Middle East, Persia, and even the Trans-Caucasus when its main enemies, the empires of Germany, Russia, and the Ottomans, collapsed in stunning simultaneity. The newly created League of Nations had lent its support to the jerry-rigged and illegitimate Mandate System[14] and through it, the British gained control over the former Middle Eastern possessions of the Ottoman Empire in Iraq, Palestine, the Arabian Peninsula, and Transjordan. In addition, the British also cemented their control over Egypt where they had informally exercised power since 1882 and more formally as a Protectorate since 1914. However, the powerful ideas about national self-determination that both Woodrow Wilson and Lenin had provided to the world, and a weak economy that was proving unequal to supporting imperial over-reach forced the British Empire to adopt a framework of tutelary nationhood in the Middle East. The

British promised the colonized peoples eventual independence once they had proved that they were ready for its heavy burden.[15]

Following the Second World War, the Soviet Empire, in turn, used the rhetoric of a people's democracy to acquire domination in the countries of Eastern Europe and institute Soviet systems that included the nationalization of the economy, one-party control, and the suppression of public opinion and local culture. But the Soviet Union not only kept intact the national forms of their colonies in Eastern Europe, but also inadvertently provided nationalist content for claims of independence in Poland, Yugoslavia, Hungary, and other countries of Eastern Europe. By creating the concept of a peoples' democracy, the Soviet Union undercut its own imperialistic policies in Eastern Europe.[16]

As empires go, the British excursus into the Middle East and Soviet imperialism in Eastern Europe were relatively brief and, for the most part, extremely ineffective. John Darwin has even argued that if the British had focused on maintaining their possessions in Asia and Africa, without trying to connect them by adding significant territory in the Middle East, the British Empire might have survived longer.[17] And for the Soviet Union, the occupation of Eastern Europe led to the delegitimization of the Soviet system not only in the world but also within the Soviet Union itself. A handful of Soviet dissidents famously demonstrated against the Soviet invasion of Czechoslovakia in Moscow in 1968.[18] It would be hard to imagine the collapse of the Soviet Union in 1991 without the fall of the Berlin Wall in 1989. Both empires came to an end for the most part in the face of determined local resistance and, strangely enough, the United States played a major role in hastening their imperial collapse. Finally, the Soviet Union and the British Empire left behind a reinvigorated religious identity in their former colonies that served as the intellectual matrix of resistance to imperialism. This religious identity shaped the evolution of the postcolonial nations of Egypt and Poland.

In this chapter, I will analyze British imperial policies in the Middle East, especially in Egypt, and compare them to Soviet policies in Eastern Europe, with an emphasis on Poland in the post–Second World War era. I will compare how these empires tried to manage the problem of emerging nation-states and nationalism by inventing new forms of imperial control such as the Mandate Territory and the People's Democracy. In the last part of the chapter, by reflecting on the writings of the Islamic feminist Zainab Al-Ghazali and the Catholic theologian Dr. Urszula Dudziak, I will show that religious language and identity provided important tools of resistance to empire. The rise of conservative Islam in Egypt and conservative Catholicism in Poland are often seen as right-wing or even fascist movements that arose inexplicably in the aftermath of independence. But religious nationalism gained popular legitimacy through its grassroots resistance to imperialism, and, as such, the phenomenon needs to be read in the historical context of the transition from empire to nation.

The British Empire in the Middle East: The Strange Case of Egyptian Independence

The occupation of Egypt in 1882 served as the lynchpin of the British Empire in East Africa and the Middle East and connected the colonial capitals of Cape Town, Cairo, Baghdad, Calcutta, Singapore, Wellington, and beyond. From 1869 the newly constructed Suez Canal had served as the key shipping point for British military and commercial sea traffic from Europe to East Africa, to the crown jewel, India, and beyond to the Far East. The British established a veiled protectorate not only over Egypt but over Sudan as well where the headwaters of the Nile River are located. And Churchill was to get his taste for imperial wars in the famous British victory or massacre, depending on one's perspective, led by the British General Kitchener over the Mahdi in the Battle of Omdurman in Sudan, in 1898.[19] Before the establishment of a formal protectorate in 1914, Egypt, nominally a province of the Ottoman Empire, was ruled informally by a series of British proconsuls. The talented Evelyn Baring, Earl of Cromer, ruled the longest, and between 1883 and 1907 he turned Egypt into a giant cotton-producing colony for British textile mills. Baring also built the first Aswan Dam on the Nile River, as large water resources were necessary for the cultivation of cotton. Baring also managed to establish complete control over Egyptian finances, the transportation system, and the armed forces. As someone who had seen firsthand how modern education in India led to the rise of a broad nationalist movement, Baring was resolutely opposed to building institutions of learning for Egyptians. His short-sighted policies were going to fuel the rise of Islamic nationalism in Egypt in the twentieth century. And Islam was going to provide much of the language for anti-imperialism in the Arab world in the twentieth century.[20]

British rule in Egypt was formalized in 1914 with the onset of the war against the Ottoman Empire. Troops from British India were used to maintain control of the vitally important Suez Canal during the First World War, and they played a significant role in the defeat of the Ottoman forces. But the fall of the Ottoman Empire in 1918 led to the unexpected rise of Arab nationalism, and the British faced a wave of determined resistance in Iraq, the Arabian Peninsula, Transjordan, Palestine, and Egypt. The infamous Article 22 of the Covenant of the League of Nations declared, to those colonies and territories which as a consequence of the late war have ceased to be under the sovereignty of the States which formerly governed them and which are inhabited by peoples not yet able to stand by themselves under the strenuous conditions of the modern world, there should be applied the principle that the well-being and development of such peoples form a sacred trust of civilization and that securities for the performance of this trust should be embodied in this Covenant. Certain communities formerly belonging to the Turkish Empire have reached a stage of development where their existence as independent nations can be provisionally recognized subject to the rendering of administrative advice and assistance by a Mandatory until such time as they are able to stand alone. The wishes of these communities must be a principal consideration in the selection of the Mandatory.[21]

The Class A Mandate Territories formed from the dismembered Ottoman Empire however did not feel that their "wishes" were being taken into consideration. They believed that they could not only 'stand alone,' but that European supervision was contributing very little either to the well-being or development of their peoples. Emerging nations across the Middle East rejected the basic premise of the League of Nations system: that the advanced nations had an obligation and duty to develop backward nations and supervise them until they came of age. In their experience words such as "tutelage," "development," and "civilization's responsibilities" were nothing but euphemisms for the colonial extraction of labor and resources, the oppression of local sentiments and culture, and the use of territory for further imperial and military adventures. Nationalism and a desire for freedom from colonial rule also allowed the old feudal and commercial elites to merge with the newly emerging professionals, members of the middle class, and the peasantry to create cross-class movements that were opposed to imperial control.

The British were unprepared for the depth of mass resistance that they faced in their Protectorates and Mandate Territories. With dwindling financial resources, coupled with the rise of independence movements in Ireland and India, they chose different strategies of containment in each locale.[22] The most notorious of all was the aerial bombing of the Sunni-Shia uprising in Baghdad and other provinces of Iraq in 1920 that led to an estimated 6,000 to 10,000 civilian casualties. Churchill as the British War Secretary had authorized the bombing of Iraqi tribesmen by the Royal Air Force as a cost-saving measure that was designed to contain movements for national independence in the Middle East. The prolonged use of troops from India was proving to be increasingly expensive after the First World War, and there were limits to just how much the Indian peasant could be taxed to pay for British holdings in the

Middle East. As Priya Satia has argued, the aerial bombardment was also a curiously "invisible" system of colonial control as opposed to the crassness of ground troops and tanks that imperial publics in Britain were beginning to abhor in the aftermath of the First World War.[23] Subsequently, this policy of aerial bombing or "air control" was used extensively during the Second World War against Germany. After the massacre of the freedom fighters in Iraq, King Faysal I, a pro-British Sunni Arab, was installed and the Shia population was blocked from accessing power in Iraq for almost a hundred years until the fall of Saddam Hussein's government in 2003. Although Iraq received formal independence in 1932, the British continued to enjoy transit rights through the territory and maintained their military bases in Iraq till 1954. A similar model of alliances with conservative elites was instituted in the Transjordan.

In Egypt, the nationalist movement led by Said Zaghlul, the leader of the nationalist Wafd Party, proved to be much more powerful than the British had anticipated. The language of nationalism changed as the earlier opposition movement that was spearheaded by the Egyptian aristocracy expanded, and became a broad urban movement led by lawyers, traders, and public servants. The new Egyptian nationalist movement drew on the support of clerics, workers, and peasants. Egyptian feminism came of age in the 1919 Revolution when women marched in the streets of Cairo and Alexandria demanding independence. Law and order was restored at the point of the gun but as the casualties mounted it was clear to the British that they could not contain the independence movement in Egypt. It grew exponentially despite the subsequent imposition of martial law. Egypt was granted formal independence on February 28, 1922, but the British continued to control Egypt's destiny along with its foreign affairs and internal administration. Between 1922 and 1956 when the Anglo-French forces invaded Egypt, the country was continually in turmoil because of the British occupation that was legitimized by the Mandate System.

The language of the *Allenby Declaration* that gave de jure independence to Egypt in 1922 is a noteworthy example of the language of imperial nationalism and its many legal obfuscations. It is especially instructive when we read this document together with the Anglo-Egyptian Treaty of 1936. In 1922 Britain solemnly declared that the British Protectorate over Egypt was terminated and the country was to be "an independent sovereign state." At the same time, the agreement stipulated that the territory of Sudan, Egyptian defense, foreign policy, and communications throughout the territories were to remain under British control.[24] Under the terms of the Anglo-Egyptian Treaty of 1936, Egypt was once again declared to be a sovereign and independent country that was to receive "assistance" to receive membership in the League of Nations. The British, however, remained responsible for Sudanese welfare, maintained their control of the naval base of Alexandria, and retained the right to station 10,000 troops including an air force in the vicinity of the Suez Canal. Britain also retained the right to impose martial law and censorship in times of emergency. Members of the British armed forces and other representatives enjoyed immunity from Egyptian law.[25] Egypt was responsible for maintaining roads in good repair to allow for the easy transit of British forces. Despite Egypt's official independence, it was used extensively as an Allied military base during the Second World War. Egyptians realized to their bitter cost that there could be no national independence within the British Empire, and the status of a Mandate Territory merely prolonged their subjugation and dependence.

Matters came to a head after the Second World War when the British were forced to retreat from most of their bases in the Middle East, starting with their abrupt departure from Palestine in 1948. In 1952 the Egyptian monarchy was overthrown and Gamal Abdul Nasser, the new military leader of Egypt, took a hard line against the stationing of British forces in Egypt. He also challenged the British control of the Suez Canal. The last of the remaining British military detachments left in 1956. Nasser was a supporter of the Non-Aligned Movement of Third World countries, a promoter of Pan-Arabism, and was very critical of Anglo-American Cold War policies in the Middle East. When the United States reneged on a promise to fund the construction of the new Aswan High Dam, a project that was supposed to control the flooding of the Nile, promote Egyptian agriculture, and produce cheap electricity, Nasser unilaterally nationalized the Anglo-French owned Suez Canal. He also turned to the Soviet Union for armaments and economic help. In response, British, French, and Israeli forces launched an uncoordinated military attack to reoccupy the Sinai and the Suez Canal. At that point in time much of the oil exported from Iraq and the Gulf states to the United States and Western Europe was shipped through the Suez Canal, and therefore the control of the canal was crucial for the economic health of the Western world.[26]

The Suez Crisis was a comedy of errors from start to finish, and at one point President Eisenhower famously questioned the very sanity of Anthony Eden, the British prime minister under whose watch the botched plan of invasion was launched.[27] Khrushchev, who had authorized the crushing of the workers' uprising in Poland in 1956, and had sent Soviet troops to Hungary the same year when they tried to leave the Warsaw Pact, used the Suez Crisis to deflect attention from Soviet imperialism in Eastern Europe. Khrushchev attributed the uprisings in Eastern Europe to imperialist and anti-Soviet forces. He also took great pleasure in posing as a champion of the Arab states against European imperialism. In his memoirs, Khrushchev claimed that low-ranking Western diplomats approached their Soviet counterparts and offered to bury their condemnation of Soviet policies in Hungary and Poland if the Soviet Union, in turn, turned a blind eye to the invasion of the Suez Canal.[28] Of course, Khrushchev added self-righteously that the Soviet Union rejected the crafty plans of the imperialists, and upheld the right of colonial countries to achieve national independence!

The United States was forced to agree with the Soviet Union in demanding that the British, French, and Israeli forces withdraw unilaterally from the Suez Canal under the auspices of the United Nations. The United States found it impossible to simultaneously criticize the Soviet interventions in Poland and Hungary while condoning the Anglo-French invasion of Egypt. European imperialistic practices were to prove extremely costly for the United States. In 1960 the Soviet Union pushed the famous General Assembly Resolution 1514, *Declaration on the Granting of Independence to Colonial Countries and People*, through the United Nations. Drawing heavily on the language of the Non-Aligned Afro-Asian Bandung Conference of 1955, the Resolution called for immediate decolonization and the affirmation of national sovereignty worldwide. But member countries dropped the many anti-Western references that the Soviet delegate had suggested for inclusion in the document. During the discussion that ensued in the General Assembly, both the British and the American delegates accused the Soviet Union of practicing "a new and lethal colonialism" in Eastern Europe and the Baltics while intentionally misusing the words "democratic" and "autonomous" in their description of their rule.[29] In the final vote on the Resolution, Eisenhower reluctantly acceded to the request of the British prime minister Harold Macmillan that the United States abstain from voting on the declaration on decolonization.[30] It is important to remember that Eisenhower took this step against the advice of the entire American delegation to the United Nations whose members wanted to support the resolution. In 1958 the pro-British monarchy in Iraq was overthrown by an Arab nationalist uprising, and in the same year the Anglo-Iranian Oil Company was forced to relocate to Aden on the Persian Gulf. In the following two decades the British would leave Kuwait in 1961, Aden in 1967, and give independence to its Gulf Protectorates in 1971.[31] British withdrawal from its African colonies was also hastened by the unexpected turn of events following the Suez invasion of 1956.[32]

Soviet Eastern Europe and the Strange Fate of the People's Democracies

While British rule in the Middle East softened during the twentieth century, in Eastern Europe the reverse proved to be true as the Soviet Union tightened its grip over its satellite states exponentially. This was a territory that the Soviets knew well as the Russian Empire had exercised hegemony in Eastern Europe and the Balkans for many centuries. Furthermore, parts of Poland and the states of Finland, Lithuania, Latvia, and Estonia had been a part of the Russian Empire until the end of the First World War.[33] Russian knowledge of Eastern Europe had been accrued over the centuries through conflict with the Lithuanian, Polish, Swedish, German, Austro-Hungarian, and Ottoman Empires much like the British knowledge of the Middle East had grown through its interactions with the Romanov, Ottoman, and Iranian Empires. During the Cold War, Soviet policies, as Vladislav Zubok has argued, were a strange amalgamation of pre-revolutionary Russian imperialism and Soviet ideas about revolution and socialist modernization.[34] Similar to the nations in the Middle East that were carved out of the erstwhile Ottoman Empire by the Great Powers, Eastern European nations came into existence because of the simultaneous collapse of the Romanov, Ottoman, and Hapsburg Empires during the First World War. Lacking any natural boundaries on the western frontier, Russia and the Soviet Union had long regarded Eastern Europe to be their primary security corridor. Between 1914 and 1941, Germany had launched two devastating attacks on Russia and the Soviet Union using Polish territories as a passage for its armies. Stalin was particularly insistent that the Soviets have a free hand to reshape postwar Poland, and, for the most part, the Western Powers appeared to concede this demand during the dark days of the Second World War.[35]

Both Roosevelt and Churchill had agreed with Stalin at the Tehran Conference of November 1944 and again at the Yalta Conference of February 1945 that Eastern Europe would belong to the Soviet sphere of influence. They had tacitly legitimized the Soviet incorporation of Polish territory to the east, an event that had occurred soon after the signing of the Molotov-Ribbentrop Pact of 1939.[36] In 1944 at the Fourth Moscow Conference in October 1944, Churchill discussed the infamous percentages agreement with Stalin about the future of Eastern Europe, the Balkans, and the Eastern Mediterranean. This meeting was a throwback to nineteenth-century imperial practices and should be considered on par with the infamous Partition of Africa in 1884–5 when European leaders had negotiated the fate of millions and redrawn international boundaries of an entire continent with impunity. As Ivan Maisky, a senior Soviet diplomat, had perceptively noted in his memorandum to V. Molotov, the Soviet foreign minister in January 1944, the British Empire had become a conservative empire, anxious to maintain its imperial holdings rather than prepare for a new round of annexations. Maisky observed that the weakened British wanted to maintain their primacy as a global sea power, rather than expand their holdings on land.[37] Churchill assured Stalin that the Soviet Union would have primacy in most of the countries of Eastern Europe, except for Yugoslavia. The Soviets were also promised increased influence in the Black Sea region, the old hunting grounds of the Russian Empire. In return, Churchill asked that the Soviet Union respect British supremacy in the Eastern

Mediterranean especially around the Suez Canal, the conduit of all oil supplies to the West, and the gateway to Asian colonies.[38] Stalin could afford to be patient and even collaborate with local left-wing parties in Eastern Europe for the time being. After all the Western acquiescence to the Soviet sphere of influence in Eastern Europe was predicated on the holding of free elections and the installation of democratic governments.

Between 1945 and 1948, instead of nationalizing all private property at once in their colonies in Eastern Europe, large sectors of the economy such as banking, transportation, and industry were slowly brought under state control. Land reforms involved the breaking up of feudal estates, rather than the imposition of Soviet-style collectivization of agriculture. Many small businesses were allowed to function. Moreover, Soviet policies varied dramatically across the states, causing scholars to even speak of self-Sovietization in certain countries by local communists seeking to curry favor with Moscow.[39] But the so-called national road to communism did not yield the results that it was supposed to, and the Soviet-backed communist parties failed to win major electoral victories except in Yugoslavia under Marshall Tito.[40]

A grudging commitment to the national form, whether for purely hypocritical or pragmatic reasons, lay at the heart of this new Soviet Empire. Unfortunately, this resulted in problems for both the rulers and the ruled. Despite the redrawing of the map of Soviet-Polish borders and population transfers between Ukraine and Poland, the nation-states that had been created in Eastern Europe in the aftermath of the First World War were kept largely intact. For the most part citizens in Albania, Czechoslovakia, and even Eastern Germany developed a distinct national identity under Soviet rule.[41] Terms such as "people's democracy," "economic development," and "national liberation" were used to dispel the perception that the Soviet Union was imposing a collective identity in the countries of Eastern Europe.[42] If the ambiguous definition of the Mandate Territories in the Middle East by the League of Nations caused endless semantic and geopolitical confusion, the Soviets were equally unclear as to what a "people's democracy" actually meant. Since the Soviets retained the right to intervene militarily in these areas, it made a mockery of the sovereignty of the so-called peoples' democracies. By 1949 most of the states, except Yugoslavia, were firmly under the control of Soviet-backed communist parties.[43]

In his seminal "two camps speech" delivered at the founding of the Cominform in 1947, Zhdanov spoke about the struggle for national liberation and economic development in the people's democracies, even as the Soviet and Yugoslav delegates called for an end to cooperation with all non-socialist and non-communist parties.[44] Other speakers at the conference such as Władysław Gomułka, the General Secretary of the Polish Workers' Party, also emphasized the "national" and "democratic" communist movement in

Poland that arose organically in opposition to German fascist imperialism. He claimed that the people's democracies were created from below and that there was a Polish path to socialist development that was different from the roads chosen by Yugoslavia, Czechoslovakia, or Bulgaria.[45] Gomułka reiterated that each country should choose its path to socialism based on its internal situation.

With the defection of Yugoslavia from the Soviet bloc in 1949 under Marshall Tito, the Soviet Empire cleared up the semantic confusion and clarified the actual nature of the "people's democracy" that the countries in Eastern Europe were living under. Eastern Europeans had been appalled by the brutal behavior of their Red Army liberators, by the forced population transfers, by the ethnic cleansing, and by the extortionate reparations regime that the Soviets instituted in countries such as East Germany, Poland, and Romania.[46] By the end of the decade, it was becoming increasingly clear that the countries in Eastern Europe were being inexorably drawn into the Soviet orbit through the strategic use of military force, the use of terror unleashed by the secret services that included deportations to the Soviet gulag, and the open support that was given to pro-Soviet communist parties and leaders hand-picked by Moscow. After 1948, from East Germany to Albania, countries behind the Iron Curtain saw the nationalization of industry, economic coordination with the Soviet Union under the Comecon or the Council for Mutual Economic Aid that was formed in 1949. The intermittent attempts to enforce collectivization of agricultural lands, the complete Sovietization of the army, and the imposition of a Soviet cultural hegemony that impugned both secular and religious sensibilities further enraged the inhabitants of Eastern Europe.[47]

With the hardening of Soviet control of Eastern Europe, Soviet authorities removed Gomułka from the post of Secretary General in 1948 in Poland. He was accused of right-nationalist deviation and imprisoned in 1951. The death of Stalin in 1953 led to hopes that Soviet control would loosen in Eastern Europe and these were further buoyed by Khrushchev's secret speech delivered at the Twentieth Party Congress in February 1956 in which he attacked both Stalin and the cult of Stalinism. Although Khrushchev was careful to concentrate exclusively on Stalin's crimes against the communist party, without mentioning the existence of the Soviet Empire in Eastern Europe, the wide circulation of the text of his speech led many to believe that changes were imminent. But Eastern Europeans were soon to be rapidly disabused of their misconceptions.

In 1953 Soviet troops crushed the workers' uprisings in East Germany and arrested thousands for protesting against the catastrophic fall in living standards, the collectivization of agriculture, and cultural oppression. In Poland, Soviet troops were sent in to quell the workers' uprisings in the city of Poznań in June 1956. But by October that year, the Soviets decided to use a less confrontational approach and brought back Gomułka once again to develop his national road to communism. The Soviet Union forgave many of the Polish debts, private farming was gradually restored, and the number of collective farms fell. Most importantly, there was a rapprochement with the Catholic Church, and Cardinal Wyszynski was released.[48] In Hungary, later that year, the mass uprising was less successful as Soviet tanks rolled in early November even as people shouted: "Russians go home." Almost 2,500 Hungarians were killed in the uprising, and approximately 22,000 were arrested in the following months. Over 200,000 refugees fled the nation as the Soviet Union inexorably tightened control over the Eastern Bloc.[49] The United Kingdom embroiled in their imperial misadventure in the Suez Canal proved incapable of stopping the Soviet aggression in Eastern Europe.[50] And the United States, despite the encouragement given to anti-Soviet dissidents through the circulation of audio and printed liberation propaganda, was unable to proffer any actual help or military assistance to either the Poles or the Hungarians.[51] Charles Gati has argued that the timing of the Soviet military intervention in Hungary was influenced by the ongoing Suez Crisis, and it allowed the Soviet Union to act with impunity in Eastern Europe.[52]

Recently independent nations were shocked by the juxtaposition of the Hungarian and the Suez crises and were quick to recognize the imperial lineages that united both events. While the Western press condemned the Soviet invasion of Hungary, and the Soviet press criticized the imperialism inherent in the Suez invasion, very few connected these events during that time.

Not surprisingly, the Western press criticized Jawaharlal Nehru, the prime minister of India for his refusal to support the UN resolution of November 4, 1956, condemning the Soviet invasion of Hungary. In his subsequent public speeches, Nehru, who sought advice from Marshall Tito of Yugoslavia about the situation, was extremely critical about the Soviet affront to Hungarian nationalism.[53] The Soviets themselves were apprehensive that their image had taken a severe beating in Third World countries such as India, Pakistan, and Sri Lanka on account of their role in suppressing the Polish and Hungarian uprisings.[54] It was both strange and awkward that the Soviet Union, the self-styled leader of the global anti-imperialist camp that Zhdanov had described in such glorious terms in his 1947 Cominform speech, had been caught savagely suppressing so-called anti-Soviet elements in not one but three of the "people's democracies" of Eastern Europe. The Soviet Empire survived in Eastern Europe till 1989 when another wave of uprisings convulsed the region. But in 1989 the revolutions from below unexpectedly coincided with the thinking at the highest level of Soviet leadership. Like the British in the previous two decades, the Soviets had begun to question the value of holding on to an "outer empire" in Eastern Europe. More importantly, the Soviet Union had second thoughts about supporting conservative and aging satraps such as Erich Honecker in East Germany or Gustav Husak in Czechoslovakia, especially since they seemed incapable of understanding the new Soviet policies of perestroika and glasnost.[55]

Religious Dimensions of Anti-Imperialism

The challenges to British and Soviet imperialism were seen primarily as modern movements, led by a pantheon of secular, nationalist, and left-liberal heroes. In the scholarly world, anti-imperial resistance is usually coded as modern and progressive. To resist is to be a middle-class intellectual, a left-wing journalist, a musician, an artist, a university student, or, better still, a feminist who has joined "the carnival of revolution" seeking civil rights and a secular and liberal community.[56] Occasionally, resistance is represented as a class-conscious worker of the famous Solidarity movement that grew in Poland under Soviet rule. But when anti-imperialism is expressed in the form of religious nationalism, and through a religious idiom of pro-natalism, and heteronormative marriage codes, it induces acute analytical discomfort among scholars. The rise of conservative religious values that seem to grow organically around the desire to control women's bodies and actions in a colonial context defy our modern expectations that the end of empire should inexorably lead to secular progress and liberalism.[57] And since 1989 it has become almost axiomatic that internationalism, liberal democracy, free markets, and gender equality should follow in the aftermath of imperial collapse.[58] In the last section of the chapter, I analyze the rise of religious feminism in postcolonial Poland and Egypt, not as a resurgence of Catholic and Islamic faith per se, but as a set of beliefs, discourses, and community building practices that should be understood in terms of anti-imperial resistance. Religious feminists often see their work as an important way to recuperate the fragile nation, whose very existence has been threatened by colonialism and the imposition of alien values.

Comparing the political trajectory of Zainab Al-Ghazali—a national feminist leader in Egypt, a close associate of Hasan al-Banna, and the founder of the Muslim Brotherhood movement in Egypt—and Urszula Dudziak—a Catholic theologian and an academic in post-Soviet Poland, who is closely linked with the Catholic Church and the anti-communist Law and Justice Party—one finds a remarkable set of political convergences in these two postcolonial locations. Neither woman looked back to a supposedly golden age of religion but were and are consciously building the utopia of the future where the individual will be reintegrated in a righteous and free nation. They believe that a strong family is the basis of a healthy community. And that a nation cannot prosper in the absence of strong families and communities. Al-Ghazali's politics challenged the core principles of liberal feminism that developed among elite feminists, who were anxious to secure their political rights as women under British rule in Egypt. And Al-Ghazali continued her fight, perhaps mistakenly, with the socialist feminist policies that were sponsored by the state in postcolonial Egypt under Nasser. The bureaucratic states that were created in Nasserite Egypt and Soviet Poland tried to control civil society by secularizing the educational system and downgrading religious learning in the process. Led by modern and rational principles of enlightened patriarchy, these states guaranteed women equal status under the law. They also tried to draw women into educational institutions and the labor force through a series of material incentives such as maternity leave, state-funded childcare service, and quota systems that guaranteed the labor rights of women.[59] Instead of applauding these advances in women's rights, religious institutions were horrified by the overt attempts to create an intimate relationship between the atomized individual and the beneficent state, a process that Hannah Arendt described as totalitarian. The institutions of state feminism threatened to subvert the authority of religion and religious figures who saw themselves as crucial to the building of the family and community at the grassroots level. Instead of giving women a Bill of Rights, Al-Ghazali and Dudziak presented them with a Bill of Obligations and Duties which when completed would revive the community and the nation.

Zainab Al-Ghazali, who was born in 1902 to a well-to-do Egyptian family, received a good education early in life. Originally, she had worked with Egyptian liberals such as Huda Shurawi, but she left the Egyptian Feminist Union. Al-Ghazali was convinced that the liberal individualism of Western feminism offered few solutions to an Islamic Egypt that was rooted in the ummah or the vitality of the Islamic community. For the rest of her life, Al-Ghazali was committed to unearthing an Islamic feminist vocabulary of rights and responsibilities from the intellectual tradition that she knew best. She refused to cede to the British any measure of intellectual authority in how to define the successful evolution of Egyptian women's movements. Her anti-imperial struggle was closely tied to the rejection of the Western vocabulary of progress, and Western prescriptions on how to define the life trajectory of a woman. Al-Ghazali argued that Egyptians had to look for solutions to the problem of women's rights and emancipation within their native intellectual traditions. Although Al Ghazali had links with the religious establishment of Saudi Arabia, she did not believe that any Muslim nation had been able to create a truly Islamic society. Rather than build a transnational Islamic community, she dedicated her life to creating a virtuous Egyptian nation that would be worthy of the Islamic precepts that it formally subscribed to. Al-Ghazali was an Islamic scholar of repute and was one of the few women to have published a two-volume commentary on the Qur'an. She gave innumerable interviews and edited and published a woman's magazine *al-Daw'wa*. She was also a brilliant preacher drawing crowds numbering in the thousands to the Ibn Tulun Mosque in Cairo.[60]

In 1920, Al-Ghazali formed the Muslim Women's Association, an organization that existed until its formal dissolution in 1964. It was dedicated to philanthropy, educational outreach, and most importantly finding employment and housing for families of the Muslim Brotherhood. The Muslim Brotherhood was an important political presence and the secular Nasserite state arrested thousands of members in a desperate bid to blunt its appeal. The Muslim Women's Association created deep community bonds by extending support to family members in neighborhoods and small towns. Despite her formal piety, Al-Ghazali had a mind of her own and when asked to merge her women's organization with that of the powerful Muslim Brotherhood, Al-Ghazali initially refused. She only agreed to do so when the Brotherhood was banned by the state and Hassan al-Banna, the founder, executed in 1948.[61] Al-Ghazali, who miraculously escaped imprisonment under British rule, was savagely tortured in the prison of the Nasserite state that rose after the end of British rule in 1952.[62] She not only survived her term of imprisonment from 1965 to 1970 but went on to create a national movement of Islamic feminism. She started by first creating circles and neighborhood clubs comprised of women in Cairo, but gradually her movement spread throughout Egypt. Her political methods in building grassroots women's organizations resonated throughout the wider Muslim world and inspired millions. Al-Ghazali saw herself primarily as a builder of local communities, and even in prison she claimed that she was able to create Islamic networks of resistance. Her faith gave her stoicism, and her ability to resist physical torture inspired fellow prisoners to follow her example.

As a charismatic Islamic preacher, Al-Ghazali sought to empower ordinary women to learn about Islam by participating in small, intimate communities of learning. She spoke of the importance of instituting religious practices and precepts in one's daily life. But Al-Ghazali did not consider that accepting Islam was submission to a long-forgotten religious tradition. Instead she argued that religion helped her achieve the radical act of feminist self-transformation. Al-Ghazali advocated that a woman should be educated about Islam, world politics, current events, science, and technology, and this knowledge would enable her to be a good wife and mother. Since the family is the basic unit of the Islamic state, the woman's primary duty was to marry and bear children. Once she had fulfilled these primary duties, a woman could work for the welfare of the community, find employment, and spread the message of Islam in the public sphere. Rejecting all varieties of liberal feminism, Al-Ghazali argued that women would only experience a full range of rights and freedoms in a truly Islamic nation. Her mission was to prepare a populace that could morally inhabit an Islamic civilization by discharging their duties and obligations to the family, the nation, and religion.[63]

If the Egyptian nation had been preserved by Islamic thought through the centuries of oppression by the Mongols, the Mamelukes, the Ottomans, the British, and, subsequently, Nasserite socialism, then the Catholic Church had provided the same function in Poland. Catholicism had saved Poland from centuries of German, Austrian, Russian, and Soviet rule, or so the majority of the people believed. The Holocaust of the Second World War era and the subsequent population transfers had created an abnormally homogenous nation in Poland, in which the Catholic Church emerged as one of the main centers of oppositional politics through the period of Soviet occupation.[64] The election of the Polish priest Karol Józef Wojtyła as Pope John Paul II in 1978 was a major catalyst for Polish labor politicians such as Lech Walesa. Walesa was brilliant in that he seamlessly fused the people's veneration for the Catholic Church with an anti-imperial labor movement.[65] The Pope's triumphal visit to a socialist Poland in 1979 when he turned his outdoor speech into an impromptu mass replete with a makeshift altar marked an important signpost in the long road to Polish religious nationalism. This subsequently culminated in the election of the conservative Law and Justice Party in 2015.[66] The Solidarity Project was politically progressive but also socially conservative in many ways. This was especially apparent in its attitudes toward women. After the revolutions of 1989 in Eastern Europe and the collapse of the Soviet Union in 1991, Poland became a conservative country where Catholic ideas about womanhood, family, abortion rights, and feminism began to gain increasing resonance.[67]

In the decades since the collapse of Soviet rule, Western feminism and the mandates of a liberal European Union have replaced the image of the Soviet colonizer among the supporters of the Law and Justice Party. That coupling is not as strange as it seems as both liberal and Marxist feminism share the same commitment to equality, rights of individuals, and an increase in the participation of women in the public sphere.[68]

Urszula Dudziak, a psychologist and theologian, is employed as a faculty member in the John Paul II Catholic University of Lublin.[69] She is a popular speaker on the conservative radio show, Radio Maryja, and appears frequently on Polish television. Dudziak serves as an expert on education in family life, a euphemism for sex education, in the National Ministry of Education in Poland, and has been closely associated with the Law and Justice Party since their first electoral victory in 2015. The Law and Justice Party, which is openly against liberal feminism, has also positioned itself against the LGBTQ+ movement. It has been trying to outlaw abortion in Poland since 2016 and derives its strength and popularity from conservative members, both men and women. The Party and its vociferous members are not only viscerally opposed to Poland's communist legacy but has clashed repeatedly with the European Union about the liberal values and the immigration policies that it is trying to impose on Poland.

Dudziak's life trajectory and her professional affiliation with the John Paul Catholic University represent the curious culmination of Catholic nationalism and religious feminism that were incubated as modes of resistance under decades of Russian and Soviet rule. Dudziak is dedicated to the preservation and growth of the Polish-Catholic family. Working for the National Ministry of Education, Dudziak has created a manual for sex education that promotes sexual restraint, Christian marriage, monogamy, and natural family planning methods among the students. She is an anti-abortion activist, who has condemned the use of the "morning-after pills." Dudziak, channeling Pope John Paul II's well-known views about marriage and family,[70] considers heterosexual marriage to be a spiritual union that is part of a divine plan. John Paul II famously put the family at the center of his "civilization of love." He argued that men and women learned about spirituality, holiness, and selflessness while taking care of each other and raising children together. As a chaplain to university students in Krakow where he mentored several families, John Paul II realized that the communist state was destroying the family by celebrating individualism. But far from strengthening the individual, communism encouraged an overwhelming dependence on the state to address all problems. John Paul II believed that local community organizations like the church would revitalize the individual and the community.

For Dudziak and others like her who believe that marriage is an institution sanctioned by God, the religious prohibition on sexual relations and reproduction outside of marriage is admirable. She has condemned in-vitro fertilization as an unnatural method of inducing pregnancy,[71] and has even claimed that the use of contraception causes addiction to sex.[72] Paralleling Al-Ghazali's claims about Islam and the family, Dudziak argues that the Catholic family is the basic unit of a Polish-Catholic civilization and it is imperative to strengthen this unit through any means necessary.[73] Since the very existence of Poland and Polish culture was threatened by decades of Soviet communism, Polish women have the grave responsibility of preserving the nation through cultural and physical reproduction. Dudziak would argue that women's bodies are not merely the site of individual rights but offer the best hope of national continuity. Therefore, Polish women also have to physically produce the next generation of soldiers and citizens of Poland.

In the eyes of Al-Ghazali and Dudziak national identity is inextricably tied to religious identity and the attempt to unyoke this "natural coupling" will lead to civilizational and demographic collapse. They argue that the family constitutes the primary unit of a nation, as it ensures not only the physical reproduction of its members but also the survival and continuity of national values. Furthermore, both women claim that only religious institutions can be trusted to create conditions in which families can flourish, grow, and multiply. The liberal and the socialist state is concerned with giving rights to women as individuals, but the undue emphasis on women's rights rather than responsibilities can lead to the destruction of the family and by extension that of the nation. Islam and Christianity, on the other hand, are concerned with women's duties, especially reproductive and familial ones, to the family and society. A responsible woman who fulfills her obligations as a wife, a mother, and as a builder of community is the most important citizen of the nation whose activities should be supported by state subsidies.[74]

In a colonial context where the state is seen as an alien entity, people put their faith in religious institutions that respond to grassroots needs and concerns, and in religious practices that help bring a community together in the face of colonial exploitation. Religious authorities are seen as the natural guardians of a civilizational and national identity that imperialism constantly threatens to subsume under a set of imported ideas. The recuperation of an essentialist religious identity is often a political response to the condition of imperialism that seeks to erase the particular and the local in favor of a unilateral universalism. Finally, the struggle for national liberation and the recovery of identity and values threatened by imperialism is an emotional journey of transcendence in which a person's obligation and duty to the cause takes precedence over their rights as an individual. While liberal/socialist feminism emphasizes the individual rights of women, religious feminists appeal to the idea that women are distinguished by their duties to the family and the nation. One ideology promises individual self-fulfillment and self-expression, the other entices with a vision of heroic selflessness that promises to rescue the nation from oblivion.

This chapter has tried to do two things: first, uncover the imperial dimensions of the Cold War; second, document the crucial link between religious revival and anti-colonial resistance. The ideological reading of the Cold War as a global battle between the American system of capitalism and the Soviet system of communism has obscured three important phenomena that shaped this period. The British colonization of the Middle East after the First World War and the Soviet colonization of Eastern Europe after the Second World War are comparable stories of imperial misadventures that need to be highlighted in the histories of the Cold War. Second, the British Empire and the Soviet Union had to deal with the potent force of nationalism in the twentieth century, and their curious attempts to co-opt and manage nationalism through the invention of the concept of the Mandate Territory and the People's Democracy are well worth comparing. Finally, the rise of religious nationalism during and after independence is a trans-imperial phenomenon that needs to be studied in a comparative context rather than as a postcolonial regression to either fascism or Islamic terrorism.

7

Who Should a Woman Speak For in a Post-World Order?

Anna Politkovskaya, Arundhati Roy, and Lisa Kirschenbaum

In this last chapter, I take the liberty of straying from the main interpretive framework of this book that thus far has compared episodes of British and Russian imperialism in the nineteenth and twentieth centuries. Instead, I turn to the challenges and complications that have arisen in post-imperial space and time. The paths and byways of imperial decline and collapse not only influence the way historians approach the subject of empire but also shape the subsequent stories about the rise and fall of the empire. Collapsing empires are dangerous places that leave treacherous eddies and shoals in their wake. These continue to shape geopolitics long after the empires have officially vanished from the global map. And we have learned repeatedly from history that empires have long memories, and they hold on tenaciously to ideas about their so-called imperial destiny. In the twentieth and twenty-first centuries we have seen many a demagogue use the trope of imperial revival to fuel a successful political career. Therefore, most obituaries of empire are premature and should be read with a healthy dose of skepticism.

At the other end of the imperial spectrum, we saw the rise of numerous postcolonial states in Asia, Africa, the Middle East, the Caribbean, and the Pacific as the European Empires collapsed in a highly orchestrated manner in the second half of the twentieth century. India became independent only in 1947, and Australia attained full sovereignty with the passing of the Australia Act as late as 1986. Citizens of postcolonial states celebrate their newfound independence avidly and, for the most part, are keen to distance themselves from the supposed benefits and boons bestowed by former European overlords. There is a newfound interest in the history of national origin and an exaggerated concern with stories of racial and cultural purity, even if they fly against empirical evidence. But the marshaling of historical facts is a poor counter-argument to the emotional and psychological mindset of post-colonialism, a historical phenomenon that needs further comparative research and analysis. The tales of imperial oppression and exploitation are an important political tool that helps bind together the citizens of a newly formed nation-state through memories of shared suffering. The traumatic past of colonialism is especially important as it helps distract attention from the problems of inequality, coercion, and exploitation that persist long after the formal attainment of independence. The "imagined community" provides the basis of self-identification among the members and offers a way to differentiate themselves from others.[1]

But as Klyuchevsky and Trevelyan so wisely warned us, the nation-state is never an innocent endeavor. Whenever a sizable population is bound together by a coherent message (secular or religious), a shared vision, and a set of remembered experiences that took place in a delimited geographical space, it becomes the basis of a polity that can grow exponentially and become extremely powerful in the future. Recently decolonized states, with tangible memories of imperial capture and cultural dilution, are therefore the most likely to promote nationalism, civic unity, and a closing of ranks against enemies from within and without. When this habit and discourse of identity fractures, whether due to globalization or other forms of imperialism, the polity loses its political potency and its will to act. Waning empires therefore also borrow from the script of national regeneration in the aftermath of collapse. In the sections that follow, I will analyze the twined story of imperial collapse and national resurgence in Russia and India by considering two famous critics of waning imperialism and ascending nationalism: Anna Politkovskaya and Arundhati Roy.

By the end of the twentieth century, the British Empire had all but vanished and the Soviet Union was severely truncated in terms of land as well as power. The Russian wars in Chechnya demonstrated neither its might nor its military ability, but rather its diplomatic ability to pick local warlords in the periphery who found it advantageous to work with Moscow. India, a colony that had contributed greatly to the material basis for the rise of imperial Britain, and had been completely impoverished by the processes of colonialism, is emerging as a rising Asian power. Many in the West believe that India might be useful to counter the growing might of the other global behemoth, China. India believes that it must strike the right balance in its friendship with Russia and the West, in order to preserve its territories from Chinese encroachment and its economy from Western and Chinese exploitation. Breaking free of British imperial control was relatively easy compared to the insurmountable task of creating a unified Indian nation on a subcontinent that is home to a bewildering array of languages, cultures, and ethnicities. The building of the Indian nation was a proto-imperial project from the very beginning, and the arguments about the defense of the nation are being increasingly twined with the extension of centralized control in the peripheries. All this was vastly complicated by the terrorist attacks of September 11, 2001, on select targets in the United States that set off a worldwide conflagration entitled the War on Terror, one that is still raging in many parts of the globe.

The United States was late to the struggle, having covertly supported armed Islamic organizations for years in both Afghanistan and Pakistan to offset the collateral effects of the Iranian Islamic Revolution of 1979 and the Soviet invasion of Afghanistan shortly thereafter. Other countries, notably the Soviet Union and India, that had been battling radical groups for much of the 1980s and 1990s, had analyzed the international ramifications of this global threat long before the official US declaration of the War on Terror.[2] The Soviet Union, later Russia, and India had tried to call attention to call attention to the destructive potential of terrorists who exploited the teachings of Islam to gain legitimacy for almost two decades before 2001.

Within Russia and India, the majority of the citizens, outraged by repeated terrorist attacks on civilian populations in the 1990s and 2000s, overwhelmingly supported the role of the Russian state in the two Chechen Wars and the Indian military response to the prolonged insurgency in Kashmir. Safeguarding the borders and upholding national honor has been a matter of extreme political urgency in Russia and India in the last two decades—especially among elites, resident and diaspora, who have used the nation-state as a vehicle for their global ambitions. And this is also true for vast sections of the newly formed middle class whose sense of national belonging is being increasingly shaped by sophisticated media and social media platforms. In post-Soviet Russia, the loss of empire was felt keenly by large sections of the population; and Putin's promises to revive national greatness have been as effective a strategy as that pursued by the ruling Bharatiya Janata Party in India.

Two women, defying the political consensus on the use of armed forces to deal with terrorism and secession, took an anti-imperial and anti-national stance that echoed very loudly around the globe. They challenged the right of the nation-state to suppress minority groups that wanted to either secede or seek political autonomy within the federative framework of Russia and India. Anna Politkovskaya and Arundhati Roy, internationally renowned journalists and writers, rather than stand with their nation, in a strange twist of logic championed the rights of Chechen and Kashmiri civilians who suffered greatly during these prolonged conflicts. They fought hard, using their incendiary journalism to win recognition for the enormous collateral damage caused by the state-sanctioned wars in Chechnya and Kashmir. Defying the efforts of the nationalist media to either silence or shame her as a "hysterical woman," Politkovskaya became a global celebrity while she reported on gross human rights abuses and widespread civilian deaths in Chechnya. And more recently, Roy, a latecomer to the national conversation on Kashmir, has used her considerable international renown to shine a light on the atrocities committed by the Indian army in this remote mountainous region bordering Pakistan and China, which is a gateway for India's trade ambitions with Central Asia and beyond.

In the process of explicating the secessionist politics of Chechnya and Kashmir, Roy and Politkovskaya have also called unwelcome attention to the growing authoritarianism of the Russian and the Indian states. Their critique of state power has proved to be more subversive and challenging to the authorities than the reportage on the military atrocities committed in these breakaway regions of Chechnya and Kashmir. Roy and Politkovskaya's writings have helped world organizations such as Amnesty International, the United Nations, and the International Court of Justice in The Hague to get involved in what both Russia and India both regard as strictly domestic affairs.[3]

As a result, both women have been widely reviled as traitors and denigrated in the Russian and Indian media for their lack of patriotism. They have been called naïve and irresponsible, extremist and misguided, and criticized widely for their inability to understand the radical nature of Islamic terrorism and its embedded threat to women's rights and modern civilization. The criticism from state officials, journalists, and intellectuals failed to silence neither Politkovskaya nor Roy. In fact throughout their respective careers, both Politkovskaya and Roy became more defiant, more outspoken, and more critical of the state. And in certain cases, they took such hardline and extreme positions that they alienated even the more progressive members of the intelligentsia in Russia and India. While Politkovskaya and Roy are polarizing women at home, they hold an enviable position in the global mediascape. In universities, in the liberal media of Western Europe, the United States, Canada, Australia, and other Anglophone countries such as India and South Africa, they are admired as tireless human rights activists and as perceptive transnational journalists.

In this last chapter, I analyze the lives and writings of these two complex and driven women from two opposing perspectives: the nationalist critique generated from sections within Russia and India, and the self-understanding and self-articulation of Roy and Politkovskaya who claim to function outside the boundaries of the nation-state. Are they good "citizens of the earth,"[4] or traitors to the nation-state? Are they intellectuals defining a decentralized and distributive model of global development and conflict resolution? Or, as their critics aver, are they simply unthinking pawns in a Western-directed movement and discourse about human rights, one that threatens the national integrity of Russia and India? Where should a woman's allegiance lie, to herself, to her family, to the nation, or the world?

The problem of ensuring a woman's political loyalty is not a new one, and this has recurred serially since recorded history. In the fifth century BC, Sophocles examined the many contradictions between a woman's political duty as a member of a polis or city-state and her responsibilities to the members of her family. In his powerful play *Antigone*, Sophocles raised many important questions, and instead of providing definitive answers or even a dramatic resolution, he presented the speeches of Antigone and Creon as two sides of an unresolved debate. The debate is still ongoing many centuries later. Antigone, the daughter born of Oedipus's unnatural sexual relationship with his mother, Jocasta, captured the imagination of the ancient world by her bravery, her eloquence, and her tragic death. Antigone defied Creon, the ruler of Thebes, and the laws that forbade people from burying traitors who had harmed the interests of the city-state. The unburied and rotting corpses of the traitors reminded the citizens about their civic obligations and about the power of the city-state.

Antigone challenged the laws of Thebes and buried her treacherous brother Polynices with full honors. She argued that the laws of God existed before the laws of men, and that a woman's duty was to her family rather than the state. When punished by Creon, she showed neither humility nor remorse at her actions. Instead, and with incredible arrogance, Antigone called into question the very legitimacy of the state and its legal structures. She mounted a full-throated defense of her actions, and her arguments still ring true many centuries later. Sophocles was too intelligent a playwright to provide any definitive evaluation about the morality of Antigone's actions. As a result, through the centuries we have debated Antigone's character and the nature of her actions. Was she good or evil, was she a true patriot who sought to strengthen the moral foundations of the state, or was she a criminal, who transgressed both law and civic customs? Finally, the play brings up the central question: is it possible for an individual to exist outside a polity?

Are Arundhati Roy and Anna Politkovskaya the modern-day incarnations of Antigone? In this chapter, a comparison and an analysis of Roy and Politkovskaya's national and transnational politics also allow me to raise larger questions about women's history and its relationship to the history of the state. In conclusion, I append an interview conducted with Lisa Kirschenbaum, an eminent historian of the Soviet Union. Kirschenbaum examines the complicated relationship that has evolved between transnational intellectuals and the nation-state in the twenty-first century, especially those who are caught between the demands of the home, the state, and the world. Kirschenbaum answers important questions about historical philosophy, methodology, and politics, and explains how her work has been shaped by both global and national currents. I thank my readers for their patience as they navigate the arguments presented in this chapter.

Anna Politkovskaya and Post-Soviet Russia

Chechnya, a Muslim-majority Republic led by a highly decorated general from the Soviet army, Dzhokhar Dudayev, tried to break away from Russian control after the collapse of the Soviet Union in 1991, leading to the First Chechen War between 1994 and 1996. The demoralized post-Soviet army performed poorly against Chechen fighters who fought brilliantly on the mountainous territory that they knew well. Composed of only a million people but possessing deep oil reserves, the significance of Chechnya lies in its strategic geopolitical location: it is the conduit to Moscow's control of the Southern Caucasus, especially the post-Soviet states of Georgia and Armenia.

The Russian Empire spent many decades between the 1780s and the formal incorporation of this region in 1862 fighting the independent peoples that lived in isolated villages in this difficult and mountainous terrain. During the Russian Revolution of 1917, the area briefly gained independence only to be reincorporated by military force in 1921. During the Second World War, almost half a million Chechens were deported to labor camps in Central Asia because of their purported sympathy with the Nazi army. They were only allowed to return in 1957 when the Chechen-Ingush Autonomous Soviet Republic was reestablished after the death of Stalin.[5] Many have accused Stalin of practicing genocide against the Chechen peoples.

The Second Chechen War broke out in 1999 when under the leadership of Shamil Basaev an Islamic-based Chechen force attacked Dagestan, a neighboring province to build an Islamic caliphate. Vladimir Putin ascended to power by playing an important role in the Second Chechen War.[6] Putin used the invasion of Dagestan to frame the war in Chechnya as a military response to Islamic terrorism, anticipating the strategy that the United States was going to adopt during its own War on Terror. Russia declared the right to respond to terroristic acts with unilateral military measures unconstrained by the rule of constitutional law. Many terrorist incidents such as the Moscow Apartment bombings of 1999, the hostage crisis at the Nord-Ost Theater in Moscow in 2002, the kidnappings of Russian armed personnel, the hostage crisis of school children in Beslan in 2004, and the bombings at the Moscow metro in 2010 and the Moscow airport in 2011 all contributed to a sense of fear and panic among citizens. Many of them believed that the Russian state was justified in its retaliatory acts against Muslim peoples in the Caucasus.

The war in Chechnya took a bizarre turn after the initial military invasion when the Russian government chose the strong man Akhmet Kadyrov to attack Islamic fundamentalists in the North Caucasus. And after the death of Akhmet Kadyrov, his son, Ramzan Kadyrov, has played a willing role as Moscow's man in this region. The Russian army used Chechnya as a springboard to control Islamic-inspired violent movements in neighboring Ingushetia and Dagestan. The Kadyrov family benefited economically and militarily from their alliance with Moscow, and Chechnya has omerged as a highly profitable center of arms trafficking, oil smuggling, and the drug trade. Ramzan Kadyrov lives an ostentatious lifestyle, engaging publicly with celebrities and Western actors such as Jean Claude Van Damme and Gerard Depardieu. In 2011, the famed violinist Vanessa Mae performed at Kadyrov's birthday celebrations in the capital of Grozny. Despite his playboy image, Kadyrov has supported a return to the traditional forms of a decentralized Sufi Islam in Chechnya that is based on the veneration of individual charismatic leaders and local saints. He has adopted these policies to dismantle the appeal of a transnational Sunni ideology that seeks to resurrect a global Islamic caliphate. While Kadyrov has been criticized for following socially conservative policies toward women and using pro-natalism as a way to offset catastrophic demographic losses sustained during the war, Chechnya under his leadership has recovered economically from the two devastating wars that caused enormous destruction. During the last two decades, there has been a building boom in this war-torn country, and the Kadyrov administration has carried out extensive restorations in the badly damaged capital, Grozny. At the same time, Kadyrov has used Moscow's largesse to enormously strengthen his power: to build a private militia and to silence opposition by intimidation, arrests, and extrajudicial torture and killings.

Anna Politkovskaya came of age during the collapse of the Soviet Union.[7] Born to a Ukrainian family of diplomats in New York, Politkovskaya identified herself as Soviet/Russian. Despite her university education, Politkovskaya focused on raising her two children while her husband, host of the famous television talk show *Vzgliad* (Point of View) Sasha Politkovskii, played a crucial role during the media boom made possible by Gorbachev's policies of *glasnost*. Politkovskii became famous while covering the nuclear disaster in Chernobyl, and his fame grew following his other pioneering exposés. In the 1990s Politkovskaya, who had trained at the famous Soviet newspaper *Izvestiia*, turned her hand toward investigative journalism. Within a decade of entering this profession, she became a star reporter for the *Novaya Gazeta*, one of Russia's most liberal and outspoken newspapers.[8] But Politkovskaya found her voice reporting on the two Chechen wars, in this war-torn region of Europe. Unlike Roy, Politkovskaya was not a gifted writer, nor did she have the ability to endow her interviewees with subjectivity and individualism. But as you read Politkovskaya's impressionistic accounts of starving Chechens in refugee camps, beset with lice and disease; of Russian soldiers forced to survive on spoiled rations and endure brutal hazing rituals; of orphaned Chechen children, listless and hungry, obligated to write celebratory essays about the "Russian Motherland" in shabby tents that masquerade as schools, you feel her urgency and visceral anger at the Russian government. On every page, you encounter her boundless empathy and her breaking heart as she is unable to help the innocent victims of war. Her angry words, artless and without literary quality, burn the pages that they are written on.

Politkovskaya wrote in the brutal staccato of a drill sergeant: she wrote as if she wanted to shake the uncomprehending and uncaring public by the shoulders and shame them into demanding accountability from the Putin administration. She wrote about the *zachistki*, or cleaning operations, an anti-terrorist terrorist strategy followed by the Russian army. Villages would be blockaded for days on end, and young men arrested, tortured, and killed with little or no evidence. Those wishing to leave the village would be forced to pay enormous bribes. Politkovskaya also uncovered a brisk trade in dead bodies where Chechen relatives paid outrageous sums for the mutilated bodies of kidnapped men to Russian armed forces to give them a decent burial.

To Politkovskaya's credit, she was an impartial witness; and while she excoriated the violence of the Russian army, she had little sympathy for the Chechen nationalists and their brutal policies. Politkovskaya reserved her special ire for Ramzan Kadyrov and accused him of becoming a Chechen version of Stalin. Politkovskaya went into dangerous places to retrieve information on the war in Chechnya. She took on enormous risks when she traveled to interview the families of survivors. Politkovskaya was on a mission to document what she considered to be tantamount to a state-sponsored genocide. She was kidnapped by Chechen authorities; she was also beaten up by Russian armed forces, and even poisoned, but nothing deterred her in her quest for truth. In numerous hard-hitting books and articles, Politkovskaya listed the collateral damage of the two wars in Chechnya: the hungry and traumatized children, grieving mothers and widows who wept over the mutilated bodies of dead sons and husbands, burnt and incinerated schools, the bombed hospitals, and the devastated farms. She wrote about homes, in which normal people presumably once lived normal lives, flattened to rubble during the war. She also recounted the brutalization of young Russian conscripts and soldiers in the Russian army, forced to fight a war that made little sense to them.

Politkovskaya's life was cut short on October 7, 2006, when gunmen shot her dead in front of her apartment building in Moscow. She was expecting the birth of her grandchild that day. The impromptu crowds that collected at her funeral three days later were a testament to the admiration and regard that she elicited in many who knew her. Politkovskaya's raw courage and her public attacks on Putin's administration have made her a veritable icon of resistance in the West. Family members, friends, colleagues, and legions of admirers worldwide have kept her ideas alive through films, awards established in her name, the publication of her works, and the yearly commemoration of her death in Moscow.[9] The trials and mistrials of her killers have also kept Politkovskaya in the public eye but, strangely over time, Politkovskaya's research into the war crimes committed in Chechnya has faded. She is increasingly represented in the West as a voice for freedom of expression and democracy in Russia against an autocratic Russian government headed by Vladimir Putin.

Arundhati Roy and India

While Politkovskaya was concerned with human rights violations in Chechnya and the growing political authoritarianism in Russia, Arundhati Roy's critiques are more wide-ranging. Roy has spent a lot of time and ink attacking what she calls "gush-up capitalism," made possible by the global neoliberal order and assisted by a compliant IMF and the World Bank.[10] She is incensed by the unfair distribution of material rewards that has flown disproportionately to the upper reaches of society worldwide during the decades of globalization. Roy is also convinced that the recent material prosperity of the Indian middle class has further impoverished the remaining 800 million, while pro-growth policies have caused untold environmental degradation. She has strongly criticized the growing authoritarianism of right-wing Hindu nationalist organizations and political parties in India, and the disruption of peasants and indigenous peoples in the corporate quest to privatize natural resources such as mines, farms, forests, and waterways. Finally, Roy has been very vocal about the excesses committed during the US-sponsored global War on Terror, human rights abuses, and global ecocide.[11] Roy's vociferous attacks on American imperialism and consumerism, including in her now infamous essay entitled "The Algebra of Infinite Justice," published shortly after 9/11, her deep friendship with Noam Chomsky, the most celebrated dissident in the United States, and her regular rants against American corporations have made her a permanent fixture in intellectual circuits in the West exemplified by outlets such as *Democracy Now*, the *New York Times,* and *The Guardian,* and she is a much sought-after lecturer on university campuses.

Roy believes that the gospel of inclusive capitalism that has been broadcast throughout the world since the collapse of the Soviet Union hides the massive and illegal privatization of public and natural resources that animates the apparent miracle of growth engendered by the free market. Roy has led struggles against the building of large dams that threaten to displace millions of the rural poor in India. She has championed the cause of Maoist rebels in Central India by fighting corporations that want to develop the rich mines in the area by displacing indigenous peoples. Roy has spent a few months in the jungles of Chhattisgarh and Madhya Pradesh in India with Maoist insurgents who are waging a large-scale insurgency against transnational corporations. She has also condemned the Indian government's use of force against insurgents in these areas. Roy has criticized both socialism and capitalism for being anti-human and anti-democratic systems. She believes that just as socialism collapsed, capitalism will also come to a similar end because of the impoverishment and resistance that it is creating throughout the globe.

Arundhati Roy was born to a Bengali Hindu father and a Syrian Christian mother who was an activist for women's rights. She trained in architecture and dabbled in acting and screen-writing before gaining a global audience in 1996 with the publication of her blockbuster first novel, *God of Small Things*. A story about a multi-generational Indian family, the novel won the Booker Prize and went on to garner huge sales around the world. Although the novel brought her wealth and renown, a highly photogenic Roy refused to be the face of New India for the nationalistic Indian media. She cut off her long hair and decided to turn to journalism and activism on behalf of India's poor. She soon emerged as a sharp and clever critic of global capitalism and imperialism, creating endless controversy through her polemical and sometimes brilliant writings.

Roy, like Politkovskaya, is not afraid of conflict and has led attacks on India's most sacred icons, including Mohandas Gandhi and the anti-corruption activist Anna Hazare. But perhaps her most controversial act that has alienated many Indians is her open support for Kashmiri independence. At a talk delivered at a seminar "Whither Kashmir: Freedom or Enslavement," organized by Coalition of Civil Societies on October 24, 2010, Roy declared to the horror of many that Kashmir has never been a part of India and needs to be independent. She subsequently reiterated this inflammatory comment when she shared a stage with the hardline Kashmiri separatist Syed Ali Shah Geelani later that year.

Kashmir, the formerly princely state of British India, is now a disputed territory with the governments of India, China, and Pakistan laying claim to different parts of the region.[12] Like Chechnya, Kashmir's strategic location (which includes the Indian administered territories of Jammu, Kashmir, and Ladakh) strategic location is key to its geopolitical importance. Kashmir, since ancient times, has been home to Hindu and Buddhist populations and has produced many noteworthy Hindu scholars such as Vasugupta, Abhinavgupta, and the twelfth-century historian of Kashmir, Kalhana. Islam came late to Kashmir, as late as the fourteenth century, and the spread of the religion was mediated through the activities of Central Asian Sufi preachers and Indian Muslim rulers from the south. Kashmir became the crown jewel of the Mughal Empire but it was then in turn ruled by the Sikhs. Kashmir became an independent kingdom in British India under Hari Singh, a Hindu Rajput ruler. During the partition wars of 1947, both India and Pakistan laid claim to this magic kingdom of unbelievable beauty that housed a majority Muslim peasant population but was also home to a sizable population of Hindu, Buddhist, and Sikh inhabitants. Kashmir was divided between India and Pakistan during the partition, and these two countries have fought three wars over this territory in 1947, 1965, and 1990. India has jailed large numbers of separatists under the guise of security concerns, routinely dismissed democratically elected governments, and manipulated elections to bring compliant and pro-Indian politicians to power in the state of Jammu and Kashmir.

In the late 1980s and early 1990s, a mass uprising arose against the Indian control of Kashmir leading to the military occupation of the region.[13] Kashmiri insurgents, strengthened by an influx of Afghan Mujahideen fighters funneled through Pakistan, attacked government forces, vehicles, personnel, and civilians and, like their Chechen counterparts, used suicide bombers or fidayeen to reach their targets. Hundreds and thousands of Hindus, especially Kashmiri Pandits, were forced out of the region leaving behind their ancestral property, and many of them were brutally murdered. In retaliation, the Indian forces made sweeping arrests, jailed a large number of people, and engaged in torture and extrajudicial killings. Currently, in 2020, India has stationed more than 700,000 armed forces in the Kashmir Valley to bring "peace" to this war-torn region. India has claimed that both the Pakistani military and the intelligence services and Al Qaeda arms, personnel, and cash are fueling the fundamentalist insurgency. India, like Russia, has reframed the problem of Kashmiri separatism as a war on Islamic terrorism.

Unlike Politkovskaya who made the war on Chechnya her life's mission, traveling there repeatedly at considerable risk to her own life, interviewing warlords and victims, and making a wide range of contacts among the refugees and demobilized soldiers, Roy's engagement with Kashmir is more recent. Apart from a few high-level visits, talks, and the publications of a few essays, Roy has not made a prolonged study of the situation. Moreover, unlike Politkovskaya who has criticized the excesses committed by both the Russian and the Chechen sides, Roy has spoken very briefly about Islamic fundamentalism and the Sharia law that Kashmiri separatists have threatened to install in Kashmir. She has ignored the extensive ties that these groups have with Pakistani security and intelligence forces. For the most part, Roy has condemned the excesses of the Indian government and security forces but remained silent about the plight of Kashmiri Hindus who have been forced from their ancestral homes in Kashmir and are living in dire poverty in refugee camps.[14]

The Case against Politkovskaya and Roy

Did Roy and Politkovskaya's revelations of the military excesses committed in Chechnya and Kashmir only advance their reputation while damaging that of Russia and India in the global media? Did Politkovskaya and Roy bring shame, discomfort, and dishonor to their family, friends, and their respective nations by exposing human rights violations in Chechnya and Kashmir? Influential Russian-American journalists such as Keith Gessen and Masha Gessen have used Politkovskaya's murder to attack the Putin administration incessantly from safe havens in the West.[15] Nationalist critics have charged that Roy and Politkovskaya's revelations have empowered Western-dominated organizations such as Amnesty International, the United Nations, and the International Court of Justice to criticize human rights violations in Chechnya and Kashmir. While the human rights movement has taken on global urgency from the 1970s after the signing of the Helsinki Accords in 1975, the fact that it is largely based in organizations in the United States and Western Europe, and staffed predominantly by Western intellectuals or those that are based in Western universities, think tanks, and NGOs, makes the findings and recommendations suspect among domestic audiences in Russia and India. Charges of human rights violations challenge the sovereignty of recent nation-states that are insecure about their newfound independence; and they often interpret criticism as unwarranted international interference in domestic affairs.[16]

During the early years of Perestroika, Gorbachev had hoped that with the abolition of the Soviet Empire in Eastern Europe and especially the reunification of Germany, NATO, an armed coalition aimed at militarily containing the Soviet Union, would also cease to exist. But since 1991 we have seen the increase in the size and composition of NATO; and Russia continues to feel aggrieved that Western promises of the demilitarization of Europe were not kept after 1991. Russia has always been insecure about its western borders where historically the enemies of Russia have waged murderous campaigns. At the same time like other colonial powers in Western Europe, Russians mourn their loss of status after the imperial collapse of 1991.[17] Russian nationalism is often presented in terms of nostalgia for the greater Russian Empire expressed by both the extreme right and left-wing parties. Ardent nationalists such as Alexander Dugin, one of the prominent ideologues affiliated with the Putin administration, often talks about the concept of Eurasianism: Russia's natural destiny in creating a traditional Eurasian society that includes Turkic and Slavic races joined together against the liberal materialist order led by the United States and based on the Atlantic world civilizations.[18]

Putin and his foreign minister, Sergei Lavrov, have repeatedly accused the West of militarism on its borders, of drawing Poland, Czechoslovakia, and Hungary into NATO, and of erecting missile sites aimed at Russia in these countries. The entrance of the Baltic States of Latvia, Estonia, and Lithuania into the European Union in 2004 has outraged the Putin administration, and large sections of the Russian population living within these EU states are very receptive to ideas of a future reunification with Russia. The subsequent expansion of the European Union into the Balkans is considered by Russia to be a direct affront. Moscow sees the former republics as the natural Russian sphere of influence and resents Western interference into the political affairs of countries in the Baltics, Ukraine, Caucasus, and Central Asia (Georgia. For the most part, Russia has used the media and the foreign office to express its displeasure over what it terms Western infiltration through philanthropy, aid, religious missions, and the funding of civil society and pro-democracy projects.

Similarly, India since its independence in 1947 has been particularly sensitive about Western opinion about its policies as the British Empire in India was particularly corrupt and venal, and extracted human and natural resources with little attention to either human rights or civil liberties.[19] India has long argued on a variety of diplomatic platforms that Kashmir is a domestic issue, and has denied the rights of any international agency to either adjudicate or help with the creation of an equitable political solution. Although the liberal media in the West is extremely critical of Russia and India, it should be pointed out that Western governments have been quiet about the excesses committed against civilians and non-combatants in the wars in Chechnya and the occupation of Kashmir.[20] They have been silent for the most part about Russia's hardline position in Chechnya, and have stood with India on its policies in Kashmir. India is now perceived to be an important part of an emerging Indo-Pacific strategy designed to contain China's imperial ambitions.

Furthermore, have Politkovskaya and Roy used Chechnya and Kashmir to raise their status as global dissidents and profited from their activism? Strangely, neither Politkovskaya nor Roy has managed to raise world consciousness about the military situations in Chechnya or Kashmir given the strange global consensus on the War on Terror. And in many ways, the Western media has been less interested in Politkovskaya's account of human rights violations in Chechnya and more interested in using Politkovskaya's legacy to criticize Russia's domestic and foreign policies. Politkovskaya's and Roy's identities as global dissidents have become bigger than the causes they have championed. Politkovskaya has been criticized for the fact that she garnered lucrative book contracts with Western publishers, had an American passport, and received funding from numerous Western organizations and agencies. Many alleged that Politkovskaya was motivated in her anti-Russian reportage by the love of money and personal glory.[21] Similarly, Arundhati Roy's popularity among environmentalists and left-wing groups within the Western academy and media has helped Indian nationalists sharpen their arguments about her irrelevance in India. Some have even criticized her for self-aggrandizement, for her thoughtless remarks about the record of the Pakistani army during the war of Bangladeshi independence, and for taking credit for environmental activism that many poor and underserved communities have been engaged in.[22]

Third, are Politkovskaya and Roy unreliable journalists, given their sometimes-shoddy research, factual errors, and partisan judgments? Politkovskaya was regarded as an extremist during her lifetime, and many of her friends and relatives felt that her work was less about journalism, the reporting of facts, than a mission of what her husband, Sasha Politkovskii, described as "justice alarm." Among her friends and acquaintances, many felt that she lacked objectivity and disregarded facts while pursuing her conclusions.[23] Others charged that Politkovskaya's extreme antipathy to the Putin administration led her to inadvertently glorify the Chechen nationalists and legitimize terrorism. According to a poll conducted by the prestigious Levada Center soon after her assassination in 2006, many Russians professed to know little about her. Many believed that Politkovskaya had been killed by forces anxious to destabilize and discredit Russia, something that President Putin himself suggested when he was interviewed just after Politkovskaya's death during his visit to Germany in October 2006.[24] Similarly, Roy too has been accused of distorting history, of being a poor and solipsistic thinker, and of ignoring facts that get in the way of her portentous judgments.[25]

Finally, have Politkovskaya and Roy ignored the considerable growth rates and stability that both Russia and India have witnessed during the last two decades and thereby hurt the pride and sensibilities of their compatriots? Instead of celebrating the genuine progress that has taken place in economic, social, and cultural spheres in both Russia and India since 1991, especially the widespread amelioration of poverty, Roy and Politkovskaya have harped incessantly on the negative aspects of this era. They have alienated the large middle class in both countries that are justly proud of their recent material achievements and who are unwilling to entertain news that challenges the narratives of national unity and integrity that underwrite their personal stories of success.

Arundhati Roy's rock star status in the West has helped the Indian nationalist media create a story about a privileged and wealthy woman who takes on extremist positions to win more approbation abroad and enhance the sales of her books and ideas. Like Politkovskaya, Arundhati Roy makes people uncomfortable because she punctures the official narrative of "India Shining" that was promulgated by the ruling BJP party in the early 2000s when India was officially recognized as a developing economy. A rapidly developing and populous country, India sloughed off the shackles of state socialism and entered the global marketplace in 1991. In less than two decades India is now home to a substantial middle class of more than 350 million people who, like their counterparts in the West own homes, shop avidly at malls and online, have adopted a disposable lifestyle with scant regard for the environment. Many Indians travel the world looking for leisure and entertainment. Instead of celebrating the many achievements of this new capitalist India, that upper-class Indians, their political leaders, and diaspora Indians are wont to both in public and private, Roy is the awkward person at the party who asks embarrassing questions: loudly and repeatedly. Recently, Aatish Taseer, a well-known Indian novelist, has accused Roy of ignoring the genuine material gains of the Indian middle class and has charged her with wanting to doom India to picturesque poverty in the name of environmentalism.[26]

Under the long-lived Putin administration, there has been a steady improvement in the living standards of many in Russia, especially during the first decade of the 2000s. Like the New Indians, New Russians are anxious to present the best possible face to the world.[27] Many were sick of the news related to Chechnya during the oil-fueled boom of the 2000s and believed that Politkovskaya was developing a mania on the subject. According to Yevgeny Kiselyov,

> People like Politkovskaya are crusaders. She was a study in fanaticism and obsession. Sometimes it even seemed as though she was cloaked in an aura of saintliness, like many people who believe they have a mission in life that must be pursued every hour of every day and in every way possible. Politkovskaya believed that fate had given her a mission: to tell people the truth about what was actually going on in Chechnya.[28]

The middle-class lifestyles that many have achieved under policies of economic liberalization in both Russia and India have helped create a vociferous nationalist majority in both nations, which is very intolerant of dissent, especially if it is framed as a threat to the nation. Many believe that their material success is predicated on policies of liberalization adopted by the nation-state since 1991, and are content for the most part to trade the freedom of expression for the freedom of the marketplace. Politkovskaya's and Roy's journalism challenges the narratives of growth, national unity, and strength that many have become accustomed to hearing in the last two decades. In this instance, it appears that citizens share an exaggerated concern about the fragility of the nation-state, over-estimate the threats to territorial integrity, and are willing to use any means necessary for preserving national unity. The media in Russia and India have played a significant role in demonizing Politkovskaya in Russia and Roy in India.

Truth-Telling and Transnational History

Anna Politkovskaya: What am I guilty of? I have merely reported what I witnessed, nothing but the truth.[29]

Arundhati Roy: To love. To be loved. To never forget your own insignificance. To never get used to the unspeakable violence and the vulgar disparity of life around you. . . . To respect strength, never power. Above all, to watch. To try and understand. To never look away. And never, never, to forget.[30]

Michel Foucault: More precisely, parrhesia is a verbal activity in which a speaker expresses his personal relationship to truth, and risks his life because he recognizes truth-telling as a duty to improve or help other people (as well as himself). In parrhesia, the speaker uses his freedom and chooses frankness instead of persuasion, truth instead of falsehood or silence, the risk of death instead of life and security, criticism instead of flattery, and moral duty instead of self-interest and moral apathy.[31]

In his famous lecture "Discourse and Truth: The Problem of Parrhesia," Foucault argued that rather than establish logical criteria for a "truth" in the mode of analytical philosophy, he was more interested in the practice of truth-telling as an important political and moral activity, especially as it functioned in ancient Greece. Similarly, rather than evaluate Politkovskaya's and Roy's writings for truth/untruth, exaggeration or hyperbole, faulty reasoning, and factual errors that litter their speeches and writings, I would like to analyze their political practice in light of the criteria that Foucault outlined in his essay. Evaluating Politkovskaya's and Roy's politics, we find that they risked personal injury to speak the facts that they believed to be true. While Politkovskaya was ultimately killed for her truth-telling, security forces in Russia and Chechnya harassed her constantly while she was alive. Nationalist crowds in New Delhi have vandalized Roy's home. She has been arrested by the Indian government numerous times, and it has also filed cases of sedition against her in 2010 and then in 2015.

Neither Politkovskaya nor Roy has profited from their truth-telling. Politkovskaya lived a very simple life and drove a beaten-up Lada. Roy, who found enormous success as a novelist, like Tolstoy, has renounced writing popular fiction. Instead, she produces political and journalistic tracts to improve the lives of poor people. She has donated most of her earnings from the sales of her novel to fund progressive causes throughout India. Both women have a strong following among the poor, the dispossessed, and the marginalized. Politkovskaya's funeral in Moscow saw an outpouring of grief among the thousands that attended the event, and her death anniversary is still commemorated in Russia. Marina Goldosvskaya's film *A Bitter Taste of Freedom* clearly shows that she was greatly revered by Chechens who saw her as a tireless advocate. Roy's speeches in India are attended by thousands of laborers, indigenous people, students, and environmental activists. Her English language writings are translated into numerous Indian languages and read by millions around the world.

Finally, as Politkovskaya and Roy battled for what they considered to be the "truth" in the twenty-first century, I ask whose truth and whose peace is more important? Is it that of the nation-state—fueled by the aspirational nationalism of an emerging middle class, an entrenched elite, and a wealthy diaspora as it struggles to establish sovereignty and define borders using the time-hallowed weapons of violence and discursive coercion? Or that of transnational intellectuals who claim to speak for universal humanity and whose activities are now regarded by many as part of the cultural agenda of globalization, as an insidious form of imperial universalism that is funded by global corporations?[32] Politkovskaya spoke and Roy continues to speak on behalf of the civilians that are dispossessed by war, and for soldiers brutalized in wars that they do not choose to fight. Both have spoken about the plight of ordinary soldiers forced to commit unspeakable crimes, about innocent bystanders, and about ordinary people who are forced to choose sides by states and non-state actors. They have claimed the status of supranational intellectuals, bearing witness, criticizing their beloved nations while piercing the veil of ideology with their version of the truth. Both have refused the anti-national appellation and claimed to be motivated by genuine patriotism alone.

Theirs was a lonely journey. Politkovskaya described herself as a pariah and recorded the pain of being regarded as an insane woman even by people around her.[33] In 1998 Roy wrote, "I hereby declare myself an independent, mobile republic. I am a citizen of the earth. I own no territory. . . . Immigrants are welcome. You can help me design our flag."[34] Can transnational history take up this challenge and design a flag for a de-territorialized intellectual community as Politkovskaya and Roy urge us to? Whose members speak for truth and justice rather than the selfish interests of the nation-state? But on the other hand can intellectuals refuse to be a part of the nation-building project even as they profit from the many benefits that national membership brings? What are the challenges of engaging in transnational critique while living in the world of nation, borders, and passports? Finally, should our Bill of Rights also be balanced by a Bill of Duties that shore up the political entity that we belong to?

These questions are not simply academic or intellectual ones but have real resonance for me, an immigrant who voluntarily came to the United States to avail myself of the many opportunities, and the freedom of speech and inquiry that this country offers. I have worked hard to create relationships and engage in practices that accentuate my sense of belonging to my adopted home. And as an educator working with primarily first-generation and immigrant students, I see among them a similar desire for upward mobility, economic security, and emotional belonging. My students exhibit a voracious appetite for ideas and desire to know about the many ways of being in this world. I delight in the free-ranging and rambunctious debates that punctuate my class meetings. And I have learned over the years that upholding the freedom of speech and thought lies at the heart of the liberal project. I have to hear the voices that I abhor, debate with those that I disagree with, and engage with those who offend my political sensibilities. As a historian of the Soviet Union, I know well how knowledge is created, politicized, and even destroyed, and as a result, I am justly cautious about ideologues of all stripes, no matter how well-intentioned. In this last chapter I have tried to demonstrate that even when my political sympathies are firmly with Politkovskaya and Roy, I must exhibit the ability to listen to counter-arguments and engage in rational debate with points of view that are markedly different from my own to expand the dialogue and conversations.

Finally, while writing this book about intellectuals and their ideas, I have realized that the job of the scholar is not just to offer commentary, critique, and advice against inequality, oppression, and injustice everywhere. Deconstructing intellectual hierarchies is not a particularly perilous choice, especially when we live in a society like the United States where one pays almost no price for speaking the truth. Unlike Foucault, I believe that the job of the intellectual has to encompass more than truth-telling and the metaphorical tearing down of walls, boundaries, and hierarchies. The intellectual has to act on the truths that they have discovered and uphold them in their personal lives like the many characters in my book, especially Politkovskaya and Roy. There has to be a correspondence between words and deeds as Tolstoy and Tagore urged, otherwise, what then is the value of our words? And finally, we have to build, nurture, create, and uphold the community whose values we espouse.[35] Ideas about a better, more just world have power when they can be demonstrated in concrete ways. Finally, I believe that if you cannot build a home and strengthen your community (even when you address its myriad shortcomings), it is impossible to have a standing in the world.

To help us elucidate the connections between the individual, the local, the national, and the transnational, I turn to a historian of the Soviet Union, Lisa Kirschenbaum. She has written books on topics as varied as the politics of childhood in the early Soviet Union and the role that the memory of the Siege of Leningrad played in shaping postwar politics.[36] She is also a pioneer in the emerging field of Russia in world history with the publication of her monograph in 2015, *International Communism and the Spanish Civil War:*

Solidarity and Suspicion.[37] Her book is a deeply nuanced exploration of everyday life and lived experiences in the transnational world of communism during the 1920s and 1930s, and her meticulous research into the lives and activities of individuals who believed that the idea of communism was more important than the welfare of a state makes her particularly qualified to answer the questions that I have posed. Kirschenbaum is a professor of history at West Chester University of Pennsylvania, a state-funded academic institution that serves many first-generation university students.[38] She is a public intellectual in the old-fashioned sense of the term in that she speaks directly to a large community of interested listeners, a world that is largely invisible to the world of elite academia, journalism, and social media. Similar to Roy and Politkovskaya, Kirschenbaum is a transnational intellectual, but as a scholar and historian her work is held to a different set of disciplinary standards and criteria. In the following interview I ask Kirschenbaum to analyze her scholarship in relation to the demands of nationalist and transnational history.

Choi Chatterjee: How do you see yourself? As an American historian of the Russian Empire or as a transnational historian writing world history?

Lisa Kirschenbaum: I guess I'm all of these things to some extent, some by choice, some despite my best intentions. I'm clearly an "American historian" in the sense that I grew up here, went to school here, and work here. My institutional home, for better or worse, is a regional American public university. That position has all kinds of material and mental consequences from how much time and money I have for research and writing to my willingness (often born of necessity) to work as a teacher and a scholar in areas in which I'm not an authority. The more I taught world history surveys, the more I thought about Russia as part of the world. I became a transnational historian because it didn't seem worthwhile or reasonable to rope Russia off from the world. But as an individual, I don't feel transnational; I'm located in a very particular American place that informs my research and my teaching along with my way of making both somehow "transnational."

Choi Chatterjee: Was your interest in the Russian Empire shaped by the fact that the United States itself was a former imperial colony of Great Britain?

Lisa Kirschenbaum: No. As a high school student, I found American history a little dull, and I gravitated to Russian history and especially Russian literature, which by comparison seemed operatic and exciting. My initial interest in Russia had to do with its difference, so I guess it's more than a little ironic that my recent scholarly work has focused on investigating how difference gets constructed.

Choi Chatterjee: What is the value of transnational history?

Lisa Kirschenbaum: For me it's about getting beyond or around national narratives, focusing not on explaining a particular place or region but on seeing connections and networks. Rather than seeing the world in terms of bounded cultural or political spaces, transnational history gets us to focus on the in-betweens, the interchanges.

Choi Chatterjee: Does transnational history undercut the power of the nation-state?

Lisa Kirschenbaum: Well, the nation-state has a lot of staying power. But I think transnational history is a critical means of challenging national histories, and especially narratives of national exceptionalism. When we shift the focus to how people, institutions, ideas, symbols, and cultural products cross borders, then the nation becomes less central to the story.

Choi Chatterjee: Since the historian enjoys rights within a nation-state, do they have an obligation to uphold the political formation in their scholarship?

Lisa Kirschenbaum: Depends on whom you ask, I guess. States seem to think historians have this obligation. That's why you get an outcry against the US History Advanced Placement exam that supposedly ignores the "founding fathers" or against research on the Second World War in Russia that questions the veracity of legendary Soviet heroes like the Panfilovtsy. But I'd say it is the historian's responsibility to challenge such nation-building myths. The syllabus of my general education world history course says that my goal is to help students to see history not as an immutable chronicle that explains why the world—and we could add the nation—must be as it is, but as a multiplicity of contingent and shifting interactions to which a wide range of interdependent global actors contribute. I think that is the academic historian's obligation.

Choi Chatterjee: Can we build a research curriculum around a global concept of social justice and development that also addresses the needs of the local community in concrete ways?

Lisa Kirschenbaum: I think you can address this question better than I can. I hope we can. My idea of transnational history is that people make it (although never just as they please), where they happen to be using ideas and materials from all over. In my work on international communism, I tried to look at how even the most inveterate border crossers working for global change operated in and in support of some kind of "local" community.

Choi Chatterjee: Should we theorize a position of intellectual "homelessness" as the basic condition of objectivity when reporting on world affairs?

Lisa Kirschenbaum: I like this idea; although I'm not much of a theorist. I think of my position less as "homeless" than as "marginal." I have a home, but I'm at the edges of it. From the margins, the way things are "always" done can look useless or foolish, or oppressive. I don't think an oblique perspective is the same thing as objectivity. Are you suggesting that presumed powerlessness of the outsider, the "homeless" intellectual is a kind of superpower?

Choi Chatterjee: How is the "homelessness" of a woman scholar different from that of a male intellectual?

Lisa Kirschenbaum: If we see "homelessness" as akin to "marginality" then I think it's pretty clear that white male intellectuals are probably less likely to come from such a position. But I'm not sure how useful such generalizations are.

Choi Chatterjee: Should a historian address the concept of a Bill of Rights as well as a Bill of Duties in their scholarship and their teaching?

Lisa Kirschenbaum: I don't think I'd put it quite that prescriptively. But I do think academic historians need to think carefully about—and do a better job of publicly articulating—the central importance of history and the ability to think historically for citizens in a democracy.

Choi Chatterjee: How will the backlash against globalization impact the writing of transnational history?

Lisa Kirschenbaum: I had a student some years ago, who after the first day of class came up to me, very worried, and said, "I thought history was only about the US." That's not "backlash." That's the status quo. K-12 curricula have enshrined national just-so stories as history. We in the academy need to do a better job of explaining why these kinds of histories are a problem and training history teachers who can push back against them.

Conclusion

This is an intellectual history born of many decades of thinking, reading, and teaching, and powered by the simple fact that I, a product of British imperialism in India, have spent my life studying the Russian Empire while living in the United States. When you have lived your life at the intersection of three empires and traveled on many, many sub-imperial roads, it engenders a certain kind of perspective, a certain approach to history. In this book, I have argued that the British and Russian imperial experiences were more similar than previously acknowledged in the historical literature, and I hope that you have enjoyed this journey through literary works, prison systems, historical writings, left-wing ideologies, collective farms and plantations, colonial misadventures, and ideas about the development of selfhood and postcolonial nationalism in far-flung regions of the world.

The commonalities between the Russian and the British Empires have been obscured by the ferocious Anglo-Russian rivalry of the last two centuries that have shaped the world in significant ways. The West successfully created a trope about a despotic Russian Empire and its seeming backwardness that compared poorly with the development of highly profitable systems of capitalism, and the evolution of representative democracy in certain Western countries in the nineteenth and early twentieth centuries. This trope was further consolidated by the political paradigms generated by the Cold War that tethered Great Britain firmly to the winning side of freedom and democracy. By a strange twist of logic, the British Empire was described as a "liberal empire," although one would be very hard-pressed to find evidence of such liberalism in the colonies, beginning with Ireland and ending with Kenya. Instead, I have argued that these political arguments about the "liberal empire" have obscured the reality of British imperialism. British conduct in its colonies of Asia and Africa was similar to many of the colonial practices of the illiberal Russian Empire. But the overwhelming emphasis on the unfreedom of the Russian Empire was a brilliant political and ideological maneuver that deflected attention from the patently similar patterns of exploitation and oppression in the British Empire. Furthermore, I have argued that the history of Western European Empires is rarely taken into consideration when we study the history of Russia and the Soviet Union, and this has perpetuated the paradigm of Russian uniqueness. And that for the most part, the historians of Western European imperialism and globalization ignore the Russian and

Soviet experience. Without the inclusion of Russia, much of modern world history is necessarily incomplete.

When we move beyond the simple binary opposition of a free United Kingdom and an oppressive Russia, and instead compare the two empires, it reveals comparative colonial experiences. These include incarcerations of political prisoners in distant lands and islands, the elimination of the imperial past from the national histories of Russia and the United Kingdom, and the violent transformation of peasants, foragers, and nomads into exploited but modern agricultural workers. Such a historical approach also reveals many other interesting patterns of world history such as the avid embrace of modernity in places as unconnected as Kenya and Kazakhstan, the religious response to imperialism in Poland and Egypt, and the deep anti-nationalism of many important thinkers and activists.

This book is also an extended conversation about the home and the world and the ways in which we define a good society. Intellectuals such as Emma Goldman, M. N. Roy, Anna Politkovskaya, and Arundhati Roy argue that the world is ultimately more important than the home and that the nation-state is an impediment to the realization of a just world. Dudziak and Al-Ghazali argue to the contrary that internationalism and cosmopolitanism are the preserve of a highly privileged class, and this ideology fails to represent the interests of the common people in whose name they purport to speak. Furthermore, they warn that if we do not foster local cultures that are born out of religious traditions that have evolved over millennia, then the nation itself will perish. Trevelyan and Klyuchevsky believe that the nation is not defined by religion alone, but that an indelible sense of place born of one's profound engagement with the natural environment lies at the heart of nationalism. They argue that our connection to the land, the rivers, the forests, and the mountains creates an ineradicable national sentiment that has needs to be nourished anew in every generation. Mukhamet Shayakhmetov and Wangari Maathai would agree with Trevelyan's and Klyuchevksy's ideas about a love for one's nation that is rooted in the traditions of the land. Finally, Tagore and Tolstoy urge us to build a home in the image of the world that we wish to inhabit. They insist, most unreasonably, that we have to live our truths before we share them with the world, and that a correspondence between words and deeds is the hallmark of a true intellectual.

For better or for worse the contemporary world is a product of European colonization and modernization. But my cast of characters in this book proves that there were some who agreed, others who resisted, and yet others who completely changed the imperial script and produced alternative visions and realities, both in the metropole and in the colonies. I have focused on the conversations, the disagreements, the arguments, and the clash of personalities to show that while the historian may be tempted to arrive at monolithic and sweeping conclusions about the past, the desire to control the historical narrative is always undone by the historical process itself. In some cases, I have stretched the interpretive framework of this book extremely thin and purists will surely castigate me for my idiosyncratic approach to world history that stretches from Kenya to Kazakhstan, from Yasnaia Poliana to Jorasanko. And I am most deserving of their censure. But this book is intended for students of history who are open to considering unconventional arrangements of the past. If my book gives you a few hours of reading pleasure punctuated with bouts of irritation and disquietude, my years of work will have been worthwhile.

Rather than summarize the main arguments of my book in the conclusion, I thought it would be interesting to consider how these two empires have fared after decolonization. The British Empire and the Soviet Union collapsed in the second half of the twentieth century, within a few decades of each other. However, there was one important difference: while the latter's demise was peaceful for the most part, and dramatically telescoped into a matter of months and days in 1991, the British Empire did not go "gently into the good night." To paraphrase Dylan Thomas, a Welsh poet, it raged, raged against the "dying of the night" to make sure that the sun never set on the British Empire. A blind and shorn Samson, the empire nonetheless had the ability to put up a good fight till the bitter end. As a result, most postcolonial nations that were born of the British Empire came into the world bathed in blood. Civil wars, genocide, and bitter conflicts still mark many regions of the world that were formerly British colonies. The immense violence that marked the independence of India (1947), Egypt (1956), and Kenya (1963) were not isolated incidents, but part of a larger story of decolonization and imperial decline. The Soviet Union, on the other hand—the imperial power that had successfully suppressed all attempts of national independence movements within its fifteen soviet socialist republics through constant surveillance, massive schemes of imprisonment and population transfers, and the selective cooptation of local elites—was suddenly undone in 1991. When the Russian Soviet Federative Socialist Republic, the crown jewel, seceded from the Soviet Union itself under the leadership of Boris Yeltsin, the experiment in socialist imperialism ended in ignominy. The Nagorno-Karabakh conflict broke out in 1990–1 in the Caucasus, between Armenia and Azerbaijan, and there were uprisings in Lithuania and Latvia. But as Stephen Kotkin has argued, the least violent chapter of Soviet history was at the very end when the immensely militarized empire, with countless divisions and battalions, to the great surprise of its friends, foes, and legions of trained Sovietologists, I might add, "gently went into the good night."[1]

After decolonization, the British Empire transformed itself into the Commonwealth of Nations, a voluntary organization of fifty-four nations that comprise almost a third of humanity and conduct most of their business in the

English language. Despite the bitter fights over independence, postcolonial elites in the Americas, Middle East, Australasia, Asia, and Africa retain their consistent affection for the mother country and continue to educate their children in the institutions of higher education in the United Kingdom. The industrialist Ratan Tata acquired the classic British car company Jaguar as he was loathe to allow the car of his childhood to disappear from the world. In a similar manner, Mukesh Ambani has acquired the iconic British toy store Hamleys to save it from bankruptcy and plans to open 500 new stores in India alone. Nostalgia for a British imperial past apparently plays an important role in the business decisions of Indian magnates.[2] There have been very few calls for reparations and fewer still for accountability for colonial crimes outside the pages of countless historical monographs.

Russia, too, formed the Commonwealth of Independent States that is comprised of nine of the former fifteen Soviet republics. But while very few countries fear that the British Empire will reappear in the former colonies as a military power (with perhaps the possible exception of Iraq, Afghanistan, and Libya), former Soviet colonies such as Ukraine and Georgia still fear the imperial presence of a Russia that is too close by and lays too great a store by its imperial past. Ukraine has suffered from repeated imperial aggression, and its current state of independence may prove to be transitory. Postcolonial elites in former colonies in the western part of Russia, with the exception of Belarus of course, are cautious about openly expressing their affection for the mother country. Russia's ties seem to be strongest in Central Asia, with countries such as Kazakhstan. Siberia will probably emerge as a future site of a Sino-Russian conflict as an imperial China gains in strength and global confidence.

Despite Russia's enormous land size, even after losing a considerable amount of territory in 1991, the population is relatively small, but at 146 million, it has more than double the population of the comparatively tiny United Kingdom. In economic terms, however, the GDP of the United Kingdom is almost twice that of Russia. Despite the loss of its colonies, the United Kingdom is a formidable world power and ranks sixth in the global economy whereas Russia has failed to figure in the top ten countries in the ranking of world economies. British banking and financial services are still the best in the world and former colonies in the Americas, Africa, Asia, the Middle East, and Australasia avail of them liberally. Russia supplies oil and gas to most former colonies, and many historic trade and immigration routes have survived the collapse of the Soviet Union. Both countries have a strong scientific establishment and are formidable suppliers of weaponry to the world. While British foreign policy has been for the most part subsumed under American leadership during the Cold War and even more so during the War on Terror, Russia is a fiercely independent player in the world of geopolitics. Thanks to its presence on the Eurasian landmass that stretches from Eastern Europe to the Pacific, and its significant armed forces, it continues to play an important role in both Europe and Asia and is beginning to penetrate the continent of Africa as well.

The biggest difference, however, lies in the way that the political system is structured in the two countries. Despite much talk about a democratic transition in Russia after the collapse of the Soviet system in 1991, we have seen an authoritarian and centralized political structure gain strength and confidence under Putin. The growing middle class in post-Soviet Russia wants economic and political stability and, for the most part, shares the Putin administration's desire for global respect and acknowledgment. As long as there are no overt attacks on the Putin administration, Russians are free for the most part to voice their opinions and ply their everyday life. The United Kingdom on the other hand with the loss of its overseas colonies has devolved to its strong traditions of parliamentary rule, representative government, freedom of speech, and liberalism, a political project that was born in the British Isles many centuries ago. It predates the time that the empire was conceived. While British liberalism coexisted with the worst excesses of empire, it has survived the end of imperialism as a project that is worthy of our political and ethical attention. The "Little England" that intellectuals like George Trevelyan and other nationalists like him dreamed of in the late nineteenth century has become a reality. Moreover, the British parliamentary system has taken root in many former colonies stretching across the world. A system of representative government, an imperial gift, has become a global phenomenon. The popularity of the English language that has been powered by its enviable literary traditions continues to grow. This liberal tradition, despite its many shortcomings, needs to be preserved at home and exported to the rest of the world. This is to be done not by military force and proto-colonial misadventures, or by presumptions of moral superiority that are transmitted through creaky and inept world organizations; rather it is to be done by reason, dialogue, and a dedication to the free exchange of ideas first at home, and then abroad. We live as always in interesting times, and I end with the two poems that were written almost a hundred years apart. Poetry surely is the best record of historical change.

Excerpt from the "Second Coming," William Butler Yeats, 1919

Surely some revelation is at hand;
Surely the Second Coming is at hand.
The Second Coming! Hardly are those words out

When a vast image out of *Spiritus Mundi*
Troubles my sight: somewhere in sands of the desert
A shape with lion body and the head of a man,
A gaze blank and pitiless as the sun,
Is moving its slow thighs, while all about it
Reel shadows of the indignant desert birds.
The darkness drops again; but now I know
That twenty centuries of stony sleep
Were vexed to nightmare by a rocking cradle,
And what rough beast, its hour come round at last,
Slouches towards Bethlehem to be born?[3]

"March 20th" Ilya Senmenenko-Basin, 2016

A bright ray of sunshine illuminated
girls' faces, girls who were bent over their papers
at a long table
in a room on the ninth floor of the ugly ancient house.
And there was nothing, nothing
that I could call my own,
the center of my little universe
where my interests and rights reign.
But only the sun
the sun reminded me of myself by unsettling me
with its too early spring warmth.
* * *

there's a point on the horizon,
that I'm interested in
or rather, it's interested in me
and perhaps I'm not the center of the universe
and maybe the center is not here, where I'm standing
but at this point on the horizon
in that hardly visible dot
is the center that attracts me.
where were we going?[4]
* * *

Notes

Introduction

1 Clare Anderson, "The British Indian India, 1789–1939," in Clare Anderson ed., *A Global History of Convicts and Penal Colonies* (London: Bloomsbury, 2018), 212–45.

2 Ian R. Christie, *The Benthams in Russia 1780–1791* (Oxford: Berg, 1993); and Alessandro Stanziani, "The Traveling Panopticon: Labor Institutions and Labor Practices in Russia and Britain in the Eighteenth and Nineteenth Centuries," *Comparative Studies in Society and History*, vol. 51, no. 4 (2009): 715–41.

3 Simon Werrett, "The Panopticon in the Garden: Samuel Bentham's Inspection House and Noble Theatricality in Eighteenth-Century Russia," *Ab Imperio*, no. 3 (2008): 47–70.

4 Padraic Kenney, *Dance in Chains: Political Imprisonment in the Modern World* (New York: Oxford University Press, 2017).

5 Michael David-Fox, *Showcasing the Great Experiment: Cultural Diplomacy and Western Visitors to the Soviet Union, 1921–1941* (New York: Oxford University Press, 2012); David Charles Engerman, *Know Your Enemy: The Rise and Fall of America's Soviet Experts* (New York: Oxford University, 2009); David Foglesong, *The American Mission and the "Evil Empire": The Crusade for a "Free Russia" since 1881* (New York: Cambridge University Press, 2007); Martin Malia, *Russia Under Western Eyes: From the Bronze Horseman to the Lenin Mausoleum* (Cambridge, MA: The Belknap Press of Harvard University Press, 1999); Richard Pipes, *Russia Under the Old Regime*, rpt. edition (New York: Penguin Press, 1997); and Larry Wolff, *Inventing Eastern Europe: The Map of Civilization on the Mind of Enlightenment* (Stanford: Stanford University Press, 1994).

6 V. I. Lenin, "Two Tactics of Social-Democracy in a Democratic Revolution," in Lenin's *Collected Works*, vol. 9 (Moscow: Progress Publishers, 1962), 15–140. Lenin derived these ideas from Peter Struve, a famous Marxist economist. See Richard Pipes, *Richard Struve: Liberal on the Left* (Cambridge, MA: Harvard University Press, 1970), 193–6. I thank Jane Burbank for this citation and many others in this text.

7 Robert Edelman, *Proletarian Peasants: The Revolution of 1905 in Russia's Southwest* (Ithaca, NY: Cornell University Press, 1987).

8 Paul Miliukov, *Russia Today and Tomorrow* (London: Macmillan and Co. Limited, 1922).

9   Jonathan Daly, "Russian Punishments in the European Mirror," in Susan
       McCaffray and Michael Melancon eds., *Russia in the European Context,
       1789–1914: A Member of the Family* (New York: Palgrave Macmillan, 2005),
       161–88.

10 Jane Burbank and Frederick Cooper, *Empires in World History: Power and
       the Politics of Difference* (Princeton, NJ: Princeton University Press, 2011);
       Krishan Kumar, *Visions of Empire: How Five Imperial Regimes Shaped the
       World* (Princeton, NJ: Princeton University Press, 2017); Dominic Lieven,
       Russian Empire and its Rivals (New Haven, CT: Yale University Press, 2002);
       Ilya Gerasimov, Sergey Glebov, Marina Mogilner, and Alexander Semyonov
       eds., *Novaia imperskaia istoriia postsovetskogo prostranstva* (Kazan, Russia:
       Tsentr Issledovaniia Natsionalizma i Imperii, 2004); Alexander Morrison,
       Russian Rule in Samarkand, 1868-1910: A Comparison with British India
       (Oxford, UK: Oxford University Press, 2008); Alexander Semyonov, "Imperial
       Parliament for a Hybrid Empire: Representative Experiments in the early
       20th-century Russian Empire," *Journal of Eurasian Studies*, vol. 11, no. 1
       (2020): 30–9; and Alessandro Stanziani, "Bondage: Labor and Rights in
       Eurasia from the Sixteenth to the Early Twentieth Centuries," *International
       Studies in Social History*, vol. 24 (New York: Berghahn Books, 2018).

11 Alexander Etkind, *Internal Colonization: Russia's Imperial Experiences*
       (Cambridge: Polity Press, 2011).

12 Luke Kelly, "British Humanitarianism and the Russian Famine, 1891–92,"
       Historical Research, vol. 89, no. 246 (November 2016): 824–45; and Richard
       Robbins, *Famine in Russia, 1891-92* (New York: Columbia University Press,
       1975).

13 Mike Davis, *Late Victorian Holocausts: The El Nino Famines and the
       Making of the Third World* (London: Verso, 2001); and Amartya Sen, *Poverty
       and Famines: An Essay on Entitlement and Deprivation* (Oxford: Oxford
       University Press, 1981).

14 Steven Marks, *How Russia Shaped the Modern World: From Art to Anti-
       Semitism, Ballet to Bolshevism* (Princeton, NJ: Princeton University Press,
       2003); Choi Chatterjee, Steven G. Marks, Mary Neuburger, and Steven
       Sabol, eds., *The Global Impacts of Russia's Great War and Revolution,* Book
       2*: The Wider Arc of Revolution*, Parts 1 and 2 (Bloomington, IN: Slavica
       Publishers, 2019).

15 Jennifer Pitts, *A Turn to Empire: The Rise of Imperial Liberalism in Britain
       and France* (Princeton, NJ: Princeton University Press, 2005); Uday Mehta,
       Liberalism and Empire: A Study in Nineteenth Century British Liberal Thought
       (Chicago, IL: University of Chicago Press, 1999); and Edward Said, *Culture
       and Imperialism* (New York: Vintage Books, 1994);

16 Andreas Kappeler, *The Russian Empire: A Multi-Ethnic Empire*, trans. by
       Alfred Clayton (New York: Routledge Press, 2001); Geoffrey Hosking, *Russia,
       and Russians: A History*, second edition (Cambridge, MA: Belknap Press of
       Harvard University Press, 2011); Harsha Ram, *Imperial Sublime: The Russian
       Poetics of Empire* (Madison, WI: University of Wisconsin Press, 2003); and
       David Schimmelpenninck van der Oye, *Russian Orientalism: Asia in the
       Russian Mind from Peter the Great to Emigration* (New Haven, CT: Yale
       University Press, 2010).

17 Jack P. Greene ed., *Exclusionary Empire: English Liberty Overseas* (New York: Cambridge University Press, 2010).

18 Antoinette Burton, *The Trouble with Empire: Challenges to Modern British Imperialism* (New York: Oxford University Press, 2105); Niall Ferguson, *Empire: How Britain Made the Modern World* (New York: Penguin Books Ltd., 2018); and Vijay Prashad, *The Darker Nations: The People's History of the Third World,* rpt. edition (New York: The New Press, 2008).

19 Laura Engelstein, *Slavophile Empire: Imperial Russia's Illiberal Path* (Ithaca: Cornell University Press, 2009).

20 Artemy Kalinovksy, *Laboratory of Socialist Development: Cold War Politics and Decolonization in Soviet Tadjikistan* (Ithaca, NY: Cornell University Press, 2018); and Jie Hyun-Lim, "Nationalizing the Bolshevik Revolution Transnationally: Non-Western Modernization Among 'Proletarian' Nations," in Choi Chatterjee, Steven Marks, Mary Neuberger, and Steve Sabol edited, *The Global Impacts of Russia's Great War and Revolution: The Wider Arc of Revolution*, Part I, vol. 2 (Slavica Publishers, Indiana University, Bloomington, 2019), 177-199.

21 Christopher Bayly, *Birth of the Modern World, 1780-1914* (New York: Wiley-Blackwell, 2003); Dipesh Chakrabarty, *Provincializing Europe: Postcolonial Thought and Historical Difference* (Princeton, NJ: Princeton University Press, 2000); Pankaj Mishra, *From the Ruins of Empire: The Intellectuals Who Remade Asia* (New York: Farrar, Strauss and Giroux, 2012); Sanjay Subrahmanyam, *Empires Between Islam and Christianity* (Albany, NY: SUNY Press, 2020); and Jurgen Osterhammel, *the Transformation of the World: The Global History of the Nineteenth Century* (Princeton, NJ: Princeton University Press, 2014).

22 John Darwin, *After Tamerlane: The Rise and Fall of Global Empires, 1400-2000* (New York: Bloomsbury Press, 2008). Other noteworthy world history approaches within the field of Russian history include Lisa Kirschenbaum, *International Communism, and the Spanish Civil War: Solidarity and Suspicion* (New York: Cambridge University Press, 2015); Silvio Pons, *The Global Revolution: The History of International Communism, 1917-1991*, trans. Allan Cameron (Oxford: Oxford University Press, 2014); Stephen Smith, *Revolution and the People in Russia and China: A Comparative History* (New York: Cambridge University Press, 2008); and Gregory Afinogenov, *Spies and Scholars. Chinese Secrets and Imperial Russia's Quest for World Power* (Cambridge, MA: Harvard University Press, 2020).

23 For an excellent use of individual stories in the history of imperialism see, Nicholas Breyfogle, Abby Schraeder, and Willard Sunderland eds, *Peopling the Russian Periphery: Borderland Colonization in Eurasian History* (London and New York: Routledge, 2007).

24 See Kate Brown's insertion of individual narratives into the structures of history, *A Biography of No Place: From Ethnic Borderland to Soviet Heartland* (Cambridge, MA: Harvard University Press, 2009).

25 James Scott, *Against the Grain: A Deep State of the Earliest States* (New Haven, CT: Yale University Press, 2017).

Chapter 1

1 Charlotte Alston, *Tolstoy and His Disciples: The History of a Radical International Movement* (London: I.B. Tauris, 2015); and William Nickell, *The Death of Tolstoy: Russia on the Eve, Astapova Station, 1910* (Ithaca, NY: Cornell University Press, 2010).

2 Branko Milanovic, *Global Inequality: A New Approach for the Age of Globalization* (Cambridge, MA: Harvard University Press, 2016); and Steven Radelet, *The Great Surge: The Ascent of the Developing World* (New York: Simon and Schuster, 2015).

3 Anthony Atkinson, *Inequality: What Can Be Done* (Cambridge, MA: Harvard University Press 2015); David Brady, *Rich Democracies: Poor People. How Politics Explain Politics* (New York: Oxford University Press 2008); Matthew Eagleton-Pierce, *Neoliberalism: The Key Concepts* (New York, 2016); Thomas Piketty, *Capital in the Twenty First Century* (Cambridge, MA: Belknap Press, Harvard University Press, 2014): and Arundhati Roy, *Capitalism: A Ghost Story* (Chicago, IL, 2014).

4 Adam K. Webb, "The Counter-Modern Movement: A World Historical Perspective on the Thought of Rabindranath Tagore, Allama Iqbal and Liang Shuming," *Journal of World History*, vol. 19, no. 2 (June, 2008): 189–212; According to the eminent Bengali poet, Buddhadev Bose, Tagore was a master at describing feelings but lacked philosophical and theological depth and sophistication. *Tagore, Portrait of a Poet* (Bombay: Bombay University Press, 1962).

5 Martin E. Malia, "Adulthood Refracted: Russia and Leo Tolstoi," *Daedalus*, vol. 105, no. (Spring, 1976): 181.

6 See welcome exceptions and recent work by Alexandre Christoyannopoulos, *Tolstoy's Political Thought* (Andover: Routledge, 2014); and Michael Collins, *Empire, Nationalism and the Postcolonial World: Rabindranath Tagore's Writings on History, Politics and Society* (New York: Routledge, 2012).

7 Isaiah Berlin, *Russian Thinkers,* edited by Henry Hardy and Aileen Kelly (New York: Viking Press, 1978); and Isaiah Berlin, "Rabindranath Tagore and the Consciousness of Nationality," in *The Sense of Reality: Studies in Ideas and their History*, edited by Henry Hardy (New York: Farrar, Straus and Giroux, 1997).

8 Krishna Dutta and Andrew Robinson ed., *Selected Letters of Rabindranath Tagore* (New York: Cambridge University Press, 1997), 43. Later in his life Tolstoy expressed his disgust with the "dreary and vulgar Anna," cited in Irina Paperno, *"Who, What Am I?" Tolstoy Struggles to Narrate the Self* (Ithaca, NY: Cornell University Press, 2014). Tagore's strictures on *Anna Karenina* notwithstanding, Tolstoy was greatly admired in India and continues to find a wide readership at all levels of society. See Radha Balasubramanian's excellent study, *The Influence on India on Leo Tolstoy and Tolstoy's Influence on India: A Study of Reciprocal Receptions* (Lewiston, NY: Edwin Mellen Press, 2013).

9 Tagore jokes about prophets being stoned to death in a letter to his friend, Charles Andrews. Charles F. Andrews, ed., *Letters to a Friend*

(Rabindranath Tagore) (London: G. Allen and Unwin, 1928); and Maxim Gorky was completely taken aback when Tolstoy boasted about his sexual prowess. *Reminiscences of Lev Nikolaevich Tolstoy* (New York: B.W. Huebsch, 1920).

10 Tolstoy believed that all political parties would use force to stay in power and invent new forms of slavery. See *Kingdom of God Is Within You* (1894). See Tagore's letter to Dilip Roy where he refuses to accept the primacy of organized politics as the only methodology for social and national redemption. Cited in Reba Shom, *Rabindranath Tagore: The Singer and His Song* (New Delhi: Penguin Group India, 2009), 86.

11 Bhabatosh Chatterjee has described Tagore thus, "an artist is a lonely traveller, walking through the crowd, responding to stimulations from outside, assimilating the experiences of many minds which extend beyond the segregated regions of a particular country, the experiences that cannot be classified or catalogued," and I believe that this image fits Tolstoy equally well. Bhabatosh Chatterjee, *Rabindranath and Modern Sensibility* (New Delhi: Oxford University Press, 1996), 75.

12 Rabindranath Tagore, "Crisis in Civilization," in Sisir Kumar Das ed., *The English Writings of Rabindranath Tagore*, vol. 3 (New Delhi: Sahitya Akademi, 2002), 722–8; and Rini Bhattacharya Mehta, "In the Shadow of the Nations: Dissent as Discourse in Rabindranath Tagore's Political Writings, 1914–1941," *South Asia: Journal of South Asian Studies*, vol 35, no. 1 (2012): 172–91.

13 Ironically, both Tolstoy and Tagore were subsequently claimed and appropriated as icons of Russian and Indian nationalism respectively, their philosophical heritage shorn of its universalism, and their perceptive analyses of power and property buried. See Rosamund Bartlett's excellent epilogue on the fate of Tolstoy in Soviet times in her masterly *Tolstoy: A Russian Life* (Boston and New York: Houghton, Mifflin, Harcourt, 2011).

14 Nirad Chaudhuri in the second volume of his memoir, *Thy Hand Great Anarch* (Reading, PA: Addison-Wesley Publishing Co., 1987), has a searing chapter analyzing the many reasons that the literati and nationalists in India hated Tagore.

15 *Tolstoy and Education*, translated by Leo Weiner (Chicago: University of Chicago Press, 1967). See Also Tolstoy's brilliant *Childhood* (1852), *Boyhood* (1854), and *Youth* (1857) for his adventures within the world of formal education. Uma Das Gupta ed., *Tagore. Selected Writings on Education and Nationalism* (New Delhi: Oxford University Press, 2009); and Uma Das Gupta ed., *Rabindranath Tagore: My Life in My Words* (New Delhi: Penguin Books, 2009). See also Tagore, *Reminiscences* (1912), *Boyhood Days* (1940), and the short story parodying modern educational methods in "A Parrot's Training" (1924).

16 See Tolstoy's famous essay, "What Is Art?" (1897), and Tagore's famous collection of essays entitled, "Literature" (1907).

17 *The Diaries of Sofia Tolstoy*, trans. by Cathy Porter (New York: Harper Perennial, 1985); and Aruna Chakravarti, *Jorasanko* (New Delhi: Harper Collins, 2014) contains excellent information on the women in the Tagore family.

18 Sabyasachi Bhattacharya, *Rabindranath Tagore: An Interpretation* (New Delhi: Penguin Books India, 2011), 48–53; See Irina Paperno's brilliant analysis of Tolstoy's fascination with death in chapter 6 of her *"Who, What am I?" Tolstoy Struggles to Narrate the Self* (Ithaca, NY: Cornell University Press, 2014).

19 Tolstoy writes, "Rid of individualism . . . my consciousness will be consciousness of everything." Tolstoy, *Polnoe Sobranie Sochenenii (PSS). Dnevnik I Zapisnye knizhki, 1890*, vol. 51, http://tolstoy.ru/online/90/51/, accessed June 6, 2016. "It's a sort of moral sickness like leprosy—it doesn't destroy any one part but it disfigures the whole—it insinuates itself gradually and imperceptibly and then develops throughout the whole organism; there is no manifestation of life which it doesn't infect; it's like a venereal disease—if it's driven out of one part it appears with greater force in another." R. F. Christian, *Tolstoy's Diaries,* vol. 1 (New York: Charles Scribner's Sons, 1985), 44. "Vanity is . . . a sort of self-love transferred to the opinion of others—a vain man loves himself not as he is, but as he appears to others." R. F. Christian, *Tolstoy's Diaries* vol. 1 (New York: Charles Scribner's Sons, 1985), 44. See Richard Gustafson's brilliant work *Leo Tolstoy, Resident and Stranger: A Study in Fiction and Theology* (Princeton: Princeton University Press, 1986) in which he analyzes Tolstoy's desires to belong to a community, but argues that Tolstoy's self-centeredness prevents him from reaching his goal of the selflessness necessary to belong to a community.

20 In *Kingdon Of God Is Within You* Tolstoy compares luxury, honor, and fame to fleeting clouds, which upon attainment, appear to be insubstantial. Of course the problem is that very few of us actually attain these heights of achievement and therefore one cannot readily understand Tolstoy's trans-material philosophy using either a liberal or a utilitarian framework. But perhaps the anthropological notion of potlatch is an important consideration here. See Marcel Mauss, *The Gift: The Form and Reason for Exchange in Archaic Societies*, translated by W. D. Halls (New York: W. W. Norton, 1990).

21 Dragan Milivojevic, "Tolstoy's Views on Buddhism," *Tolstoy Studies Journal*, vol. 3 (1990): 62–75. http://sites.utoronto.ca/tolstoy/vol3/pages %2062-75%20criticism%20volume%203.pdf. last accessed March 21, 2016.

22 "Problem of Self," in *The Essential Tagore*, edited by Fakrul Ahmad and Radha Chakravarty (Cambridge MA: Belknap Press of Harvard University Press, 2011), 59–60.

23 Hugh McLean, "Rousseau's God and Tolstoy's," *Tolstoy Studies Journal*, vol. 9 (1997): 25–35, http://media.wix.com/ugd/dab097_6841cbb5d2a749169c c8e2d19e36086b.pd last accessed March 23, 2016. Tolstoy writes in a letter to N. N. Strakhov (April 26, 1895), "I don't know who I pray to nor who will answer my prayers, but know that it is the best and the most important thing that I can do, and that it is not a mere act of weakness. Leo Tolstoy, *PSS,* vol. 68, Letter no. 75, http://tolstoy.ru/online/90/68/ last accessed September 28, 2016.

24 Pål Kolstø, "'For Here We Do Not Have an Enduring City': Tolstoy and the Strannik Tradition in Russian Culture," *The Russian Review*, vol. 69, no. 1 (January 2010): 119–34, argues that Tolstoy's seeming apostasy represented an established Eastern Orthodox Church practice.

25 There is considerable difference of scholarly opinion about Tolstoy's conception of religion. While scholars such as Richard Gustafson are critical of the aesthetic failures of Tolstoy's religious writings, Medzhibovskaya in her recent book argues against the division between Tolstoy as a good novelist and Tolstoy the bad theologian and social critic. Instead she brilliantly demonstrates that Tolstoy's religious and philosophical concerns haunted him throughout his life. Inessa Medzhibovskaya, *Tolstoy and the Religious Culture of His Time—A Biography of a Long Conversion, 1845–1887* (Lanham, MD: Lexington Books, 2008). Richard F. Gustafson, Leo Tolstoy, *Resident and Stranger: A Study in Fiction and Theology* (Princeton, NJ: Princeton University Press, 1986); and Hugh McLean on Tolstoy and Jesus in, *In Quest of Tolstoy* (Boston, MA: Academic Studies Press, 2008), 117–42.

26 *Promode dhaliya dinu mon* (1883).

27 See Reba Shom's fine analysis of the pleasure/pain principle in Tagore's music. *Rabindranath Tagore: The Singer and His Song* (New Delhi: Penguin Group India, 2009).

28 "Letter to Bireshwar Goswami," November 24, 1906, in Sukanta Chaudhuri (ed.), *The Oxford Tagore Translations, Selected Poems: Rabindranath Tagore* (New Delhi: Oxford University Press, 2004), 382.

29 *Nirjharer Swapna Bhango* (A Waterfall Awakens), 1883.

30 Princess Maria Bolkonskaya in *War and Peace* is one of the few characters in Tolstoy's fiction who embodies love and forgives all who offend her.

31 Samir Dayal, "Repositioning India: Tagore's Passionate Politics of Love," *positions: east asia cultures critique*, vol. 15, no. 1 (Spring 2007): 165–208.

32 See Tagore's drama, *Prakriti's Pratishodh* (1884) in which an ascetic realizes that the path to liberation lies through engaging the world, and not renouncing it.

33 Rabindranath Tagore, *Sadhana: The Realisation of Life* (New York: Macmillan Co., 1925), 48.

34 Krishna Kripalani, *Tagore: A Life*, second edition (Calcutta, India: Calcutta Press, 1971), 47.

35 Rabindranath Tagore, *Of Myself: Atmaprichay*, Davdatta Joardar and Joe Winter trans. (London: Anvil Press, 2006), 27.

36 Rabindranath Tagore, *Religion of Man* (New York: Macmillan and Co., 1931).

37 Partha Chatterjee, *Nationalist Thought and the Colonia World: A Derivative Discourse* (Minneapolis, MN: University of Minnesota Press, 1993).

38 Susan Layton, *Russian Literature and Empire: Conquest of the Caucasus from Pushkin to Tolstoy* (Cambridge: Cambridge University Press, 1994);

John Burt Foster, *Transnational Tolstoy: Between the West and the World* (New York: Academic Bloomsbury, 2013); and Harsha Ram, *The Imperial Sublime: A Russian Poetics of Empire* (Madison: University of Wisconsin Press, 2003).

39 Leo Tolstoy, "The Law of Violence and the Law of Love," in James Edie et al. eds., *Russian Philosophy*, vol. II (Chicago: Quadrangle Books, 1965), 232. This work was not published in Russia due to censorship.

40 See also Tolstoy's earlier short story, "Prisoner of the Caucasus" (1870).

41 See for example Ayad Akhtar's play, *Disgraced* (2012).

42 Tolstoy's nuanced understanding of modern conquest has been strangely validated by postcolonial historical research in the twenty-first century. Bruce Grant, *The Captive and the Gift: Cultural Histories of Sovereignty in Russia and the Caucasus* (Ithaca, NY: Cornell University Press, 2009); Charles King, *The Ghost of Freedom: A History of the Caucasus* (Oxford: Oxford University Press, 2008); Michael Khodarkovsky, *Bitter Choices: Loyalty and Betrayal in the Russian Conquest of the North Caucasus* (Ithaca, Cornell: Cornell University Press, 2011); Eric Mathew Souder, *The Circassian Thistle: Tolstoy's Khadzhi Murat and the Evolving Russian Empire* (PhD diss., University of Miami, Ohio, 2014); and Rebecca Gould, "The Topographies of Anticolonialism: The Ecopoetical Sublime from Tolstoy to Makaev," *Comparative Literature Studies*, vol. 50, no. 1 (2013): 87–107.

43 *Christianity and Patriotism* (1896). Tolstoy anticipated much of the twentieth-century scholarly literature on the "invention of culture" to fill the national form.

44 Choi Chatterjee, "Imperial Subjects in the Soviet Union: Rabindranath Tagore, M. N. Roy, and Re-thinking Freedom and Authoritarianism in the Twentieth Century," *Journal of Contemporary History*, vol. 54, no. 4 (October 2017), 913–34.

45 Ernst Simmons, *Leo Tolstoy* (London: John Lehmann, 1949).

46 Pankaj Mishra, *From the Ruins of Empire: Intellectuals who Remade Asia* (New York: Farrar, Strauss and Giroux, 2012); Jane Addams, *Twenty Years at Hull House with Autobiographical Notes* (New York: The Macmillan Co., 1923); and James Cracraft, *Two Shining Souls Jane Addams, Leo Tolstoy and the Quest for Global Peace* (Lanham, MD: Lexington Books, 2012).

47 See footnote 40 for an analysis of these novels.

48 "Cult of Charkha," in Sisir Kumar Das ed., *The English Writings of Rabindranath Tagore*, vol. 3 (New Delhi: Sahitya Akademi, 2002), 538–48.

49 Here I argue against Ananya Vajpeyi's excellent chapter on the role that nostalgia played in Tagore's thinking in her book, *Righteous Republic: Political Foundations of Modern India* (Cambridge, MA: Harvard University Press, 2012).

50 Tagore's lectures on the subject before he traveled to the Soviet Union translated as, *The Co-Operative Principle* (Calcutta, India: Visva Bharati, 1963); Tapati Dasgupta, *Social Thought of Rabindranath Tagore: A Historical Analysis* (New Delhi: Abhinav Publications, 1993); S. Radhakrishna, *The Philosophy of Rabindranath Tagore* (London: Macmillan and Co. 1918); Anjan Chakrabarti and Anup Kumar Dhar, "Development, Capitalism, and Socialism: A Marxian Encounter with Rabindranath Tagore's Ideas on the Cooperative Principle," in *Rethinking Marxism: A Journal of Economics, Culture & Society*, vol. 20, no. 3 (June 2008): 487–89; and Uma Das Gupta, *Rabindranath Tagore: A Biography* (New Delhi: Oxford University Press, 2004).

51 Rebecca Gould, "Topographies of Anti-Colonialism: The Ecopoetical Sublime in the Caucasus from Tolstoy to Mamakaev," *Comparative Literature Studies*, vol. 50, no. 1 (2013): 87–107.

52 "City and Village," in Sisir Kumar Das ed., *The English Writings of Rabindranath Tagore*, vol. 3 (New Delhi: Sahitya Akademi, 2002), 510–18.

53 *Morning of a Landowner* (1856).

54 See Tagore's important essay, "Religion of the Forest," in his essay collection, *Creative Unity* (London: Macmillan and Co., 1922), 45–68.

55 Pål Kolstø "'For Here We Do Not Have an Enduring City': Tolstoy and the Strannik Tradition in Russian Culture," *The Russian Review*, vol. 69, no. 1 (January 2010): 119–34.

Chapter 2

1 Parts of this chapter were previously published as "Imperial Incarcerations: Ekaterina Breshko-Breshkovskaia, Vinayak Damodar Savarkar and the Original Sins of Modernity," *Slavic Review*, vol. 74, no. 4 (Winter 2015): 850–72; Anna, M. Babey, *Americans in Russia 1776–1917: A Study of the American Travelers in Russia from the American Revolution to the Russian Revolution* (New York: The Comet Press, 1938); Choi Chatterjee and Beth Holmgren edited, *The Russian Experience: Americans Encountering the Enigma, 1890 to the Present* (New York: Routledge Press, 2012); David Charles Engerman, *Modernization from the Other Shore: American Intellectuals and the Romance of Russian Development* (Cambridge, MA: Harvard University Press, 2003); Michael David-Fox, *Showcasing the Great Experiment: Cultural diplomacy and Western Visitors, 1921–1941* (New York: Oxford University Press, 2012); David Foglesong, *The American Mission and the "Evil Empire": The Crusade for a Free Russia since 1881* (New York: Cambridge University Press, 2007); Aleksandr Etkind, *Tolkovanie puteshestvii: Rossia i Amerika v travelogakh i intertkstakh* (Moscow: Novoe literaturnoe obozrenie, 2001); and Aleksandr Nikolaevich Nikoliukin, *Literaturnye sviazi Rossii i SShA: stanovlenie literaturnikh kontaktov* (Moscow: Nauka, 1981).

2 Carroll Smith-Rosenberg, *Disorderly Conduct: Visions of Gender in Victorian America* (New York: Alfred Knopf, 1985).

3 Sarah Badcock, *A Prison without Walls? Eastern Siberian Exile in the Last Years of Tsarism* (Oxford: Oxford University Press, 2016); Daniel Beer, *The House of the Dead: Siberian Exile under the Tsars* (New York: Alfred A. Knopf, 2017); and Andrew A. Gentes *The Mass Deportation of Poles to Siberia, 1863–1880* (Cham: Palgrave Macmillan, 2017).

4 Evgenia Ginzburg, *Journey into the Whirlwind* (New York: Harcourt, Brace and World, 1967); Varlam Shalamov, *Kolyma Tales* (New York: W. W. Norton,

1980); Alexander Solzhenitsyn, *Gulag Archipelago 1918-1956: An Experiment in Literary Investigation* (New York: Harper and Row, 1974); Leona Toker, *Return from the Archipelago: Narratives of Gulag Survivors* (Bloomington: Indiana University Press, 2000); and Alexander Etkind, *Warped Mourning: Stories of the Undead in the Land of the Unburied* (Stanford: Stanford University Press, 2013).

5 Anne Applebaum, *Gulag: A History* (New York: Doubleday, 2003); Steven Barnes, *Death and Redemption: Gulag and the Shaping of Soviet Society* (Princeton: Princeton University Press, 2011); Oleg Khlevniuk, *The History of the Gulag: From Collectivization to the Great Terror* (New Haven, CT: Yale University Press, 2004); Alan Barenberg, *Gulag Town, Company Town: Forced Labor and Its Legacies in Vorkuta* (New Haven, CT: Yale University Press, 2014); Jeffrey S. Hardy, *The Gulag after Stalin: Redefining Punishment in Khrushchev's Soviet Union, 1953–1964* (Ithaca, NY: Cornell University Press, 2016); Golfo Alexopolous, *Illness and Inhumanity in Stalin's Gulag* (New Haven, CT: Yale University Press, 2017); Wilson T. Bell, *Stalin's Gulag at War: Forced Labour, Mass Death, and Soviet Victory in the Second World War* (Toronto: University of Toronto Press, 2018); and Aidan Forth, "Britain's Archipelago of Camps: Labor and Detention in a Liberal Empire, 1871–1903," *Kritika,* vol. 16, no. 3 (Summer 2015): 651–80.

6 Hannah Arendt, *The Origins of Totalitarianism* (New York: Shocken Books, 2004); Aimé Césaire, *Discourse on Colonialism* (New York: Monthly Review Press, 2001); and Jawaharlal Nehru, *Toward Freedom: The Biography of Jawaharlal Nehru* (Boston, MA: Beacon Press, 1941).

7 Charles Maier, "Consigning the Twentieth Century to History: Alternative Narratives for the Modern Era," *American Historical Review,* vol. 105, no. 3 (2000): 807–31, uses the term "moral narrative" to differentiate it from causal or structural analyses.

8 Recent research on Russian prisons has yielded a less negative picture than before. According to Jonathan Daly, Russia imprisoned fewer political prisoners than either France or Germany in the nineteenth century. "Political Crime in Late Imperial Russia," *The Journal of Modern History*, vol. 74, no. 1 (March 2002): 62–100. Bruce Adams, *Politics of Punishment: Prison Reform in Russia, 1866–1917* (Dekalb, IL: Northern Illinois University Press, 1996); Jonathan Daly, *Autocracy under Siege: Security Police and Opposition in Russia, 1866-1905* (Dekalb, IL: Northern Illinois University Press, 1998); Andrew Gentes, *Exile to Siberia, 1590-1822* (New York: Palgrave Macmillan, 2008); Ana Siljak, *Angel of Vengeance: The "Girl Assassin," the Governor of St. Petersburg, and Russia's Revolutionary World* (New York: St. Martin's Press, 2008); and Abby M. Schrader, *Languages of the Lash: Corporal Punishment and Identity in Imperial Russia* (DeKalb, IL: Northern Illinois University Press, 2002).

9 "Political exile in Siberia," *The Times*, December 25, 1903, 3, http://find.gal egroup.com/ttda/infomark.do?&source=gale&prodId=TTDA&userGroupNam e=calstate&tabID=T003&docPage=article&searchType=AdvancedSearchFo rm&docId=CS51441049&type=multipage&contentSet=LTO&version=1.0, accessed September 5, 2013.

10 *Bengalee,* April 27, 1912; R. C. Majumdar, *Penal Settlement in Andamans* (New Delhi: Gazetteers Unit, Ministry of Culture and Social Welfare, 1975). Bannerjea was opposed to armed resistance to British rule and condemned acts of "anarchism." See the coverage of cases involving anti-British violence in the *Bengalee*, 1908–1913.

11 P. A. Kropotkin, *Memoirs of a Revolutionist* (Boston, MA: Houghton Mifflin and Co., 1899) was also serialized in the journal, the *Atlantic Monthly* in 1898–99: Vera Figner, *Memoirs of a Revolutionist* (Dekalb: Northern Illinois University Press, 1991); Leo Deutsch, *Sixteen Years in Siberia: Some Experiences of a Russian Revolutionist*, trans. Helen Chisholm (Westport, CO. Hyperion Press, 1977); For the influence of Russian revolutionaries abroad, see Steven Marks's excellent account, *How Russia Shaped the Modern World* (Princeton: Princeton University Press, 2004); Anthony Anemone ed., *Just Assassins? The Culture of Russian Terrorism* (Dekalb, IL: Northwestern University Press, 2010); and N. Pirumova, *Russia and the West: Nineteenth Century* (Moscow: Progress Publishers, 1990).

12 Jane E. Good and David R. Jones, *Babushka: The Life of the Russian Revolutionary Ekaterina K. Breshko-Breshkovskaia (1844–1934)* (Newtonville, MA: Oriental Research Partners, 1991); Daniel Field, "Vospominaniia E. K. Breshko-Breshkovskoi o 'khozhdenii v narod', v 1870-kh godakh. Opyt istochniovedenogo analiza," in *P. A. Zainonchkovskii 1904-1983gg. Stat'ii, publikatsii i vospominaniia o nem,*" (Moscow: Rosspen, 1998), 320–34; E. I. Frolova, "Istoricheskie portrety. Ekaterina Konstatinovana Breshko-Breshkovskaia," *Voprosy istorii,* no. 8 (2004): 70–82. Margaret Maxwell, *Narodniki Women: Russian Women Who Sacrificed Themselves for the Dream of Freedom* (New York: Pergammon Press, 1990), 122–57; and Shannon Smith, "From Relief to Revolution: American Women and the Russian-American Relationship, 1890-1917," *Diplomatic History,* vol. 19, no. 4 (1995): 601–16.

13 George Kennan, *Siberia and the Exile System* vols. 1 and 2 (New York: Century Company), 1891; Frederick F. Travis, *George Kennan and the American-Russian Relationship, 1865–1924* (Athens: Ohio University Press, 1990); David Foglesong, *The American Mission and the "Evil Empire,"* 12–18; and Norman Saul, *Concord and Conflict: The United States and Russia, 1867–1914* (Lawrence: University of Kansas Press, 1996).

14 George Kennan, *Tent Life in Siberia: A New Account of an Old Undertaking* (New York: Arno Press, 1970).

15 Alice Stone Blackwell edited, *The Little Grandmother of the Russian Revolution: Reminiscences and Letters of Catherine Breshkovsky* (Boston: Little, Brown, and Company, 1918), 100–1.

16 Kennan, *Siberia and the Exile System*, 1891, vol. 2, 121–2.

17 Ernest Poole, *Katherine Breshkovsky* (Chicago, IL: Charles H. Kerr Co., 1905); Ernest Poole, *The Bridge: My Own Story* (New York: The Macmillan Company, 1940).

18 Derek Offord, *The Russian Revolutionary Movement in the 1880s* (Cambridge: Cambridge University Press, 1986); and Franco Venturi, *Roots of* *the Revolution: A History of Populist and Socialist Movements in Nineteenth Century Russia* (Chicago: University of Chicago, 1983);

19 Lillian Wald, *House on Henry Street* (New York: Holt and Co., 1915); and Jane E. Good, "America and the Russian Revolutionary Movement, 1880–1905," *Russian Review,* vol. 41 (July 1982): 273–87.

20 The Russian-American diaspora and émigré intellectuals such as Abraham Cahan and Emma Goldman played an important role in exacerbating anti-tsarist feelings in the United States. Paul and Karen Avrich, *Sasha and Emma: The Anarchist Odyssey of Alexander Berkman and Emma Goldman* (Cambridge, MA: Harvard University Press, 2012). Steven Cassedy, *To the Other Shore: The Russian Jewish Intellectuals Who Came to America* (Princeton: Princeton University Press, 1977); and Tony Michels, *Fire in their Hearts: Yiddish Socialists in New York* (Cambridge, MA: Harvard University Press, 2009).

21 Good and Jones, *Babushka: The Life of the Russian Revolutionary Ekaterina K. Breshko-Breshkovskaia (1844–1934)*, 88.

22 See Elaine Lownsberry's profile of Breshkovskaia in her *Saints and Rebels* (New York: Longman's Green and Co., 1937), 46–79; I have collected close to fifty articles from prestigious journals and newspapers, such as the *Century, Russian Review, Outlook, Survey, Atlantic Monthly, Nation,* and others that feature Breshkovskaia.

23 Elsa Barker, "Breshkovskaya," *Current Literature,* vol. 48 (1910): 565.

24 Alice Stone Blackwell ed., *The Little Grandmother of the Russian Revolution: Reminiscences and Letters of Catherine Breshkovsky* (Boston, MA: Little, Brown and Co.), 1918.

25 Lincoln Hutchinson, ed., *Hidden Springs of the Russian Revolution: Personal Memoirs of Katerina Breshkovskaia* (Stanford: Stanford University Press), 1931.

26 "Grandmother of the Revolution on Her Own Life," *Russian Review,* vol. 4 (1918): 101–7; Catherine Breshkovsky, *A Message to the American People* (New York: Russian Information Bureau in the US, 1919); and Elizabeth White, *The Socialist Alternative to Bolshevik Russia, 1921–1939* (London: Routledge, 2011).

27 Janaki Bakhle, "Country First? Vinayak Damodar Savarkar (1883–1966) and the Writing of Essentials of Hindutva," *Public Culture,* vol. 22, no. 1 (2010): 149–86.

28 Partha Chatterjee, *Nation and Its Fragments: Colonial and Postcolonial Histories* (Princeton: Princeton University Press, 1993); Durba Ghosh, *Gentlemanly Terrorists: Political Violence and the Colonial State in India, 1919–1947* (Cambridge: Cambridge University Press, 2017); Michael Silvestri, "The Bomb, Bhadralok, Bhagavad Gita, and Dan Breen: Terrorism in Bengal and its Relation to the European Experience," *Terrorism and Political Violence,* vol. 21, no. 1 (2009): 1–27; Peter Heehs, *The Bomb in Bengal: The Rise of Revolutionary Terrorism in India 1901-1910* (New Delhi: Oxford University Press, 1995); and Rajat Kanta Ray, *Social Conflict and Political Unrest in Bengal, 1875–1927* (New Delhi: Oxford University Press, 1984).

29 J. Chinna Durai, "Indian Prisons," *Journal of Comparative Legislation and International Law*, Third Series, vol. 11, no. 4 (1929): 245–9.

30 V. D. Savarkar, *The Story of My Transportation For Life*, trans. V. N. Naik (Bombay: Sadbhakti Publications, 1950).

31 Abraham Ascher, *The Revolution of 1905* (Stanford: Stanford University Press, 1992); and Gerald Surh, *1905 in St. Petersburg: Labor, Society, Revolution* (Stanford: Stanford University Press, 1989).

32 Tirtha Mandal, *Women Revolutionaries of Bengal, 1905–1939* (Calcutta: Minerva Press, 1991).

33 Upendranath Banerjee, *Memoirs of a Revolutionary* (Calcutta: K. L. Chakravarty, 1924); Ulaskar Dutt, *Ten Years of Prison Life* (Calcutta: Arya Publishing House, 1924); Aurobindo Ghosh, *Tales of Prison Life*, translated by Sisir Kumar Ghosh (Calcutta: Sri Aurobindo Pathamandir, 1974); Barindra Kumar Ghosh, *Tale of My Exile* (Pondicherry: Arya Press, 1922); and P. K. Ray, *Down Memory Lane: Reminiscences of a Bengali Revolutionary* (New Delhi: Gian Publishing House, 1990).

34 Dhananjay Keer, *Veer Savarkar* (Bombay: Popular Prakashan, 1966); and Harindra Srivastav, *Five Stormy Years: Savarkar in London June 1906-June 1911* (New Delhi: Allied Publishers, 1983), 141.

35 John Pincince, "V. D. Savarkar and the *Indian War of Independence*: Contrasting Perspectives of an Emergent Composite State," unpublished paper delivered at the conference, "'Mutiny at the Margins': New Perspectives on the Indian uprising of 1857," at the Centre for South Asian Studies, University of Edinburgh, Scotland, July 23–26, 2007. http://www.csas.ed.ac.uk/mutiny/confpapers/Pincince-Paper.pdf, last accessed August 31, 2015.

36 Vinayak Chaturvedi, "Rethinking Knowledge with Action: V. D. Savarkar, The Bhagavad Gita and Histories of Warfare," *Modern Intellectual History*, vol. 7, no. 2 (August 2010): 417–35.

37 Trial of DHINGRA, Madar Lal (25, student), No. t19090719-55, July 19, 1909, *Old Bailey Proceedings Online*, at http://www.oldbaileyonline.org/browse.jsp?id=t19090719-55&div=t19090719-55&terms=Dhingra#highlight (accessed September 15, 2013.

38 John Pincince, *On the Verge of Hindutva: V.D. Savarkar, Revolutionary, Convict, Ideologue, C. 1905—1924*, PhD dissertation, University of Hawaii at Manoa, 2007.

39 Clare Anderson, *Convicts in the Indian Ocean: Transportation from South Asia to Mauritius, 1815-53* (Basingstoke: Macmillan, 2000); Clare Anderson, *The Indian Uprising of 1857-8. Prisons, Prisoners and Rebellion* (New York: Anthem Press, 2007); David Arnold, "The Colonial Prison: Power, Knowledge and Penology in Nineteenth-Century India," in David Arnold and David Hardiman ed., *Subaltern Studies VIII: Essays in Honor of Ranajit Guha* (New York, Oxford University Press, 1994), 148–87; Satadru Sen, *Disciplining Punishment: Colonialism and Convict Society in the Andaman Islands* (New York: Oxford University Press, 2000); and Aparna Vaidik, *Imperial Andamans. Colonial Encounter and Island History* (New York: Palgrave Macmillan, 2010).

40 Vinayak Damodar Savarkar, *An Echo From Andamans: Letters Written by Br. Savarkar to His Brother Dr. Savarkar* (Nagpur: Vishvanath Vinayak Kelkar, 1920).

41 Surendranath Bannerjea, *A Nation in Making; Being the Reminiscences of Fifty Years in Public Life* (Oxford: Oxford University Press, 1925), 69–78.

42 David Arnold, "The Self and the Cell: Indian Prison Narratives as Life Histories," in David Arnold and Stuart Blackburn edited, *Telling Lives in India. Biography, Autobiography and Life History* (Bloomington, IN: Indiana University Press, 2004), 29–53; and Kris Manjapra, *M .N. Roy. Marxism and Colonial Cosmopolitanism* (New York: Routledge, 2010).

43 Leon Trotsky, *My Life: An Attempt at an Autobiography* (New York: Pathfinder Press, 1970).

44 Guy Aldred, "The Savarkar Conspiracy," *The Herald of Revolt* vol. 2, no. 10 (October, 1912): 97–101 at http://www.savarkar.org/files/u1/Savarkar_special_Herald_of_the_Revolt 1912.pdf, last accessed September 18, 2014.

45 *The Times*, January 5, 1911, 6.

46 *New York Times,* February 25, 1911, 3; *The Sun*, January 31, 1911.

47 Stepniak [Sergei Stepniak-Kravchinskii], *Underground Russia: Revolutionary Profiles and Sketches from Life.* With a Preface by Peter Lavroff. Translated from Italian (New York: John W. Lovell Co., 1883); James W. Hulse, *Revolutionists in London: A Study of Five Unorthodox Socialists* (New York: Oxford University Press, 1970), Donald Senese, *S. M. Stepniak Kravchinskii, the London Years* (Newtonville, MA: Oriental Research Partners, 1987); Lynn Ellen Patyk, "Remembering 'The Terrorism': Sergei Stepniak-Kravchinskii's 'Underground Russia,'" *Slavic Review*, vol. 68, no. 4 (Winter, 2009): 758-781; and Lynn Ellen Patyk, *Written in Blood: Revolutionary Terrorism and Russian Literary Culture*, 1861–1881 (Madison, WI: University of Wisconsin Press, 2017).

48 My assessments are based on numerous articles in American journals and newspapers such as *The Nation, Outlook, Russian Review, New York Times*, as well as the *London Times.*

49 Robert Service, "Russian Marxism and its London Colony before the October 1917 Revolution," *The Slavonic and East European Review*, vol. 88, nos. 1/2 (January/April 2010): 359–76.

50 Vasily Klyuchevsky and Paul Miliukov, unlike the Whig historians of England such as George Trevelyan who expunged empire from the English past, wrote colonization and imperial expansion into the heart of the Russian historical narrative. See the following chapter for an elaboration of this point of view. Susan Layton, *Russian Literature and Empire: Conquest of the Caucasus from Pushkin to Tolstoy* (New York: Cambridge University Press, 2005); and Jennifer Pitts, *A Turn to Empire: The Rise of Imperial Liberalism in Britain and France* (Princeton: Princeton University Press, 2005).

51 Richard J. Popplewell, *Intelligence and Imperial Defence: British Intelligence and the Defence of the Indian Empire, 1904–1924* (London: Frank Cass and Co. LTD), 1995; and Keith Neilson, *Britain and the Last Tsar: British Policy and Russia, 1894–1917* (Oxford: Oxford University Press, 1995).

52 Joshua A. Sanborn, *Imperial Apocalypse: The Great War and the Destruction of the Russian Empire* (Oxford: Oxford University Press, 2014).

53 See footnote 25 as well as Marks, *How Russia Shaped the Modern World*, 7–37; and Hari Vasudevan, "India and the October Revolution: Nationalist Revolutionaries, Bolshevik Power, and "Lord Curzon's Nightmare,"" in Choi Chatterjee, Steven Marks, Mary Neuberger and Steve Sabol edited, *The Global Impacts of Russia's Great War and Revolution: The Wider Arc of Revolution*, Part I, vol. 2 (Bloomington, IN: Slavica Publishers, Indiana University, 2019), 299–324.

54 Michael Hughes, "British Opinion and Russian Terrorism in the 1880s," *European History Quarterly*, vol. 41, no. 2 (2011): 255–77, and Anna Geifman, *Thou Shalt Kill: Revolutionary Terrorism in Russia, 1894–1917* (Princeton: Princeton University Press, 1993).

55 Sir Valentine Chirol, *Indian Unrest* (London: MacMillan and Co., 1910).

56 Nicholas Owen, *The British Left and India: Metropolitan Anti-Imperialism, 1885–1947* (New York: Oxford University Press, 2007), 54.

57 Cited in Diwakar P. Singh, "American Official Views of Indian Nationalism, 1905-1929," *Journal of Indian History*, vol. 50, 149 (October, 1972): 265–77.

58 See for example Sydney Brooks, "American Opinion and British Rule in India," The North American Review, vol. 190, no. 649 (December, 1909): 773–84; William Jennings Bryan, *British Rule in India* (Reprinted from "India," of July 20, 1906); Jabez T. Sutherland, "The New Nationalist Movement in India," *Atlantic Monthly,* October 1, 1908, http://www.theatlantic.com/mag azine/archive/1908/10/the-new-nationalist-movement-in-india/304893/2/, last accessed August 15, 2014; and William Digby, *Prosperous British India; A Revelation from Official Records* (London: T. Fisher Unwin, 1901).

59 Frank Ninkovich, *Global Dawn: The Cultural Foundation of American Internationalism, 1865*–1890 (Cambridge MA: Harvard University Press, 2009), 233–7; and Diwakar Prasad Singh, *American Attitudes towards the Indian Nationalist Movement* (New Delhi: Munshiram Manoharlal, 1970).

60 *Some American Opinions on the British Empire* (London: T. Fisher Unwin, 1900s); and Paul Teed, "Race Against Memory: Katherine Mayo, Jabez Sunderland, and Indian Independence," *American Studies*, vol. 44, no. 1/2 (Spring/Summer 2003): 35–57.

61 Joan Jensen, *Passage From India: Asian Immigrants in North America* (New Haven: Yale University Press, 1988); and Seema Sohi, "Race, Surveillance, and Indian Anticolonialism in the Transnational Western U.S.-Canadian Borderlands," *Journal of American History*, vol. 98, no. 2 (September 2011): 420–36.

62 According to Steven Marks, while there was a limited audience for news about India, the large number of Russian immigrants in the United States formed an important constituency for news about Russia. Personal communication, November 23, 2013.

63 Nasser Hussain, *The Jurisprudence of Emergency: Colonialism and the Rule of Law* (Ann Arbor: University of Michigan Press, 2003).

64 Choi Chatterjee, "Transnational Romance, Terror and Heroism: Russia in American Popular Fiction, 1860–1917," *Comparative Studies in Society and History*, vol. 50, no. 3 (July 2008): 753–77.

65 Elinor Conlin Casella, "Prisoner of His Majesty: Postcoloniality and the Archaeology of British Penal Transportation," *World Archaeology*, vol. 37, no. 3 (2005): 453–67; and Helen Dampier, "'Everyday life' in Boer Women's Testimonies of the Concentration Camps of the South African War, 1899–1902," in Barry S. Godfrey and Graeme Dunstall eds., *Crime and Justice in Local and Global Context* (Portland: Willan Publishing, 2005), 202–23.

66 Bernard Cohn, *Colonialism and Its Forms of Knowledge: The British in India* (Princeton: Princeton University Press, 1996); Frederick Cooper and Ann Laura Stoler, *Tensions of Empire: Colonial Cultures in a Bourgeois World* (Berkeley: California University Press, 1997); Phillipa Levine and Antoinette Burton, *Gender and* Empire (Oxford: Oxford University Press, 2004); Anne McClintock, *Race, Gender and Sexuality in Colonial Context* (New York: Routledge, 1995), and Edward Said, *Culture and Imperialism* (New York: Knopf, 1993).

67 Jane Burbank, Mark Von Hagen and A. V. Remnev, eds., *Russian Empire: Space, People, Power, 1700-1930* (Bloomington: Indiana University Press, 2007); Alexander Morrison, *Russian Rule in Samarkand 1868-1910: A Comparison with British India* (Oxford: Oxford University Press, 2008); Willard Sunderland, *Colonization and Empire: Taming the Wild Field* (Ithaca: Cornell University Press, 2004); and Jeff Sahadeo, "Visions of Empire: Russia's Place in an Imperial World," *Kritika,* vol. 11, no. 2 (Spring 2010): 381–409.

68 Alexander Etkind, in his recent publication, *Warped Mourning*, has charged that there has been insufficient research into the crimes of the gulag.

69 Caroline Elkins, *Imperial Reckoning: The Untold Story of Britain's Gulag in Kenya* (New York: Henry Holt and Company, 2005).

70 Niall Ferguson, "Home Truths about Famine, War and Genocide," *Independent*, June 14, 2006, http://www.independent.co.uk/voices/comm entators/niall-ferguson-home-truths-about-famine-war-and-genocide-482314 .html, accessed October 8, 2013.

71 Richard Gott, *Britain's Empire: Resistance, Repression and Revolt* (New York: Verso Books, 2011); Kwasi Kwarteng, *Ghosts of Empire: Britain's Legacies in the Modern World* (New York: Public Affairs, 2012); Pankaj Mishra, *From the Ruins of Empire: The Intellectuals Who Remade Asia* (New York: Farrar, Strauss and Giroux, 2012); Priya Satia, *Spies in Arabia: The Great War and the Cultural Foundations of Britain's Covert Empire in the Middle East* (New York: Oxford University Press, 2009): and Shashi Tharoor, *An Era of Darkness: The British Empire in India* (New Delhi, India: Aleph Book Company, 2016).

72 Caroline Elkins, "Britain Has Said Sorry to the Mau Mau: The Rest of the Empire Is Still Waiting," *Guardian*, June 7, 2013, at www.theguardian.com/ commentisfree/2013/ jun/06/britain-maumau-empire-waiting, last accessed September 1, 2015.

73 Clare Anderson, "Convicts and Coolies: Rethinking Indentured Labor in the Nineteenth Century," *Slavery and Abolition,* vol. 30, no. 1 (March 2009): 93–109.

74 Padraic Kenny, "'I Felt a Kind of Pleasure in Seeing them Treat Us Brutally.' The Emergence of the Political Prisoner, 1865–1910," *Comparative Studies in Society and History,* vol. 54, no. 4 (2012): 863–89.

75 Ujjwal Kumar Singh, *Political Prisoners in India* (New Delhi: Oxford University Press, 1998); and Manas Mohapatra, "Learning Lessons from India: The Recent History of Antiterrorist Legislation on the Subcontinent," *The Journal of Criminal Law and Criminology*, vol. 95, no. 1 (Autumn, 2004): 315–44.

76 Clare Anderson ed., *A Global History of Convicts and Penal Colonies* (London: Bloomsbury Academic, 2018); Alfred McCoy, *Policing America's Empire: The United States, the Philippines and the Rise of the Surveillance State* (Madison, WI: University of Wisconsin Press, 2009); Darius Rejali, *Democracy and Torture* (Princeton: Princeton University Press, 2009); Vicente L. Rafael, ed., *Figures of Criminality in Indonesia, the Philippines, and Colonial* Vietnam (Ithaca, NY: Southeast Asia Program Publications, 1999) 152–74; and Peter Zinoman, *The Colonial Bastille: The History of Imprisonment in Indochina, 1862–1940* (Berkeley: University of California Press, 2001).

77 Larry Wolff, 1994.

Chapter 3

1 I apologize in advance to scholars who will object to my use of the term "nation," taken out of its West European and nineteenth-century context where it originated. Jane Burbank in particular has advised me to replace "nationalist" with "patriotic," "nationalism" with "patriotism," and "nation" with "country" or "people" (personal communication from the author May 20, 2021). I use the term "nation" to denote a geographical unit that has inspired a defined consciousness of belonging, and has given rise to a shared identity and culture that has endured over time. For Russian nationalism before the nineteenth century, see James Cracraft, "Empire vs Nation: Russian Political theory under Peter the Great," *Harvard Ukrainian Studies*, vol. 10, no. 3/4 (December 1986): 524–41.

2 Krishan Kumar, "Nation and Empire: English and British National Identity in Comparative Perspective," *Theory and Society*, vol. 29, no. 5 (October, 2000): 575–608; Emil Pain, "The Imperial Syndrome and its Influence on Russian Nationalism," in Pål Kolstø and Helge Blakkisrud ed., *The New Russian Nationalism: Imperialism, Ethnicity and Authoritarianism 2000–2015* (Edinburgh: Edinburgh University Press, 2016), 46–74; and Kevin Colclough, *Imperial Nationalism: Nationalism and the Empire in Late Nineteenth Century Scotland and British Canada* (Edinburgh: Edinburgh University Press, 2006).

3 Stefan Berger and Aleksei Miller eds., *Nationalizing Empire* (New York: Central European Press, 2015); Frederick Cooper, *Colonialism in Question: Theory, Knowledge, History* (Berkeley: University of California Press, 2005); and Krishan Kumar, "Nation-States as Empires, Empires as Nation-States: Two Principles, One Practice?" *Theory and Society*, vol. 39, no. 2 (March 2010): 119–43.

4 Yuri Lotman's idea of a semiosphere that refers to both geographical typology and metaphorical space is very relevant to this context. *Universe* *of the Mind*, trans. by Ann Shukman, rpt. edition (Bloomington, IN: Indiana University Press, 2001).

5 Ernest Renan, "What Is a Nation" (Lecture at Sorbonne, March 11, 1882) in Geoff Eley and Ronald Grigor Suny ed., *Becoming National: A Reader* (New York and Oxford: Oxford University Press, 1996), 53; and Anthony Brundage and Richard A. Cosgrove, *British Historians and National Identity: From Hume to Churchill* (Brookfield, VY: Pickering and Chatto, 2014), 161–78.

6 Hayden White, "Introduction: The Poetics of History," in *Metahistory: The Historical Imagination in Nineteenth Century Europe* (Baltimore, MD: Johns Hopkins University Press, 1973), 1–38; *Tropics of Discourse: Essays in Cultural Criticism* (Baltimore, MD: Johns Hopkins University Press, 1978), chs. 2–5; and "The Question of Narrative in Contemporary Political Theory," *History and Theory*, vol. 23, no. 1 (February 1984), 1–33.

7 V. O. Kliuchevskii, *Sochineniia v vosm'i tomakh*, vol. 1 (Moscow: Gosudarstvennoe izdatel'stvo politicheskoi literatury, 1956), Lecture 2, 44.

8 David Armitage, *The Ideological Origins of the British Empire* (New York: Cambridge University Press, 2004).

9 G. M. Trevelyan, "Clio, A Muse," in *Clio, A Muse and Other Essays*, rpt. edition (Freeport NY: Books for Libraries Press, 1968), 140–76; and Joseph M. Hernon, Jr., "The Last Whig Historian and Consensus History: George Macaulay Trevelyan, 1876–1962," *The American Historical Review*, vol. 81, no. 1 (February 1976): 66–97.

10 G. M. Trevelyan, "Bias in History," Presidential Address to the Historical Association, January 1947 reprinted in *An Autobiography and Other Essays* (London: Longmans Green and Co., 1949), 68–82.

11 Trevelyan, "Autobiography of a Historian," ibid., 23–4.

12 *The Working Men's College Journal*, vol. 10 issues 166-188 (1907). It appears that Trevelyan also arranged for students from this institution to visit colleges in Cambridge. See Mary Moorman, *George Macaulay Trevelyan: A Memoir* (London: Hamish Hamilton, Ltd, 1980), 70–4.

13 G. M. Trevelyan, "The College and the Older Universities," in Rev. J. Llewelyn Davies ed., *The Working Men's College 1854–1904* (London: The Macmillan Company, 1904), 189.

14 Ibid., 192.

15 G. M. Trevelyan, "History and Fiction," *Clio, A Muse, and Other Essays*, rpt. edition (Freeport, NY: Books for Libraries Press, 1968), 92.

16 G. M. Trevelyan, *English Literature and its Readers* (London: English Association, 1951); See Brian Doyle, *English and Englishness* (New York: Routledge, 1989) for a relationship between nationalism and English literature in the nineteenth and twentieth century.

17 I will also reference *The History of England* (London: Longmans, Green and Co., 1926) that was the precursor to *English Social History* (London: Longmans, Green, and Co., 1944). The former text contained the political history that Trevelyan left out of the second work.

18 "I owe a debt to *English Social History*. From Athens to Delhi, Istanbul to
Tokyo, and from Sydney to Beijing, complete strangers . . . tell me how much
they love it, what it taught them about England, and how captivated they
are by George's story-telling," in Laura Trevelyan, *A Very British Family: The
Trevelyans and their World* (New York: I.B. Tauris and Co., 2006), 185; and J. H.
Plumb, "G.M. Trevelyan," in *The Making of a Historian: The Collected Essays of
J. H. Plumb*, vol. 1 (Athens: The University of Georgia Press, 1988), 182–204.

19 In his first published work, *England in the Age of Wycliffe* (New York:
Longman's Green and Company, 1900), G. M. Trevelyan depicted John
Wycliffe as an early English Protestant who challenged the authority of the
Latinate Pope, and the peasants as proto Englishmen who fought against
feudal lords for their freedom.

20 David Cannadine, *G. M. Trevelyan: A Life in History* (New York: W. W. Norton
& Company, 1997).

21 To the contrary, Winston Churchill, in his four-volume *History of the
English Speaking Peoples* (London: Dodd Mead, 1956-58), emphasized the
accomplishments of the rich, the famous, and those of the members of his
own family in great detail.

22 *English Social History*, note 1, 586.

23 G. M. Trevelyan, *The Glorious Revolution 1688-1689* (New York: Oxford
University Press, 1965).

24 Anthony Smith, *National Identity* (New York, Penguin, 1991); See Linda
Colley's *Britons: Forging the Nations, 1707–1837* (New Haven, CT: Yale
University Press, 1992); and Krishan Kumar, *The Making of English National
Identity* (New York: Cambridge University Press, 2003) for an explanation of
English versus British nationalism.

25 *History of England*, chapters 1–8.

26 See Herbert Butterfield's bitter criticisms of the body of works that formed
the Whig Interpretation of English history as providential, progressive, and
utterly self-congratulatory. *Whig Interpretation of History* (London: Bell, 1931).

27 *History of England*, 140.

28 Sir J. R. Seeley, *The Expansion of England: Two Courses of Lectures* (Boston,
MA: Little, Brown, and Company, 1922).

29 G. M. Trevelyan, *History of England,* rpt. Edition (London: Longmans, Green,
and CO. LTD., 1947), 673.

30 Both David Cannadine and Alastair McLachlan see Trevelyan as a liberal
internationalist but I respectfully disagree with this perspective. David
Cannadine, *G. M. Trevelyan: A Life in History*, 92: and Alastair McLachlan,
"Intersecting and Contrasting Lives: G. M. Trevelyan and Lytton Strachey,"
in Doug Munro and John G. Reid eds., *Clio's Lives: Biographies and
Autobiographies of Historians* (Acton: Australian National University Press,
2017), 137–71. Trevelyan devotes four pages to the British role in South Africa
in his *History of England*, 667–71

31 *English Social History*, 583.

32 Bill Schwarz, "Englishry: The Histories of G. M. Trevelyan," in Catherine Hall and Keith McClelland eds., *Race, Nation, and Empire: Making Histories 1750 to the Present* (New York: Manchester University Press, 2010), 117–22.

33 Ibid.

34 Laurie Manchester, *Holy Fathers, Secular Sons: Clergy, Intelligentsia, and the Modern Self in Revolutionary Russia* (DeKalb, IL: Northern Illinois University Press, 2008).

35 See Robert Byrnes's excellent biography, *V. O. Kliuchevskii: Historian of Russia* (Bloomington: Indiana University Press, 1995).

36 Anatole Mazour, "V. O. Klyuchevsky. Making of a Historian," *The Russian Review*, vol. 31, no. 4 (October 1972): 345–59.

37 Alexander Kiesewetter, "Klyuchevsky and His Course of Russian History," *The Slavonic Review*, vol. 1, no. 3 (March 1923): 519. Kiesewetter, Klyuchevsky's student, was an important member of the Constitutional Democratic Party, and an accomplished historian in his own right.

38 V. O. Kliuchevskii, *Pis'ma, dnevniki, aforizmy i mysli ob istorii* (Moscow: Nauka, 1968), 388.

39 Theodore R. Weeks, *Nation and State in Late Imperial Russia: Nationalism and Russification on Russia's Western Frontier 1863-1914* (Dekalb, IL: Northern Illinois University Press, 1996); and Serhii Plokhy, *Origins of the Slavic Nations: Premodern Identities in Russia, Ukraine, and Belarus* (Cambridge, MA: Cambridge University Press, 2006).

40 Andreas Kappeler, *The Russian Empire: A Multi-Ethnic History* (New York: Routledge, 2001); Michael Khodarkovsky, *Russia's Steppe Frontier: The Making of a Colonial Empire* (Bloomington, IN: Indiana University Press, 2004); and David Moon, *The Plough that Broke the Steppes: Agriculture and Environment on Russia's Grasslands* (New York: Oxford University Press, 2013); and Robert Byrnes attributes Klyuchevsky's indifference to questions of empire to his strong Russian patriotism.

41 V. O. Kliuchevskii, *Socheneniia v vos'mi tomakh,* vol. I (Moscow: Gospolitizdat, 1956-59), Lecture 2, 43. His sentiments were to be echoed later by Geoffrey Hosking who argued that considerations of empire led to the insufficient development of Russian nationalism. *Russia: People and Empire* (Cambridge, MA: Harvard University Press, 1997).

42 V. O. Kliuchevskii, *Socheneniia v vos'mi tomakh,* vol. I (Moscow: Gospolitizdat, 1956–59), Lecture 2, 36.

43 Afanasy Schapov, a historian of Siberian origin, earlier than Klyuchevsky analyzed the role of geography in the evolution of Russian history but emphasized its regional characteristics rather than the composite picture that Klyuchevsky created a few decades later. A S. Madzharov, *Afanasii Prokop'evich Schapov: istoriia zhizni (1831–1876) i zhini istorii* (Irkutsk: OOO Press, 2005); For an excellent analysis of Schapov and other intellectual influences on Klyuchevsky, see A. A. Zimin, "Formirovanie istoricheskikh vzgliadov V. O. Kliuchevskogo," reprinted in in *V. O. Kliuchevskii: Pro i kontra* (St. Petersburg: Nevskaia Perspektiva, 2013), 793–820.

44 V. O. Kliuchevskii, *Socheneniia v vos'mi tomakh,* vol. I (Moscow: Gospolitizdat, 1956–59), Lecture 12, 205. Klyuchevsky was interested primarily in the core Russian lands of European Russia, not in the non-Russian imperial lands. See K. J. Mjør, "Russian History and European Ideas. The Historical Vision of Vasilii Kliuchevskii," *Vestnik Permskogo Universiteta,* vol 4, no. 27 (2014): 194–204. The core lands included Ukraine and Belarus as Kiev was the "mother of all Russia."

45 Anatole Mazour calls Klyuchevsky's approach "common sense realism," see his article, "V.O. Klyuchevsky: Scholar Teacher," *The Russian Review,* vol. 32, no. 1 (January 1973): 23; According to George P. Fedotov, Klyuchevsky, with his emphasis on socioeconomic forces in history, paved the way for the rise of Marxist historiography. See his "Klyuchevskii's Russia," in Marc Raeff ed., "Klyuchevskii's Russia: Critical Studies," *Canadian American Slavic Studies* (twentieth anniversary volume, pt. 2), vol. 20, nos 3–4 (Fall and Winter, 1986): 221; V. O. Kliuchevskii, *Pis'ma, dnevniki, aforizmy i mysli ob istorii* (Moscow: Nauka, 1968), 282–85; and M. V. Nechkina, Iunye gody V. O. Kliuchevskogo," *Voprosy Istorii,* no. 9 (1969): 67–90.

46 Klyuchevsky was going against the grain of Russian folklore and cultural history where the heroism of the knight-errant, bogatyr, was widely celebrated. Moreover, as the son of an Orthodox priest, he probably understood the term "*podvig*" in its ecclesiastical sense of spiritual struggle rather than as a daring deed or great achievement that was going to become very popular in the Soviet period. Here I respectfully disagree with Marc Raeff's characterization of Klyuchevsky as celebrating great Russian nationalism. See footnote 38.

47 Mark Bassin, "Turner, Solov'ev and the 'Turner Hypothesis': The Nationalist Signification of Open Spaces," *The Journal of Modern History,* vol. 65, no. 3 (September 1993): 473–511; See also Willard Sunderland, *Taming the Wild Field. Colonization and Empire on the Wild Steppe* (Ithaca: Cornell University Press, 2004), 168–74.

48 A. A. Kizevetter, "V.O. Kliuchevskii kak uchenyi istorik rossii," *Russkie vedomosti,* no. 110 (14 March, 1911), partially reprinted in *V.O. Kliuchevskii: Pro i kontra* (St. Petersburg: Nevskaia Perspektiva, 2013), 117.

49 V. O. Kliuchevskii, *Socheneniia v vos'mi tomakh,* vol. I (Moscow: Gospolitizdat, 1956-59), Lecture 17, 292–315.

50 V. O. Kliuchevskii, *Socheneniia v vos'mi tomakh,* vol. I (Moscow: Gospolitizdat, 1956-59), Lecture 4, 66.

51 Christopher Ely, *This Meager Nature: Landscape and National Identity in Imperial Russia* (Dekalb, IL: Northern Illinois University Press, 2002).

52 According to David Ransel, "Kliuchevkii may have believed this idea, which was a favorite of liberal historians of the tsarist era, but subsequent research sees the towns as having a different character, a competition between powerful families, whose workers and retainers sometimes fought in the streets on behalf of their patrons. Liberals read their hopes back into these events in their eagerness to find that Russia had a democratic tradition." Personal communication from the author, October 24, 2019.

53 V. O. Kliuchevskii, *Socheneniia v vos'mi tomakh,* vol. 2 (Moscow: Gospolitizdat, 1956–59), Lecture 34, 244–62.

54 Lecture 17 see note 41. At a time when populist and left-wing Russian thinkers, as well as famous Western observes such as August von Haxthausen, stressed the communal nature of the Russian peasantry some admiringly and others in the spirit of derogation, Klyuchevsky's insistence on Russian individuality was an unusual stance to take. It probably reflected his own intellectual independence from the many camps of Russian politics in the decades leading to the revolution of 1917. August von Haxthausen, *Studies on the Interior of Russia*, trans., Eleanore L. M. Schmidt (Chicago: University of Chicago Press, 1972).

55 Richard Pipes, trans., *Karamzin's Memoir of Ancient and Modern Russia: A Translation and an Analysis* (Ann Arbor: University of Michigan Press, 2004).

56 Klyuchevsky was very critical of Karamzin and accused him of lacking the sense of historic periodization and the ability for literary characterization. He also accused Karamzin of underestimating the influence of geography. "N. M. Karamzin," in M. V. Nechkina, ed., *V. O. Kliuchevskii, Neopublikovannye priozvedeniia* (Moscow: Nauka, 1983), 133–6.

57 V. O. Kliuchevskii, *Socheneniia v vos'mi tomakh,* vol. I (Moscow: Gospolitizdat, 1956-59), Lecture 23, 243.

58 Most of Book 4 is devoted to the history of Peter's reign. Unlike the four other volumes of Klyuchevsky's *Course of Russian History* that were based on his lecture notes, he rewrote this section in the year and a half before his death. V. O. Kliuchevskii, *Socheneniia v vos'mi tomakh,* vol. IV (Moscow: Gospolitizdat, 1956-59). See James Cracraft's excellent essay, "Kliuchevskii on Peter the Great," in Marc Raeff ed., "Kliuchevksii's Russia: Critical Studies," *Canadian American Slavic Studies* (twentieth anniversary volume, pt. 2), vol. 20, nos. 3–4 (Fall and Winter, 1986): 367–83.

59 V. O. Kliuchevskii, *Pis'ma, dnevniki, aforizmy i mysli ob istorii* (Moscow: Nauka, 1968), 392–4; Nicholas Riasanovsky, *The Image of Peter the Great in Russian History and Thought* (New York: Oxford University Press, 1985).

60 V. O. Kliuchevskii, *Sochineniia v devyati tomakh*, vol. 7 (Moscow: Mysl', 1989), 163–4.

61 "Evgeny Onegin and his Ancestors," in *V. O. Kliuchesvky. From Peter the Great to Pushkin*, trans. and edited Marshall Shatz (Idyllwild, CA: Charles Shlacks Publisher, 2009), 241. In contrast to these confused elites, Klyuchevsky offered as examples his heroes such as Minin and Pozharsky, the historian I. N. Boltin, the publisher, Nikolai Novikov. Ibid., 145–204. See also his articles "Dobrye liudi drevnei' Rusi," in V. O. Kliuchevskii, *O nravstevennosti i russkoi kul'ture* (Moscow: Institut Rossiskoi istorii RAN, 1998), 71–92; and V. O. Kliuchevskii, *Pis'ma, dnevniki, aforizmy i mysli ob istorii* (Moscow: Nauka, 1968).

62 See Alexander Etkind's insightful and original work that builds on Klyuchevsky's initial insights into Russian history and colonization, *Internal Colonization: Russia's Imperial Experience* (Malden, MA: Polity Press, 2011).

63 P. A. Kireeva, ed., *V. O. Kliuchevskii. Lektsii po Istorii Zapadnoi Evropy v Sviazi s Istoriei Rossii* (Moscow: Russkaia Panorama, 2012), Abastuman Lectures 13–15, 386–409.

64 M. N. Pokrovsky, *Istoricheskaia nauka i bor'ba klassov*, vol. 1 (Moscow-Leningrad: Sotsekizd, 1933), 48–58; and N. L. Rubinshtein, "Burzhuaznyi ekonomizm Kliuchevskoi" in *V.O. Kliuchevskii: Pro i kontra* (St. Petersburg: Nevskaia Perspektiva, 2013), 759–87.

65 Korine Amacher, "Mikhail N. Pokrovsky and Ukraine: A Normative Marxist Between History and Politics," *Ab Imperio*, no. 1 (2018): 101–32.

66 David Brandenberger, *National Bolshevism: Stalinist Mass Culture and the Formation of Modern Russian National Identity 1931-1956* (Cambridge, MA: Harvard University Press, 2002).

67 M. V. Nechkina, *V. O. Kliuchevksii. Zhizn i tvorchestvo* (Moscow: Izdatel'stvo Nauka, 1974).

68 Despite their revolutionary historical research agenda, Hill and Thompson, like Trevelyan, were equally indifferent to the history of British imperialism.

69 Harvey J. Kaye, *British Marxist Historians: An Introductory Analysis*, rpt. edition (New York: St. Martin's Press, 1995); Eric Hobsbawm, *Interesting Times: A Twentieth Century Life 2003* (London: Allen Lane, 2002); and Michael Bentley, *Modernizing England's Past: English Historiography in the Age of Modernism* (New York: Cambridge University Press, 2005).

70 V. O. Kliuchevskii, *Sochineniia v vosm'i tomakh*, vol. 1 (Moscow: Gosudarstvennoe izdatel'stvo politicheskoi literatury, 1956), Lecture 2, 44; and G. M. Trevelyan, "Clio a Muse," in *Clio, A Muse and Other Essays*, rpt. edition (Freeport NY: Books for Libraries Press, 1968), 152.

71 We can see Trevelyan's rehabilitation in works such as David Cannadine's, *G. M. Trevelyan: A Life in History* (New York: W. W. Norton & Company, 1997); and in Julia Stapleton, *Political Intellectuals and Public Identities in Britain since 1850* (Manchester: Manchester University Press, 2001); Klyuchevsky's completed works were reprinted several times in the late 1980s and 1990s, and his popularity is unrivaled in contemporary Russia. See the online display at the Presidential Library in Russia to mark his 175th birth anniversary, https://www.prlib.ru/en/collection_klyuchevskii, last accessed October 18, 2019.

Chapter 4

1 The section on M. N. Roy was previously published as "'Imperial Subjects in the Soviet Union', Rabindranath Tagore, M. N. Roy, and Re-thinking Freedom and Authoritarianism in the Twentieth Century," in the *Journal of Contemporary History*, 52, no. 4 (October 2017), 913–34.

2 Kevin McDermott and Jeremy Agnew, *The Comintern: A History of International Communism from Lenin to Stalin* (New York: Palgrave, 1997); Silvio Pons, *The Global Revolution: The History of International Communism,*

1917–1991, trans. Allan Cameron (Oxford: Oxford University Press, 2014); Silvio Pons and Stephen Smith eds., *World Revolution and Socialism in One Country 1917–1941* (Cambridge: Cambridge University Press, 2017); Robert Service, *Comrades! A History of World Communism* (Cambridge MA: Harvard University Press, 2007); Steven Smith ed., *The Oxford Handbook of the History of Communism* (Oxford: Oxford University Press, 2014); and Aleksandr Vatlin, *Komintern: ideii, reshenie, sud'by* (Moscow: ROSSPEN, 2007).

3 Paul Avrich, *The Russian Anarchists* (Princeton: Princeton University Press, 1967), and *Kronstadt, 1921* (Princeton: Princeton University Press, 1970); Marks, 2003; and Kate Sharpley Library, *Bolshevik Repression of the Anarchists after 1917*, https://www.katesharpleylibrary.net/xpnx76, last accessed November 9, 2018.

4 Geoffrey Eley, *Forging Democracy: History of the Left in Europe, 1850–2000* (New York: Oxford University Press, 2002); For other egalitarian visions, see Aishwary Kumar, *Radical Equality: Ambedkar, Gandhi, and the Risk of Democracy* (Stanford: Stanford University Press, 2015); Maia Ramnath, *Decolonizing Anarchism: An Anti-Authoritarian History of India's Liberation Struggle* (Oakland, CA: AK Press, 2011); and Barry Maxwell and Raymond Craib ed., *No Gods, No Masters, No Peripheries: Global Anarchisms* (Dexter, MI: PM Press, 2015).

5 Oz Frankel, "Whatever Happened to 'Red Emma'? Emma Goldman, from Alien Rebel to American Icon," *The Journal of American History*, vol. 83, no. 3 (December 1996): 903–42.

6 Alexander Rabinowich, *The Bolsheviks in Power: The First Year of Soviet Rule in Petrograd* (Bloomington, IN: Indiana University Press, 2007).

7 Emma Goldman, "What I Believe," published in the New York World, July 19, 1908, http://dwardmac.pitzer.edu/Anarchist_Archives/goldman/whatibelieve.html, last accessed November 12, 2018.

8 Emma Goldman, *Living My Life*, two volumes (New York: Dover Publications, 1931).

9 Robert K. Murray, *Red Scare: A Study in National Hysteria, 1919–1920* (Minneapolis, MN: University of Minnesota Press, 1955); and Julia Rose, "Kraut Global Anti-Anarchism: The Origins of Ideological Deportation and the Suppression of Expression," *Indiana Journal of Global Legal Studies*, vol. 19, no. 1 (Winter, 2012): 169–93.

10 Paul Avrich, *Sasha and Emma: The Anarchist Odyssey of Alexander Berkman and Emma Goldman* (Cambridge, MA: Harvard University Press, 2012); Mary Jo Buhle et al., eds., *The American Radical* (New York: Routledge, 1994); Richard Drinnon, *A Rebel in Paradise: A Biography of Emma Goldman* (Boston, MA: Beacon Press, 1961); Candace Falk, *Love, Anarchy and Emma Goldman* (New York: Holt, Rinehart and Winston, 1984); Martha Solomon, *Emma Goldman* (Boston, MA: Twayne, 1987); and Alice Wexler, *Emma Goldman: An Intimate Life* (New York: Pantheon Books, 1984).

11 http://www.lib.berkeley.edu/goldman/ last accessed February 11, 2020.

12 American historians have produced most of the literature on Goldman's revolutionary politics. See for example, Marion Morton's excellent work,

Emma Goldman and the American Left: "Nowhere at Home" (New York: Twayne Publishers, 1992); Kathy Ferguson, *Emma Goldman: Political Thinking in the Streets* (Lanham, MD: Rowman and Littlefield, 2011); and Bernice A. Carroll, "Emma Goldman and the Theory of Revolution," in Penny A. Weiss and Loretta Kensinger eds., *Feminist Interpretations of Emma Goldman* (University Park, PA: Pennsylvania State University Press, 2007).

13 Peter Filene, *Americans and the Soviet Experiment, 1917–1933* (Cambridge, MA: Harvard University Press, 1967), 147–8. For exceptions, see excellent essays by Harold J. Goldberg, "Goldman and Berkman View the Bolshevik Regime," *The Slavonic and East European Review*, vol. 53, no. 131 (April 1975): 272–6.

14 See articles in the pages of her journal, *Mother Earth*, for Goldman's references to anarchist thought.

15 Emma Goldman, *The Individual, State and Society* (Chicago, IL: Free Society Forum, 1940).

16 Emma Goldman, "Anarchism. What It Really Stands For," in *Anarchism and Other Essays* (New York: Mother Earth Publishing, 1910); and Yuri Slezkine, *The Jewish Century* (Princeton, NJ: Princeton University Press, 2006).

17 See correspondence with niece, Stella Ballantine in Emma Goldman Papers at the International Institute of Social History, vol. 4. https://search.socialhist ory.org/Record/ARCH00520/ArchiveContentList#110 last accessed July 22, 2017.

18 Jim MacLaughlin, *Kropotkin and the Anarchist Intellectual Tradition* (London: Pluto Press, 2016).

19 Avrich, *The Russian Anarchists*; B. I. Kolonitskii, *Simvoly vlasti i bor'ba za vlast': K izucheniiu politicheskoi kul'tury rossiiskoi revoliutsii* (St Petersburg: Dmitrii Bulanin, 2001); Eduard Burdzhalov, *Russia's Second Revolution: The February 1917 Uprising in Petrograd,* trans. Donald Raleigh (Bloomington: Indiana University Press, 1987); Ziva Galili y Garcia, *The Menshevik Leaders in the Russian Revolution: Social Realities and Political Strategies* (Princeton: Princeton University Press, 1989); Orlando Figes and Boris Kolonitskii, *Interpreting the Russian Revolution: The Language and Symbols of 1917* (New Haven, CT: Yale University Press, 1999); William Rosenberg, *Liberals in the Russian Revolution: The Constitutional Democratic Party, 1917–1921* (Princeton: Princeton University Press, 1974); Oliver Radkey, *Sickle Under the Hammer: The Russian Socialist Revolutionaries in the Early Months of Soviet Rule* (New York: Columbia University Press, 1963); Scott Smith, *Captives of Revolution: The Socialist-Revolutionaries and the Bolshevik Dictatorship, 1918–1921* (Pittsburgh: University of Pittsburgh Press, 2013); Rochelle Ruthchild, *Equality and Revolution: Women's Rights in the Russian Revolution, 1905–1917* (Pittsburgh: University of Pittsburgh Press, 2010); Steven Smith, *Red Petrograd. Revolution in the Factories* (Cambridge: Cambridge University Press, 1983); Richard Stites, *Revolutionary Dreams. Utopian Vision and Experimental Life in the Russian Revolution* (New York: Oxford University Press, 1989); and Allan Wildman, *The End of the Russian Imperial Army:*

The Old Army and the Soldiers' Revolt (Princeton: Princeton University Press, 1980).

20 Peter Kropotkin, *Ethics: Origin and Development* (London: George G. Harrap and Co., Ltd., 1924); See also his "Letter to the Workers of Western Europe," April 28, 1918, in Roger Baldwin ed., *Kropotkin's Revolutionary Pamphlets* (New York: Dover, 1927), 252–60.

21 Sally Boniece, "Spiridonova Case, 1906: Terror, Myth, and Martyrdom," *Kritika: Explorations in Russian and Eurasian History,* vol. 4, no. 3 (2003): 571–606; and Nestor Makhno, *Vospominaniia* (Moscow: Izd- vo Respublika, 1992).

22 See the text of Goldman's article on Kropotkin from 1921 in Emma Goldman Papers, International Institute of Social History, vol. 5, https://search.socia lhistory.org/Record/ARCH00520/ArchiveContentList#97, last accessed August 25, 2017.

23 Eric Homberger, *John Reed* (Manchester: Manchester University Press, 1990), 214.

24 Goldman, *My Disillusionment in Russia,* 168.

25 Paul Avrich, *Kronstadt, 1921* (Princeton: Princeton University Press, 1970).

26 Wexler, *Emma Goldman in Exile*, 78–9.

27 Goldman, *My Disillusionment in Russia,* 14.

28 "Was My Life Worth Living?" in Alix Kate Shulman, ed., *Red Emma Speaks. An Emma Goldman Reader* (New York: Shocken Books, 1983), 439.

29 Marion Morton, *Emma Goldman and the American Left. "Nowhere at Home"* (New York: Twayne Publishers, 1992).

30 Paul Hollander, *Political Pilgrims: Travels of Western Intellectuals to the Soviet Union, China and Cuba, 1928–1978* (New York: Oxford University Press, 1981); David Caute, *The Fellow-Travellers: Intellectual Friends of Communism* (New Haven, CT: Yale University Press, 1988); Chatterjee and Holmgren, eds, *Americans Experience Russia: Americans Encountering the Enigma, 1890 to the Present* (New York: Routledge, 2012); Katerina Clark, *Moscow the Fourth Rome: Stalinism, Cosmopolitanism and the Evolution of Soviet Culture, 1931–1941* (Cambridge, MA: Harvard University Press, 2011); Michael David-Fox, *Showcasing the Great Experiment: Cultural Diplomacy and Western Visitors to the Soviet Union, 1921–1941* (New York: Oxford University Press, 2012); Engerman, *Modernization from the Other Shore*; Aleksandr Etkind, *Tolkovanie puteshestvii: Rossiia i Amerika v travelogakh i intertekstakh* (Moscow: Novoe literaturnoe obozrenie, 2003); Foglesong, The *American Mission and the "Evil Empire"*; Malia, *Under Western Eyes*; and Ludmila Stern, *Western Intellectuals and the Soviet Union, 1920–1940: From Red Square to Left Bank* (New York: Routledge, 2007).

31 Gornick, *Emma Goldman: Revolution as a Way of Life, 118–119.*

32 Alice Wexler, *Emma Goldman in Exile* (Boston, MA: Beacon Press, 1989), 84.

33 Richard Crossman ed., *The God That Failed* (New York: Harper and Brothers, 1949); Whittaker Chambers, *Witness* (Newark, NJ: Random House, 1952);

and Michael Kimmage, *The Conservative Turn: Lionel Trilling, Whittaker Chamber, and the Lessons of Anti-Communism* (Cambridge, MA: Harvard University Press, 2009).

34 Emma Goldman, *Individual, State and Society* (First published: by the Free Society Forum, Chicago, Illinois in 1940). https://www.marxists.org/refer ence/archive/goldman/works/1940/individual.htm, last accessed August 12, 2017.

35 V. B. Karnik, *M. N. Roy, Political Biography* (Bombay: Nav Jagriti Samaj, 1978); Kris Manjapra, *M. N. Roy: Marxism and Colonial Cosmopolitanism* (New Delhi: Routledge, 2012); and Samaren Ray, *The Twice Born Heretic: M. N. Roy and the Comintern* (Calcutta: Firma K L M, 1986), 38.

36 Maia Ramnath, *Haj to Utopia: How the Ghadar Movement Charted Global Radicalism and Attempted to Overthrow the British Empire* (Berkeley: University of California Press, 2011).

37 Charles Shipman, *It Had to Be Revolution: Memoirs of an American Radical* (Ithaca, NY: Cornell University Press, 1993), 84. I thank Lisa Kirschenbaum for this citation.

38 Sobhanlal Datta Gupta, *Comintern and the Destiny of Communism in India: 1919–1943* (Kolkata: Seribaan, 2006); and John Haithcox, *Communism and Nationalism in India: M. N. Roy and the Comintern Policy 1920–1939* (Princeton: Princeton University Press, 1971).

39 M. N. Roy, *India in Transition* (Geneva: J. B. Target, 1922); *Revolution and Counter-Revolution in China* (Calcutta: Renaissance Publisher, 1946); and *My Experience in China* (Calcutta: Renaissance Publishers, 1945). For Roy's writings, see Sibnarayan Ray ed., *Selected Works of M. N. Roy* in four volumes published by Oxford University Press.

40 Hari Vasudevan, "India and the October Revolution: Nationalist Revolutionaries, Bolshevik Power," and "Lord Curzon's Nightmare," in Choi Chatterjee, Steven Marks, Mary Neuberger, and Steve Sabol ed., *The Wider Arc of Revolution: The Global Impact of 1917,* bk. 2, part 2 (Bloomington, IN: Slavica Publishers, 2019), 299–325.

41 M. N. Roy, *Fragments of a Prisoner's Diary: Letters from Jail*, vol. 3 (Calcutta: Renaissance Publishers, 1943).

42 Oleg Khlevniuk, *Stalin: A New Biography of a Dictator*, trans. Nora Favorov (New Haven, CT: Yale University Press, 2015); Robert Service, *Stalin: A Biography* (Cambridge, MA: Harvard University Press, 2005); Eric Van Ree, *The Political Thought of Joseph Stalin* (London: Routledge, 2002); and Dmitry Volkogonov, *Stalin: Triumph and Tragedy* (Rocklin, CA: Prima Publishing, 1996).

43 Kris Manjapra, *Age of Entanglement: German and Indian Intellectuals Across Empire* (Cambridge, MA: Harvard University Press, 2014).

44 Sibnarayan Ray, *In Freedom's Quest: A Study of the Life and Works of M. N. Roy, 1887–1954*, vol. III, Part I, *Against the Current, 1928–39* (Kolkata: Minerva Associates, 2005), 1–129–68.

45 Sibnarayan Ray ed., *The World Her Village: Selected Letters and Writings of Ellen Roy* (Calcutta: Ananda, 1979); See also the letter campaign waged by

Evelyn Trent from the United States to release Roy, RGASPI (Russian State Archive of Socio-Political History), fond 495, delo 213, opis 18, ll, 5–9.

46 Sibnarayan Ray, "Tagore, Gandhi and Roy: Three Twentieth Century Utopians," in Sibnarayan Ray edited, *M. N. Roy, Philosopher-Revolutionary* (Delhi: Ajanta Publications, 1995), 235–50.

47 See documents from RGASPI that contain instructions for Indian communists, fond 495, op 213, delo 18, ll 67–8.

48 M. N. Roy, *The Russian Revolution* (Calcutta: Renaissance Publishers, 1949), vii.

49 M. N. Roy, "A Critical Appreciation of Leon Trotsky" (written in 1940 after Trotsky's assassination), ibid., 62.

50 M. N. Roy, *M. N. Roy's Memoirs* (Bombay: Allied Publishers, 1964), 508–9.

51 M. N. Roy, "The Death of Stalin," *Radical Humanist*, no. XVII (March 15, 1953).

52 M.N. Roy, *If I Were Stalin* (Calcutta: Renaissance Publishers, 1988), 50.

53 Roy launched the Radical Humanist Movement in India in 1948 and in 1952 was invited to join the *International Humanist and Ethical Union*, an organization that drew membership from Europe and the United States and was dedicated to the defense of human rights globally; and M. N. Roy, *New Humanism: A Manifesto* (Calcutta: Renaissance Publishers, 1947).

54 M. N. Roy, *Politics, Power and Parties* (Calcutta: Renaissance Publishers, 1960), 54.

55 Ibid., 52.

56 It would be an interesting exercise to compare Roy's ideas with those contained in the infinitely better-known work by Ernesto Laclau and Chantal Mouffe, *Hegemony and Socialist Strategy: Towards a Radical Democratic Politics* (London: Verso, 1985), and the *Prison Writings,* of the Kurdish leader, Abdullah Öcalan (I thank Afshin Matin-Asgari for the last reference).

57 Oskar Anweiler, *Soviets: The Russian Workers, Peasants and Soldiers Councils, 1905–1921,* trans. by Hein Ruth (New York: Pantheon Books, 1975); J. H. L. Keep, *The Russian Revolution: A Study in Mass Mobilization* (New York: W. W. Norton & Co., 1977); Diane Koenker, *Moscow Workers and the 1917 Revolution* (Princeton, NJ: Princeton University Press, 1981); and S. A. Smith, *Red Petrograd: Revolution in the Factories, 1917-1918* (New York: Cambridge University Press, 1983).

58 Barbara Allen, *Alexander Shliapnikov 1885–1937: Life of an Old Bolshevik* (Boston: Haymarket Books, 2015).

59 Geoffrey Swain, *Trotsky and the Russian Revolution* (London: Routledge, 2014); Ian Thatcher, *Trotsky* (London: Routledge, 2002); and Dmitri Volkogonov, *Trotsky: Eternal Revolutionary* (London: Harper Collins, 1997).

60 V. I. Lenin, *What Is To Be Done* (1902) and *State and Revolution* (1917).

61 M. N. Roy, *Reason, Romanticism and Revolution*, vols. 1 and 2 (Calcutta: Renaissance Press, 1952 and 1957).

62 *Anarchism, A History of Libertarian Ideas and Movements*, rpt. edition (Ontario: Broadview Press, 2004), 37.

Chapter 5

1   Moshe Lewin argued that collectivization was the culmination of Soviet
    bureaucratic violence and the anti-peasant crusade that had been ongoing
    since 1917. See his seminal work, *Russian Peasants and Soviet Power: A
    Study of Collectivization*, trans. by Irene Nove (Evanston, IL: Northwestern
    University Press, 1968); and Andrea Graziosi, "The Great Soviet Peasant War.
    The Bolsheviks and the Peasants, 1917–1932," *Harvard Papers in Ukrainian
    Studies* (Cambridge, MA: Harvard University Press, 1996).

2   For differing estimates of deaths, see O. Rudnytskyi, N. Levchuk, O.
    Wolowyna, P. Shevchuk, and A. Kovbasiuk, "Demography of a Man Made
    Human Catastrophe! The Case of Massive Famine in Ukraine 1932–1933,"
    Canadian Studies in Population, vol. 42, nos. 1–2 (2015): 53–80; and R. W.
    Davies and Stephen Wheatcroft, *The Years of Hunger: Soviet Agriculture*
    (Houndmills: Palgrave Macmillan, 2010).

3   Lynne Viola, *The Unknown Gulag: The Lost World of Stalin's Special
    Settlements* (Oxford: Oxford University Press, 2007).

4   J. V. Stalin, *Works*, vol. 13 (Moscow: Foreign Languages Publishing House,
    1954), 313.

5   For comparisons between Soviet and capitalist industrial farming, see James
    Scott, "Soviet Collectivization, Capitalist Dreams," in his *Seeing Like a State:
    How Certain Schemes to Improve the Human Condition Have Failed* (New
    Haven, CT: Yale University Press, 1998), 193–222; Deborah Fitzgerald, *Every
    Farm a Factory: The Industrial Ideal in American Agriculture* (New Haven: Yale
    University Press, 2003); and Mark Tauger, "Stalin, Soviet Agriculture, and
    Collectivization," in Frank Trentmann and Fleming Just eds., *Food and Conflict
    in Europe in the Age of the Two World Wars* (New York: Palgrave Macmillan,
    2006), 109–42.

6   Walter Duranty, "Famine Toll Heavy in Southern Russia," *New York Times*,
    24 August 1933, https://timesmachine.nytimes.com/timesmachine/1933/08/2
    4/99919625.html?pageNumber=1, last accessed July 20, 2020.

7   Choi Chatterjee, "Imperial Subjects in the Soviet Union: Rabindranath Tagore,
    M. N. Roy, and Re-thinking Freedom and Authoritarianism in the Twentieth
    Century," *Journal of Contemporary History*, vol. 52, no. 4 (October 2017):
    963. Jawaharlal Nehru, the future prime minister of India was similarly
    impressed by Soviet collectivization and modernization.

8   Sir John Maynard, *The Russian Peasant and Other Studies* (London: Victor
    Gollancz, 1941), 365.

9   E. John Russell, "Sir John Maynard and his Studies of the Russian Peasant,"
    The Slavonic and East European Review, vol. 24, no. 63 (January 1946):
    56–65.

10 John Maynard, "Collective Farming in the USSR," *The Slavonic and East
    European Review*, vol. 15, no. 43 (July 1936): 47–69.

11 Maurice Dobb, *Soviet Economic Development since 1917* (London:
    Routledge and Kegan Paul Ltd, 1938), 25.

12 S. J. Taylor, *Stalin's Apologist: The New York Times's Man in Moscow* (New York: Oxford University Press, 1990), 9–14.

13 Sidney Mintz, *Sweetness and Power: The Place of Sugar in Modern History* (New York: Viking-Penguin, 1985).

14 Blair Kling, *Partner in Empire: Dwarakanath Tagore and the Age of Enterprise in Eastern India* (Berkeley, CA: University of California Press, 1977).

15 Herbert John Maynard, *Voyage to India; Stay in Central India; Life in the Punjab and Mandi and Suket States* (Adam Matthew Digital, 2018).

16 Imran Ali, *Punjab Under Imperialism, 1885*–1947 (Princeton, NJ: Princeton University Press, 1988); Ian A. Talbot, "Punjab under Colonialism: Order and Transformation in British India," *Journal of Punjab Studies,* vol. 14, no. 1 (2007): 3–10; and Ian Talbot, I. *Punjab and the Raj 1849—1947*, rpt. edition (New Delhi, India: Manohar Publishers, 2020).

17 R. W. Tawney, David Ormrod, "Agrarian Capitalism and Merchant Capitalism: Tawney, Dobb, Brenner and Beyond," in Jane Whittle ed., *Landlords and Tenants in Britain, 1440—1660: Tawney's Agrarian Problem Revisited* (Croydon: Boydell Press, 2013), 204.

18 Yujiro Hayami, "The Peasant in Economic Modernization," *American Journal of Agricultural Economics*, vol. 78, no. 5 (December, 1996): 1157–67; Sir William Arthur Lewis, a highly influential developmental economist, argued that capitalism develops by taking resources and labor from a "backward" subsistence sector until the latter is absorbed into the former. He advised countries such as Nigeria, Barbados, and Ghana to follow the English model of the agricultural revolution. See his *The Theory of Economic Growth* (Homewood, IL: Richard D. Irwin, 1955); and Giovanni Federico, *Feeding the World: An Economic History of Agriculture, 1800–2000* (Princeton: Princeton University Press, 2005).

19 V. I. Lenin, *Development of Capitalism in Russia*, in *Collected Works,* vol. 3, 4th edition (Moscow: Progress Publishers, 1964), 21–608; and Samuel H. Baron, *Plekhanov: The Father of Russian Marxism* (Stanford: Stanford University Press, 1963).

20 Esther Kingston–Mann, "Marxism and Russian Rural Development: Problems of Evidence, Experience, and Culture," *The American Historical Review*, vol. 86, no. 4 (October, 1981): 731– 752; and *In Search of the True West: Culture, Economics, and the Problems of Russian Development* (Princeton: Princeton University Press, 1999).

21 Jürgen Kocka, *Capitalism: A Short History* (Princeton: Princeton University Press, 2016), see Chapter 3.

22 See for example Alexander Chayanov's *A Theory of Peasant Cooperatives*, trans. David Wedgewood Benn (Columbus, OH: Ohio State University, 1991); and Chayanov's utopian short story, "The Journey of My Brother Alexei to the Land of Peasant Utopia," in R. E. F. Smith ed., *The Russian Peasant, 1920–1984* (London: Routledge, 1977), 78–121.

23 Karl Marx, *The 18th Brumaire of Louis Bonaparte*, December 1851–1852, 62. https://www.marxists.org/archive/marx/works/download/pdf/18th-Bru

maire.pdf, last accessed June 26, 2020; We know that Marx was going to subsequently change his opinions about the revolutionary potential of the Russian peasant commune in his correspondence with Vera Zasulich. See Kevin Anderson, *Marx at the Margins: On Nationalism, Ethnicity, and Non-Western Societies* (Chicago: University of Chicago Press, 2010); Teodor Shanin (2018) 1881 "1881 Letters of Vera Zasulich and Karl Marx," *The Journal of Peasant Studies*, vol. 45, no. 7 (October 2018): 1183–202; and Nirmal Kumar Chandra, "The Peasant Question from Marx to Lenin: The Russian Experience," *Economic and Political Weekly*, vol. 37, no. 20 (May 18–24, 2002): 1927–38.

24 The literature on the Agricultural Revolution is immense and there is great controversy on the periodization, causes, and effects. I reference a few important sources such as Robert C. Allen, *Enclosure, and the Yeoman: The Agricultural Development of the South Midlands 1450–1850* (Oxford: Clarendon Press, 1992); Mark Overton, *Agricultural Revolution in England: The Transformation of the Agrarian Economy 1500–1850* (Cambridge: University Press, 1999); and Joan Thirsk, *The Agrarian History of England and Wales* (Cambridge: Cambridge University Press: vol. IV, 1967; vol. V, 1985; vol. VI, 1989).

25 Fallowing is an ancient technique of soil rejuvenation that improves the land with the manure of wandering cattle that grazes on these unplanted fields. Fallowing allows for greater moisture retention in the soil and prevents erosion of top soil. Weeds and native plants that grow on fallowed land attract a host of pollinators that are key to successful farming. And when fallow lands are plowed under, they provided a source of green manure and essential minerals for the crops. David C. Nielsen, and, Francisco J. Calderón, "Fallow Effects on Soil" (2011). Publications from USDA-ARS / UNL Faculty. 1391. https://digitalcommons.unl.edu/usdaarsfacpub/1391, last accessed July 15, 2020.

26 Rob Bryer, "The Roots of Modern Capitalism: A Marxist Accounting History of the Origins and Consequences of Capitalist Landlords in England," *The Accounting Historians Journal*, vol. 31, no. 1 (June 2004): 1–56.

27 R. H. Tawney, *The Agrarian Revolution in the Sixteenth Century* (London: Longman, Greene and Co., 1912), 3.

28 David Kerans, *Mind and Labor on the Farm in Black Earth Russia 1861–1914* (New York: Central European University Press, 2001); and David Moon, *The Plough that Broke the Steppes: Agriculture, and Environment on Russia's Grasslands, 1700–1914* (Oxford: Oxford University Press, 2014).

29 Paul R. Gregory, *Before Command: An Economic History of Russia from Emancipation to the First Five-Year Plan* (Princeton: Princeton University Press, 1994).

30 Judith Pallot, *Land Reform in Russia, 1906-1917: Peasant Responses to Stolypin's Project of Rural Transformation* (London: Oxford University Press, 1999).

31 Orlando Figes, *Peasant War, Civil War: The Volga Countryside in Revolution, 1917–1921* (Oxford: Clarendon, 1989); Aaron B. Retish, *Russia's Peasants* *in Revolution and Civil War: Citizenship, Identity, and the Creation of the Soviet State, 1914-1922* (Cambridge: Cambridge University Press, 2008); Sarah Badcock, *Politics and the People in Revolutionary Russia: A Provincial History* (Cambridge: Cambridge University Press, 2007); Donald J. Raleigh, *Experiencing Russia's Civil War: Politics, Society, and Revolutionary Culture in Saratov, 1917–1922* (Princeton: Princeton University Press, 2002); Donald J. Raleigh, *Revolution on the Volga: 1917 in Saratov* (Ithaca, NY: Cornell University Press, 1986); I. V. Narskii, *Zhizn' v katastrofe: Budni naseleniia Urala v 1917–1922 gg* (Moscow: ROSSPEN, 2001); and Sarah Badcock, and Liudmila Novikova, eds., *Russia's Home Front in War and Revolution, 1914–1922*, bk. 1: *Russia's Revolution in Regional Perspective* (Bloomington, IN: Slavica, 2015).

32 James Heinzen, *Inventing a Soviet Countryside: State Power and the Transformation of Rural Russia, 1917–1929* (Pittsburgh: University of Pittsburgh Press, 2004), 141–6; and Zhores A. Medvedev, *Soviet Agriculture* (New York: Norton, 1987).

33 The classic program on primitive socialist accumulation of peasant surplus was formulated by the Trotskyite, Yevgeny Preobrazhensky, *The New Economics*, trans. Brian Pearce (Oxford: Clarendon Press, 1965), but was instituted by Stalin. But even Alexander Chayanov, the renowned theorist of the peasant family and the non-capitalist agrarian economy, revised his ideas about the peasant economy during the latter part of his career. He became interested in the application of American agricultural technology to vast land holdings that were to be collectivized in a non-coercive manner. See his article "Vozmozhnoe budushchee sel'skogo khoziastva," in A. Kolman ed., *Zhizn i tekhnika buduschego. Sotsial'nye nauchno-tekhnicheskie utopii* (Moscow, Leningrad: Moskovsky rabochii, 1928), 260–84. For an excellent discussion of the evolution of Chayanov's ideas, see Alexander M. Nikulin, "Reconciling Failure and Success: Soviet Elites and the Collectivized Village," *Jahrbücher für Geschichte Osteuropas*, vol. 65, no. 3 (2017): 423–44; and Danila Raskov, "Socialist Agrarian Utopia in the 1920s: Chayanov," *Œconomia* (Online), vol. 4, no. 2 (2014), http://journals.openediti on.org/oeconomia/836, last accessed August 3, 2020.

34 Viktor Petrovich Danilov, Roberta T. Manning and Lynne Viola, eds., *Tragediia Sovetskoi derevni: Kollektivizatsiia i raskulachinanie. Dokumenty i materialy v 5-kh tomakh. 1927–1939* (Moscow: Rosspen, 1999–2006), vol. 1: Mai 1927–noiabr' 1929; Sheila Fitzpatrick, *Stalin's Peasants: Resistance and Survival in the Russian Village after Collectivization* (Oxford: Oxford University Press, 1994); V. V. Kondrashin, *Golod 1932–1933 godov: Tragediia rossiiskoi derevni* (Moscow: Rosspen, 2018); Elena Osokina, *Our Daily Bread: Socialist Distribution and the Art of Survival in Stalin's Russia, 1927–1941*, trans. Kate Transchel (Armonk, NY: M. E. Sharpe, 2001); and Lynne Viola, *Peasant Rebels Under Stalin: Collectivization and the Culture of Peasant Resistance* (Oxford: Oxford University Press, 1996).

35 Anne Applebaum, *Red Famine: Stalin's War on Ukraine* (New York: Doubleday, 2017); and Robert Conquest, *Harvest of Sorrow: Soviet Collectivization and the Terror-Famine* (New York: Oxford University Press, 1986).

36 Sarah Cameron, *Hungry Steppe: Famine, Violence, and the Making of Soviet Kazakhstan* (Ithaca: Cornell University Press, 2018); Robert Kindler, *Stalin's Nomads: Power and Violence in Kazakhstan*, trans. Cynthia Klohr (Pittsburgh: University of Pittsburgh Press, 2018); Matthew J. Payne, "Seeing like a Soviet State: Settlement of Nomadic Kazakhs, 1928–1934," in Golfo Alexopoulous, Julie Hessler, and Kiril Tomoff eds., *Writing the Stalin Era: Sheila Fitzpatrick and Soviet Historiography* (New York: Palgrave Macmillan, 2011), 59–86; Niccolò Pianciola, "Famine in the Steppe: The Collectivization of Agriculture and the Kazak Herdsmen, 1928–1934," *Cahiers du Monde Russe,* vol. 45, nos. 1–2 (2004): 137–92; and Zh. B. Abylkhozin, M. K. Kozybaev, and M. B. Tatimov, "Kazakhstanskaia tragediia," *Voprosy istorii*, no. 7 (1080): 53 71.

37 Mukhamet Shayakhmetov, *The Silent Steppe: The Story of a Kazakh Nomad under Stalin*, trans. Jan Butler (London: Overlook Press, 2006); and Mukhamet Shayakhmetov, *A Kazakh Teacher's Story: Surviving the Silent Steppe*, trans. Jan Butler (London: Stacey International, 2012).

38 Mukhamet Shayakhmetov, *The Silent Steppe: The Memoir of a Kazakh Nomad under Stalin*, trans. by Jan Butler, 239.

39 Ibid., 242–3.

40 Shayakhmetov, *A Kazakh Teacher's Story*, 149.

41 Ibid., 199–200.

42 Edgar T. Thompson, *The Plantation*. Unpublished PhD thesis, Department of Sociology, University of Chicago, 1931; and Dale Tomich, "The Plantation as Problem," *Review (Fernand Braudel Center)*, vol. 34, nos 1/2 (Spring, 2011): 15–39.

43 Eric Williams, *Capitalism and Slavery* (Chapel Hill, NC: University of North Carolina, Chapel Hill, 1944), 19.

44 Klas Rönnbäck, "On the Economic Importance of the Slave Plantation Complex to the British Economy During the Eighteenth Century: A Value-Added Approach," *Journal of Global History*, vol. 13 (2018): 309–27.

45 Amiya Kumar Bagchi, "Nineteenth Century Imperialism and Structural Transformation in Colonized Countries," in A. H. Akram-Lodhi and C. Kay eds., *Peasants and Globalization: Political Economy, Rural Transformation, and the Agrarian Question* (London and New York: Routledge, 2009), 83–110; Sven Beckert, *Empire of Cotton: A Global History* (New York: Knopf, 2015); Kris Manjapra, "Plantation Dispossessions: The Global Travel of Agricultural Racial Capitalism," in Sven Beckert and Christine Desan eds., *American Capitalism: New Histories* (New York: Columbia University Press, 2018), 360–87; and Marcel Mazoyer, and Lawrence Roudart, *A History of World Agriculture: From the Neolithic Age to the Current Crisis*, trans. James H. Membrez (New York: Monthly Review Press, 2006).

46 Mohammad Saleh, "Export Booms and Labor Coercion: Evidence from the Lancashire Cotton Famine," (March 2020). *CEPR Discussion Paper* no. DP14542. Available at SSRN: https://ssrn.com/abstract=3594163; last September 1, 2020.

47 Martin S. Shanguhyia, *Population, Tradition, and Environmental Control in Colonial Kenya* (Rochester, NY; Boydell & Brewer, 2015); M. P. K. Sorrenson,

Origins of European Settlement in Kenya (Nairobi, Kenya: Oxford University Press, 1968); and Robert L. Tignor, *Colonial Transformation of Kenya: The Kamba, Kikuyu, and Maasai from 1900–1939* (Princeton: Princeton University Press, 1976).

48 A. Clayton and D. Savage, *Government and Labour in Kenya 1895–1963* (London: Frank Cass, 1974).

49 Peter Karari, "Modus Operandi of Oppressing the 'Savages': The Kenyan British Colonial Experience," *Peace and Conflict Studies*, vol. 25, no. 1 (2018): 1–20. https://nsuworks.nova.edu/pcs/vol25/iss1/2, last accessed September 2, 2020, and W. Ochieng, *Historical Studies and Social Change in Western Kenya* (Nairobi: East African Educational Publishers Ltd., 2002).

50 J. D. Overton 1988, "The Origins of the Kikuyu Land Problem: Land Alienation and Land Use in Kiambu, Kenya, 1895–1920," *African Studies Review*, vol. 31 (1988): 109–26; and H. Wolpe, "Capitalism and Cheap Labour-Power in South Africa: From Segregation to Apartheid," *Economy and Society,* vol. 1, no. 4 (1972): 425–56.

51 David Anderson, *Histories of the Hanged: The Dirty War in Kenya and the End of Empire* (London: Weidenfeld & Nicolson, 2005); Caroline Elkins, *Imperial Reckoning: The Untold Story of Britain's Gulag in Kenya* (New York, NY: Henry Holt and Company, 2005); and Caroline Elkins, *Britain's Gulag: The Brutal End of Empire in Kenya* (London: Jonathan Cape, 2005).

52 Wangari Maathai, *Unbowed: A Memoir* (New York: Alfred A. Knopf, 2006), 61–7.

53 Wangari Maathai, *The Greenbelt Movement: Sharing an Approach and an Experience*, rpt. edition (New York: Lantern Books, 2004).

54 Ali Igmen, *Speaking Soviet with an Accent: Culture and Power in Soviet Kyrgyzstan* (Pittsburgh: University of Pittsburgh Press, 2012).

Chapter 6

1 "Churchill's 'Iron Curtain' Speech, 'Sinews of Peace'," March 5, 1946, History and Public Policy Program Digital Archive, CWIHP archives. http://digitalarchiv e.wilsoncenter.org/document/116180, last accessed November 6, 2019; for the British origins of Cold War containment policy see, Anne Deighton ed., *Britain and the First Cold War* (London: Macmillan, 1990).

2 The Truman Doctrine, "Recommendation for Assistance to Greece and Turkey," March 12, 1947. https://www.ourdocuments.gov/doc_large_image. php?flash=false&doc=81, last accessed November 7, 2019.

3 Robert H. McNeal, ed., *Lenin: Stalin. Khrushchev. Voices of Bolshevism* (Englewood Cliffs: Prentice Hall, 1963), 120–3.

4 Scott Parrish, "The Marshall Plan, Soviet-American Relations, and the Division of Europe," in Norman Naimark and Leonid Gibianskii eds., *The Establishment of Communist Regimes in Eastern Europe, 1944–1949* (Boulder, CO: Westview Press, 1997), 267–90; Melvyn P. Leffler, "The

Emergence of an American Grand Strategy, 1945–1952," in Melvyn P. Leffler and Odd Arne Westad eds., *The Cambridge History of the Cold War*, vol. 1 (New York: Cambridge University Press, 2010), 67–89.

5 John Kent, "The British Empire and the Origins of the Cold War," in Anne Deighton ed., *Britain and the First Cold War* (New York: St. Martin's Press, 1990), 165–83.

6 Kees Boterbloem, *The Life and Times of Andrei Zhdanov, 1896–1948* (Ithaca, NY: McGill-Queen's University Press, 2004).

7 Text of the Zhdanov Report delivered to Session VI of the First Conference of the Cominform, 25 September 1947, in Guliano Procacci et al., eds., *The Cominform: Minutes of the Three Conferences 1947/1948/1949* (Milan: Fondazione Ginagiacomo Feltrinelli, 1994), 217–51.

8 Evgenii Varga, *Izmenenii v ekonomike kapitalizma v vtoroi mirovoi voiny* (Moscow: Gospolitizdat', 1946); and Kori Schake, *Safe Passage: The Transition from British to American Hegemony* (Cambridge MA: Harvard University Press, 2017).

9 Lawrence James, *Churchill and Empire: A Portrait of an Imperialist* (New York: Pegasus Books, 2014).

10 Sarah Ellen Graham, "American Propaganda, the Anglo-American Alliance, and the 'Delicate Question' of Indian Self-Determination," *Diplomatic History*, vol. 33, no. 2 (April, 2009): 223–59; and David Ryan and Victor Pungong, *The United States and Decolonization: Power and Freedom* (Basingstoke: Palgrave Macmillan, 2000). The United States granted independence to the Philippines to divest itself of colonial holdings and finally threatened to withhold resources from the Marshall Fund unless the Netherlands agreed to grant Indonesia independence. Robert McMahon, *Colonialism and the Cold War: The United States and the Struggle for Indonesian Independence, 1945–49* (Ithaca: Cornell University Press, 1981). But the United States pursued an inconsistent policy toward European imperial holdings: sometimes supporting national independence movements as in India and Indonesia, and in cases where they were afraid of communist penetration as in British Malay and in French Indochina, they backed the colonial powers.

11 "George Kennan's 'Long Telegram'," February 22, 1946, History and Public Policy Program Digital Archive, National Archives and Records Administration, Department of State Records (Record Group 59), Central Decimal File, 1945–1949, 861.00/2–2246; page 8, http://digitalarchive.wilsoncenter.org/document/116178, last accessed November 9, 2019.

12 George F. Kennan, *Memoirs*, 1925–1950 (Boston, MA: Little, Brown, 1967); and George F. Kennan, "The Sources of Soviet Conduct," *Foreign Affairs*, vol. 25, no. 4 (1947): 566–82.

13 Jan C. Jansen and Jurgen Osterhammel, *Decolonization: A Short History*, trans., Jeremiah Riemer (Princeton: Princeton University Press, 2013); and Dale Kennedy, *Decolonization: A Very Short Introduction* (New York: Oxford University Press, 2016).

14 The League of Nations included the British colonies of India and South Africa, as well as Canada, New Zealand, and Australia to amplify the British presence. The Soviet Union was to replicate this strategy in the United

Nations by claiming seats for Belarus and Ukraine. Initially, they claimed separate membership for all fifteen republics but desisted when the Americans wanted representation for the forty-eight states.

15 Susan Pedersen, *The Guardians: The League of Nations and the Crisis of Empire* (Cambridge, MA: Harvard University Press, 2015).

16 See Document no. 12: NSC 5608, "U.S. Policy Towards the Soviet Satellites in Eastern Europe," (excerpts), July 6, 1956, in Csaba Békés, Malcolm Byrne and János Rainer, *The 1956 Hungarian Revolution: A History in Documents* (Budapest and New York: Central European University Press, 2002), 123. The authors argue that the US foreign policy should exploit "the fact that Moscow and the satellite communist parties are giving increasing lip-service to the principle of national autonomy and diversity."

17 John Darwin, "An Undeclared Empire: The British in the Middle East, 1918–1939," *Journal of Imperial and Commonwealth History*, vol. 27, no. 2 (1999): 159–78.

18 Ludmilla Alexeyeva, *The Thaw Generation: Coming of Age in the Post–Stalin Era*, trans., Paul Goldberg (Pittsburgh: University of Pittsburgh Press, 1993), 218–20.

19 Winston Churchill, *A River War: A Historical Account of the Reconquest of the Soudan* (London: St. Augustine's Press, 1902).

20 Roger Owen, *Lord Cromer: Victorian Imperialist, Edwardian Proconsul* (New York: Oxford University Press, 2004).

21 *The Covenant of the League of Nations* (Including Amendments Adopted in 1924) https://avalon.law.yale.edu/20th_century/leagcov.asp, last accessed December 2, 2019.

22 John Darwin, *Britain, Egypt and the Middle East: Imperial Policy in the Aftermath of War 1918–1922* (London: The Macmillan Press Ltd., 1981).

23 Priya Satia, *Spies in Arabia: The Great War and the Cultural Foundations of Britain's Covert Empire in the Middle East* (New York: Oxford University Press, 2008); and Jeremy Salt, *The Unmaking of the Middle East: A History of Western Disorder in Arab Lands* (Berkeley: University of California Press, 2009).

24 *Great Britain and Egypt 1914–1951. Information Papers* No. 19, rpt. edition (London and New York: Royal Institute of International Affairs, 1952), 8.

25 *Egypt. Treaty Series no. 6 (1937), Treaty of Alliance.* https://upload.wikim edia.org/wikipedia/commons/d/de/Anglo-Egyptian_Treaty_of_1936.pdf, last accessed December 4, 2019.

26 David S. Painter, "Oil, Resources, and the Cold War," in Melvyn P. Leffler and Odd Arne Westad eds., *The Cambridge History of the Cold War*, vol. 1 (New York: Cambridge University Press, 2010), 486–507.

27 David M. Watry, *Diplomacy at the Brink: Eisenhower, Churchill, and Eden in the Cold War* (Baton Rouge: LA: Louisiana State University Press, 2014); Roger Louis, *End of British Imperialism: The Scramble for Empire, Suez and Decolonization,* second edition (London: I.B. Tauris, 2006); and Simon C. Smith ed., *Reassessing Suez 1956: New Perspectives on the Crisis and its Aftermath* (Burlington, VT: Ashgate Publishing Company, 2008).

28 N. Khrushchev, *Vremia: Liudi. Vlast'* (memoirs in 4 volumes), vol. 3. (Moscow: Moskovskie Novosti, 1999), 392–5, 397, 398, http://www.cvce.eu/

obj/nikita_khrushchev_vospominaniia_o_egypte-rue9d92e4d-d5f7-40d3-ac37-981e5bebc432.html, last accessed December 11, 2019.

29 United Nations General Assembly Resolution 1514, *Declaration on the Granting of Independence to Colonial Countries and People*, 1960. file:///Us ers/choichatterjww/Downloads/Declaration_on_the_Granting_of_Independen ce_to_Colonial_Countries_and_Peoples.pdf, last accessed December 12, 2019.

30 David Kay, "The Politics of Decolonization: The New Nations and the United Nations Political Process," *International Organization*, vol. 21, no. 4 (Autumn, 1967): 793; and James P. Hubbard, *The United States and the End of British Colonial Rule in Africa, 1941–1968* (Jefferson, NC: McFarland and Co. Inc. Publichore, 2011).

31 Robert T. Harrison, *Britain in the Middle East 1619–1971* (New York: Bloomsbury Academic, 2016).

32 John Darwin, *The End of the British Empire: The Historical Debate* (Oxford, UK: Basil Blackwell, 1991).

33 John Connelly, *From Peoples into Nations: A History of Eastern Europe* (Princeton, NJ: Princeton University Press, 2020); and Norman Naimark, *Stalin and the Fate of Eastern Europe: The Postwar Struggle for Sovereignty* (Cambridge, MA: Belknap Press, 2019).

34 Vladislav M. Zubok, *A Failed Empire: The Soviet Union in the Cold War From Stalin To Gorbachev* (Chapel Hill: The University of North Carolina Press, 2007).

35 Vojtech Mastny, *The Cold War and Soviet Insecurity: The Stalin Years* (New York: Oxford University Press, 1998).

36 Serhii Plokhy, *Yalta: The Price of Peace* (New York: Viking Press, 2010).

37 "Zapiska po voprosam budushchego i poslevoennogo ustroistva," in T. V. Volokitina et al. ed., *Sovetskii Faktor v Vostochnoi Evrope. Dokumenty*, vol. 1 (Moscow: ROSSPEN), 23–48.

38 Norman Naimark, "The Sovietization of Eastern Europe," in Melvyn P. Leffler and Odd Arne Westad eds., *The Cambridge History of the Cold War*, vol. 1 (New York: Cambridge University Press, 2010), 175–97; and Winston Churchill, *The Second World War: Triumph and Tragedy*, vol. 6 (New York: Bantam Books), 192–7.

39 T. V. Volokitina, *Narodnaia demokratiia, mif ili real'nost? Obshchestvenno-politicheskie protsessy v Vostochnoi Evrope, 1944–1948* (Moscow: Nauka, 1993).

40 Eduard Mark, "Revolution by Degrees: Stalin's National Front Strategy for Europe, 1941–47, " *Cold War International History Project*, Working Paper no. 31 (Washington, 2001).

41 T. V. Volokitina et al., eds., *Moskva i Vostochnaia Evropa: stanovlenie politicheskikh rezhimov sovetskogo tipa. Ocherki istorii* (Moscow: ROSSPEN, 2002).

42 See for example Evgenii Varga's definition of a new type of democracy in Eastern Europe as a transitional model from bourgeois capitalism to the Soviet model in the future, but he studiously avoided terms such as "collectivization" and "dictatorship of the proletariat," "Demokratiia novogo tipa," *Mirovoe Khoziaistvo i Mirovaia Politika*, no. 3 (October, 1947); While Varga's representations of capitalism were attacked in the debate that ensued after 1947, his ideas about "people's democracy" continued to have relevance even after his demotion.

43 Alfred J. Rieber, "Popular Democracy: An Illusion?" in Vladimir Tismaneanu ed., *Stalinism Revisited: The Establishment of Communist Regimes in Eastern-Central Europe* (Budapest: Central European University Press, 2009), 103–9; and Lars Haga, "Imaginer la démocratie populaire. L'Institut de l'économie mondiale et la carte mentale soviétique de l'Europe de l'Est (1944–1948)," *Vingtième Siècle. Revue d'histoire*, vol. 109, no. 1 (2011): 12–30.

44 Text of the Zhdanov Report delivered to Session VI of the First Conference of the Cominform, September 25, 1947, in Procacci et al., eds., *The Cominform: Minutes of the Three Conferences 1947/1948/1949*, 217–51.

45 Ibid, 37–63.

46 Anne Applebaum, *Iron Curtain: The Crushing of Eastern Europe, 1944–1956* (New York: Doubleday, 2012).

47 For more nuanced accounts of Soviet cultural policies in Eastern Europe see Patryk Babiracki, *Soviet Soft Power in Poland: Culture and the Making of Stalin's New Empire, 1943–1957* (Chapel Hill: University of North Carolina Press, 2015); and Rachel Applebaum, *Empire of Friends: Soviet Power and Socialist Internationalism in Cold War Czechoslovakia* (Ithaca, NY: Cornell University Press, 2019).

48 Anthony Kemp-Welch, *Poland Under Communism: A Cold War History* (New York: Cambridge University Press, 2008).

49 Kevin Mcdermott and Matthew Stibbe, *Revolution and Resistance in Eastern Europe: Challenges to Communist Europe* (London: Berg, 2006).

50 Peter G. Boyle, "The Hungarian Revolution and the Suez Crisis," *History*, vol. 90, no. 4 (October, 2005): 550–65; Anne Deighton, "A Different 1956: British Responses to the Polish events, June–November 1956," *Cold War History*, vol. 6, no. 4 (2006): 455–75; and Csaba Békés, "The 1956 Hungarian Revolution and the Great Powers," *Journal of Communist Studies and Transition Politics*, vol. 13, no. 2 (Summer, 1997): 51–66.

51 László Borhi, "Containment, Rollback, Liberation or Inaction? The United States and Hungary in the 1950s," *Journal of Cold War Studies*, vol. 1, no. 3 (Fall, 1997): 67–108; and Mark Kramer, "The Soviet Union and the 1956 Crises in Hungary and Poland: Reassessments and New Findings," *Journal of Contemporary History*, vol. 33, no. 2 (April, 1998): 163–214.

52 Charles Gati, *Hungary and the Soviet Union* (Durham, NC: Duke University Press, 1986), 153.

53 Swapna Kona Nayudu, "The Soviet Peace Offensive and Nehru's India," in Manu Bhagavan ed., *India and the Cold War* (Chapel Hill: University of North Carolina Press, 2019), 36–57.

54 "Third World Reaction to Hungary and Suez, 1956: A Soviet Foreign Ministry Analysis," December 28, 1956, History and Public Policy Program Digital

Archive, TsKhSD. Published in CWIHP Bulletin 4, 61–4. http://digitalarchive .wilsoncenter.org/document/111097, last accessed January 4, 2020.

55 It would be an interesting exercise to compare the Soviet documents on end of empire in Eastern Europe contained in Svetlana Svarankaya, Thomas Blanton, and Vladislav Zubok, eds., *The Peaceful End of the Cold War, 1989,* rpt. edition (Budapest: CEU Press, 2018) with documents about the British Empire contained in Ronald Hyam and Wm Roger Louis, eds., *The Conservative Government and the End of Empire 1957–1964*, Part 1 (London: Institute of Commonwealth Studies, University of London, 2000).

56 See Padraic Kenney's brilliant book on the revolutions of 1989, *A Carnival of Revolution: Central Europe 1989* (Princeton: Princeton University Press, 2002).

57 Partha Chatterjee, *The Nation and Its Fragments: Colonial and Postcolonial Histories* (Princeton: Princeton University Press, 1994).

58 See Paul Bett's nuanced review article on the mixed legacy of the revolutions of 1989, "1989 At Thirty: A Recast Legacy," *Past & Present*, vol. 244, no. 1 (August 2019): 271–305.

59 Mervat F. Hatem, "Economic and Political Liberation in Egypt and the Demise of State Feminism," *International Journal of Middle East Studies*, vol. 24, no. 2 (May, 1992): 231–51; Margot Badran, *Feminists, Islam and Nation: Gender and the Making of Modern Egypt* (Princeton: Princeton University Press, 1995); Laura Bier, *Revolutionary Womanhood, Feminisms, Modernity and the State in Nasser's Egypt* (Stanford: Stanford University Press, 2011); and Fidelis Małgorzata, *Women, Communism, and Industrialization in Postwar Poland* (New York: Cambridge University Press, 2010).

60 Beth Baron, "An Islamic Activist in Interwar Egypt," in Kathleen D. McCarthy ed., *Women, Philanthropy, and Civil Society* (Bloomington: Indiana University Press, 2001), 224–44; and Miriam Cooke, *Women Claim Islam: Creating Islamic Feminism through Literature* (New York: Routledge, 2000).

61 The Muslim Brotherhood started life at the forefront of the anti-British resistance in Egypt, and subsequently went on to challenge not just Nasser's vision of socialist modernity and secular pan-Arab nationalism, but also the Egyptian military's stranglehold on the country that continues today.

62 Zainab Al-Ghazali, *Return of the Pharaoh: Memoir in Nasir's Prison*, trans., Mokrane Guezzou (Leicester: The Islamic Foundation, 1994).

63 "An Islamic Activist," interview with Al-Ghazali reprinted in Roxanne L. Euben and Mohammad Qasim Zaman edited, *Princeton Readings in Islamist Thought: Texts and Contexts from Al-Bann to Bin Laden* (Princeton: Princeton University Press, 2009), 283–8.

64 Vincent C. Chrypinski, "The Catholic Church in Poland, 1944–1989," in Pedro Ramet ed., *Catholicism and Politics in Communist Societies* (Christianity Under Stress, vol. II) (Durham, NC: Duke University Press, 1990), 117–41.

65 Many on the Polish Left considered the Catholic Church to be an important ally against the undemocratic communist leadership. See Adam Michnik's 1976 essay, *The Church and the Left*, trans., David Ost (Chicago: University of Chicago Press, 1993).

66 Gracjan Kraszewski, "Catalyst for Revolution Pope John Paul II's 1979 Pilgrimage to Poland and Its Effects on Solidarity and the Fall of Communism," *The Polish Review*, vol. 57, no. 4 (2012): 27–46; Christian Caryl, *Strange Rebels: 1979 and the Birth of the Twenty-First Century* (New York: Basic Books, 2013); and George Weigel, *The Final Revolution: The Resistance Church and the Collapse of Communism* (New York: Oxford University Press, 1992).

67 Susan Gal and Gail Kligman, *Reproducing Gender: Politics, Publics, and Everyday Life after Socialism* (Princeton: Princeton University Press, 2000); and Magdalena Grabowska, "Bringing the Second World In: Conservative Revolution(s), Socialist Legacies, and Transnational Silences in the Trajectories of Polish Feminism," *Signs*, vol. 37, no. 2, *Unfinished Revolutions: A Special Issue*, ed. Phillip Rothwell (January, 2012): 385–411.

68 Agnieszka Graff and Elżbieta Korolczuk, "'Worse than Communism and Nazism Put Together': War on Gender in Poland," in Roman Kuhar and David Paternotte eds., *Anti-Gender Campaigns in Europe: Mobilizing Against Equality* (London and New York: Rowman and Littlefield, 2017), 117–33.

69 See Dr. Urszula Dudziak's academic website, https://www.kul.pl/dr-hab-ursz ula-dudziak-prof-kul,art_11878.html, last accessed January 19, 2020; Elżbieta Turlej, "Radiomaryjna specjalistka od wychowania do życia wrodzinie," *Polityka*, November 29, 2016, https://www.polityka.pl/tygodnikpolityka/spol eczenstwo/1684598,1,radiomaryjna-specjalistka-od-wychowania-do-zycia-w-r odzinie.read, last accessed January 19, 2020.

70 See his articles on the family in Karol Wojtyla, *Person and Community: Selected Essays*, trans. by Theresa Sandok (New York: Peter Lang, 1993), 314–61.

71 Urszula Dudziak, "Lies about In-Vitro," https://www.szansaspotkania.pl/klam stwa-o-in-vitro/, January 23, 2008, last accessed January 19, 2020.

72 Matthew Day, "Advisor to Government Claims Contraception Causes Sex Addiction," *Telegraph*, November 3, 2016, https://www.telegraph.co.uk/news /2016/11/03/adviser-to-polish-government-claims-contraception-causes-sex-add/, last accessed January 19, 2020.

73 Ursula Dudziak and Anna Dudziak-Kaczynska, "Transfer of Knowledge About Methods of Fertility Recognition in the Light of Experience from Poland," *Sveitkatos Mokslai*, vol. 21, no. 3 (Fall 2011): 45–9, https://sm-hs.eu/wp-conte nt/uploads/2019/02/53-177-1-PB.pdf, last accessed January 19, 2020.

74 These discourses bear a great similarity to ideas of Republican Motherhood that developed in the revolutionary United States. Linda Kerber, *Women of the Republic: Intellect and Ideology in Revolutionary America* (Chapel Hill: University of North Carolina Press, 1997).

Chapter 7

1 Benedict Anderson, *Imagined Communities: Reflections on the Origins and Spread of Nationalism*, rpt. edition (New York: Verso, 2006).

NOTES 213

2 Artemy Kalinovsky, *A Long Goodbye: The Soviet Withdrawal from Afghanistan* (Cambridge, MA: Harvard University Press, 2011); Ahmed Rashid, *Jihad: The Rise of Militant Islam in Central Asia* (New Haven, CT: Yale University Press, 2001); and Ahmed Rashid, *Descent into Chaos: How the War against Islamic Extremism is Being Lost in Pakistan, Afghanistan, and Central Asia* (London: Allen Lane, 2008).

3 "India 2019," Amnesty International https://www.amnesty.org/en/countries/asia-and-the-pacific/india/report-india/, last accessed on February 2, 2020; "Joint Statement by Human Rights Watch, Amnesty International, and Front Line Defenders, 6/3/2015," https://www.hrw.org/news/2015/06/03/joint-statement-human-rights-watch-amnesty-international-and-front-line-defenders, accessed March 2, 2016; Micheal Kugelman, "How Could the UN Help Resolve the Kashmir Dispute," http://www.dw.com/en/how-could-the-un-help-resolve-the-kashmir-dispute/a-18120254, December 10, 2014, last accessed December 1, 2015; Alexey Ilin, "Russia and the International Criminal Court: Barriers and Opportunities," July 2, 2015, https://russiancouncil.ru/en/analytics-and-comments/analytics/russia-and-the-international-criminal-court-barriers-and-opp, last accessed April 4, 2016; and Wrede Smith, "Europe to the Rescue: The Killing of Journalists in Russia and the European Court of Human Rights," *George Washington International Law Review*, vol. 43, no. 3 (2011): 493–527.

4 Arundhati Roy, "End of Imagination," August 1, 1998, http://www.ratical.org/ratville/nukes/endOfImagine.html, last accessed March 11, 2015.

5 Bruce Grant, *The Captive and the Gift: Cultural Histories of Sovereignty in Russia and the Caucasus* (Ithaca, NY: Cornell University Press, 2009); and Michael Khodarkovsky, *Bitter Choices: Loyalty and Betrayal in the Russian Conquest of the North Caucasus* (Ithaca, NY: Cornell University Press, 2011).

6 Thomas Remington, *Politics in Russia* (New York: Pearson/Longman, 2008); Emma Gilligan, *Terror in Chechnya: Russia and the Tragedy of Civilians* (Princeton: Princeton University Press, 2010); Anatol Lieven, *Chechnya: Tombstone of Russia's Power* (New Haven, CT: Yale University Press, 1998); V. A. Tishkov, *Chechnya: Life in a War-Torn Society* (Berkeley: University of California Press, 2004); George Derluguian, *Bourdieu's Secret Admirer in the Caucasus: A World System Biography* (Chicago: Chicago University Press, 2005); German Sadulaev, *I am a Chechen*, Anna Gunin, trans. (London: Harvill Secker, 2010); E. Iu. Vilenskaia ed., *Menia, kak reku surovaia epokha povernula. Sud'by rossiskikh zhenschin v period perestroika i voiny v Chechne* (St. Petersburg, 2010); and Anne Nivat, *Chienne de Guerre: A Woman Reporter Beyond the Lines of War in Chechnya* (New York: Public Affairs, 2011).

7 Anna Politkovskaya, *A Dirty War: A Russian Reporter in Chechnya* (London: Harvill, 2001); *Putin's Russia* (London: Harvill, 2004); *A Russian Diary: A Journalist's Final Account of Life, Corruption, and Death in Putin's Russia* (London: Harvill Secker: 2007); *Nothing But the Truth: Selected Dispatches* (London: Harvill Secker, 2010). For a list of Politkovskaya's articles published in *Novaya Gazeta*, see the website http://politkovskaya.novayagazeta.ru/

8 Natalia Roudakova, *Losing Pravda: Ethics and The Press in Post-Truth Russia* (Cambridge: Cambridge University Press, 2017).

9 See Marina Goldovskaya's brilliant documentary on Politkovskaya, *A Bitter Taste of Freedom* (2011).

10 Arundhati Roy, *The End of Imagination* (Kottayam, India: D.C. Books, 1998); *Capitalism: A Ghost Story* (London: Haymarket Books, 2014); *Public Power in the Age of Empire* (New York: Seven Stories Press, 2004); *Listening to Grasshoppers: Field Notes on Democracy* (New Delhi: Penguin, 2010) The Hanging of Afzal Guru and the Strange Case of the Attack on the Indian Parliament* (New Delhi: Penguin, 2013); and *Walking with the Comrades* (New Delhi: Penguin, 2011); and *My Seditious Heart: Collected Non-Fiction* (London: Haymarket Books, 2019).

11 Ibid., *Algebra of Infinite Justice* (New Delhi: Penguin, 2001).

12 Sumantra Bose, *Kashmir: Roots of Conflict, Paths to Peace* (Cambridge, MA: Harvard University Press, 2003): Pankaj Mishra, *Temptations of the West: How to be Modern in India, Pakistan, Tibet, and Beyond* (New York: Farrar, Strauss and Giroux, 2006); Marlène Laruelle and Sébastien Peyrouse, *Mapping Central Asia: Indian Perceptions and Strategies* (Farnham: Ashgate, 2011); Ian Talbott and Gurhapal Singh, *Partition of India* (New York: Cambridge University Press, 2009); Ayesha Jalal, *Partisans of Allah: Jihad in South Asia* (Cambridge, MA: Harvard University Press, 2008); and Salman Rushdie, *Shalimar the Clown* (New York: Random House, 2006).

13 Tariq Ali ed., *Kashmir: The Case for Freedom* (London: Verso, 2011); and Agha Shahid Ali, *The Country Without a Post Office* (New York: W.W. Norton, 1997).

14 Rahul Pandita, *Our Moon Has Blood Clots: The Exodus of Kashmiri Pandits* (Noida, India: Random House, 2013).

15 Masha Gessen, *Man without a Face: The Unlikely Rise of Vladimir Putin* (New York: Riverhead Books, 2012). See also numerous articles by the Gessens in influential publications such as the *New York Times, The Guardian, Newsweek,* and others.

16 Aryeh Neier, *The International Human Rights Movement: A History* (Princeton: Princeton University Press, 2012).

17 Serguei Oushakine, *The Patriotism of Despair: Nation, War, and Loss in Russia* (Ithaca: Cornell University Press, 2009).

18 Marlène Laruelle, *Russian Eurasianism: An Ideology of Empire* (Baltimore, MD: Johns Hopkins University Press, 2008).

19 But surprisingly, India has modeled its coercive laws and anti-terrorist legislation on British antecedents. An example of this is the Terrorist and Disruptive Activities Prevention Act that was applied to all of India in 1985 and whose illiberal provisions were subsequently amended and re-enshrined under the Unlawful Activities Prevention Amendment Act in 2004, and then again in 2008. Ujjwal Kumar Singh, *Political Prisoners in India* (New Delhi: Oxford University Press, 1998); and Manas Mohapatra, "Learning Lessons from India: The Recent History of Antiterrorist Legislation on the Subcontinent," *The Journal of Criminal Law and Criminology*, vol. 95, no. 1 (Autumn, 2004): 315–44.

20 In August 2019, the Indian government forcibly abrogated the special status of Jammu and Kashmir as provided under Article 370 of the Indian Constitution, and downgraded Jammu, Kashmir, and Ladakh into Union territories. Elected leaders were put under house arrest, the media restricted, and the internet suspended. Except for Pakistan and China, very few governments have criticized India's actions in Kashmir. See Christine Fair article, "India's Move in Kashmir: Unpacking the Domestic and International Motivations and Implications," *Lawfare*, August 12, 2019, https://www.law fareblog.com/indias-move-kashmir-unpacking-domestic-and-international-motivations-and-implications, last accessed October 1, 2020; and Arundhati Roy, "The Silence is the Loudest Sound," *New York Times*, August 15, 2019, https://www.nytimes.com/2019/08/15/opinion/sunday/kashmir-siege modi.h tml, last accessed February 2, 2020.

21 Konstantin Krymov, "Oderzhimaia," *Spetsnaz Rossii*, October 10, 2006, http://www.specnaz.ru/article/?967, last accessed October 4, 2016; Iulia Sokolova, "Provozashchitnitsa Politkovskaya, Isterichnaia babochka ili udachnyi media proekt," *Kompromat*, November 4, 2005, http://www.compromat.ru/page _16572.htm, last accessed February 4, 2016.

22 Julie Mullaney, "Globalizing Dissent?" Arundhati Roy, Local and Postcolonial Feminisms in the Transnational Economy," World Literature Written in English, vol. 40, no. 1 (2002-2003): 56–70; Arghya, "On Arundhati Roy," *Critical Twenties*, October 28, 2010, http://www.criticaltwenties.in/nationalpolitics/on-arundhati-roy, last accessed March 3, 2016; See interview with eminent Indian historian and environmentalist, Ramchandran Guha. Sundeep Dougal, "Arundhati Roy has Become a Joke: Ram Guha," *Outlook*, October 29, 2010, http://www.outlookindia.com/blogs/post/arundhati-roy-has-become-a-joke -ram-guha/2371/5, last accessed May 11, 2015.

23 Anna Arutunyan, "The Albat's Archipelago," *The Exile*, November 17, 2006, http://exile.ru/articles/detail.php?ARTICLE_ID=8378&IBLOCK_ID=35, last accessed October 11, 2015.

24 "Rossiyane ob ubiistve Anny Politkovskoi," October 19, 2006, http://www .levada.ru/19-10-2006/rossiyane-ob-ubiistve-anny-politkovskoi, last accessed September 12, 2015; See also Natalia Roudakova, "Post-Soviet Journalism as 'Prostitution': Russia's Reactions to Anna Politkovskaya's Murder," *Political Communication*, 26, no. 4: 412–29.

25 Venkatesan Vembu, "Arundhati Roy is Dangerously Wrong on Kashmir," October 27, 2010, http://www.dnaindia.com/analysis/column-arundhati-roy-is -dangerously-wrong-on-kashmir-1458329, last accessed August 4, 2016; and "Arundhati Roy Apologizes for 2011 video on Pakistan Army, says may have been Thoughtless," *The Print*, August 28, 2019, https://theprint.in/india/arun dhati-roy-apologises-for-2011-video-on-pakistan-army-says-may-have-been-tho ughtless/283548/, last accessed August 2, 2020.

26 "Aatish Taseer: The TNB Self-Interview," TNB, October 30, 2011, http://www .thenervousbreakdown.com/ataseer/2011/10/aatish-taseer-the-tnb-self-intervi ew/, last accessed December 11, 2015.

27 Richard Sakwa, *Putin: Russia's Choice* (New York: Routledge, 2nd edition, 2008); and Jane Zavisca, *Housing the New Russia* (Ithaca: Cornell University Press, 2012).

28 Yevgeny Kiselyov, "Politkovskaya Had One Aim: To Tell the Truth," *Moscow Times*, October 9, 2006, http://www.themoscowtimes.com/opinion/article

/politkovskaya-had-one-aim-to-tell-the-truth/201865.html, last accessed September 11, 2015.

29 Article found in Politkovskaya's computer after her death, entitled "What Am I Guilty of," in Anna Politkovskaya ed., *Is Journalism Worth Dying For?* trans. Arch Tait (New York: Melville House, 2011), 6.

30 Arundhati Roy, *The Cost of Living* (New York: Modern Library, 1999), 104.

31 Michel Foucault, *Discourse and Truth: The Problem of Parrhesia,* October 1983, http://foucault.info/documents/parrhesia/, last accessed November 15, 2015.

32 Parag Khanna, *How to Run the World: Charting a Course to the Next Renaissance* (New York: Random House, 2011).

33 See note 22.

34 Arundhati Roy, *Cost of Living* (New York: Modern Library Paperbacks, 1999), 103.

35 Choi Chatterjee, "Accidental Transnationalist: An Autobiographical Manifesto," *Ab Imperio* (4/2018): 29–41.

36 Lisa Kirschenbaum, *Small Comrades: Revolutionizing Childhood in Soviet Russia, 1917–1932* (New York: Routledge Falmer, 2001); and *The Legacy of the Siege of Leningrad, 1941–1995: Myth, Memories and Monuments* (Cambridge: Cambridge University Press, 2006).

37 Lisa Kirschenbaum, *International Communism and the Spanish Civil War: Solidarity and Suspicion* (Cambridge: Cambridge University Press, 2015).

38 For a complete list of publications, see Kirschenbaum's academic website, https://www.wcupa.edu/arts-humanities/history/LKirschenbaum.aspx.

Conclusion

1 Stephen Kotkin, *Armageddon Averted: The Soviet Collapse 1970–2000* (New York: Oxford University Press, 2001).

2 Perhaps Eliseev, the storied food emporium in Moscow, will be also saved by a billionaire from the ex-colonies.

3 William Butler Yeats, "The Second Coming" https://www.poetryfoundation.org/poems/43290/the-second-coming, last accessed April 12, 2021.

4 Ilya Senmenenko-Basin, "March 20th" Translated by Elena Dimov, available at https://pages.shanti.virginia.edu/russian/2017/02/20/russian-vers-libre-and-the-poetry-of-ilya-semenenko-basin/, last accessed April 13, 2021.

Select Bibliography

Brown, Kate. *Plutopia: Nuclear Families, Atomic Cities, And the Great Soviet and American Plutonium Disasters*. New York: Oxford University Press, 2013.

Burbank, Jane, and Frederick Cooper. *Empires in World History: Power and the Politics of Difference*. Princeton: Princeton University Press, 2011.

Burton, Antoinette. *The Trouble with Empire: Challenges to Modern British Imperialism*. New York: Oxford University Press, 2015.

Darwin, John. *After Tamerlane: The Rise and Fall of Global Empires, 1400–2000*. New York: Bloomsbury Press, 2008.

Etkind, Alexander. *Internal Colonization: Russia's Imperial Experiences*. Cambridge: Polity Press, 2011.

Kirschenbaum, Lisa. *International Communism, and the Spanish Civil War: Solidarity and Suspicion*. New York: Cambridge University Press, 2015.

Kumar, Krishan. *Visions of Empire: How Five Imperial Regimes Shaped the World*. Princeton: Princeton University Press, 2017.

Lieven, Dominic. *Russian Empire and its Rivals*. New Haven, CT: Yale University Press, 2002.

Marks, Stephen. *How Russia Shaped the Modern World: From Art to Anti-Semitism, Ballet to Bolshevism*. Princeton: Princeton University Press, 2003.

Mishra, Pankaj. *From the Ruins of Empire: The Intellectuals Who Remade Asia*. New York: Farrar, Strauss and Giroux, 2012.

Index

Page numbers followed with "n" refer to endnotes.